CHILD GROUP PSYCHOTHERAPY

CHILD GROUP PSYCHOTHERAPY

Future Tense

edited by
ALBERT E. RIESTER, Ed.D.
and
IRVIN A. KRAFT, M.D.

Monograph 3
AMERICAN GROUP PSYCHOTHERAPY ASSOCIATION
MONOGRAPH SERIES
Series Consulting Editor:
Fern J. Cramer Azima, Ph.D.

INTERNATIONAL UNIVERSITIES PRESS, INC.
Madison   Connecticut

Copyright © 1986, American Group Psychotherapy Association

Second Printing, 1989

All rights reserved. No part of this book may be reproduced by any means nor translated into a machine language, without the written permission of the publisher.

Library of Congress Cataloging in Publication Data

Child group psychotherapy.

    (Monograph series / American Group Psychotherapy Association; monograph 3)
    Includes bibliographies and index.
    1. Child psychotherapy. 2. Group psychotherapy.
I. Riester, Albert E., 1941-   . II. Kraft, Irvin A.
III. Series: Monograph series (American Group Psychotherapy Association) [DNLM: 1. Psychotherapy, Group—in infancy & childhood. 2. Psychotherapy, Group—trends. W1 M0559PU monograph 3 / WS 350.2 C536]
RJ505.G7C48 1986   618.92'89152   86-10486
ISBN 0-8236-0765-8

Manufactured in the United States of America

Contents

Acknowledgment vii

Contributors ix

Foreword by Saul Scheidlinger xi

Consulting Editor's Introduction by Fern J. Cramer Azima xiii

Part I   The Context of Child Group Psychotherapy

    Chapter 1   Past as Prologue to the Future in Child Group Psychotherapy Practice—*Irvin A. Kraft, M.D. and Albert E. Riester, Ed.D.*   3

Part II   Developmental Perspectives and the Change Process

    Chapter 2   Differential Methods of Group Therapy in Relation to Age Levels—*S. R. Slavson*   9

    Chapter 3   Differential Diagnosis and Group Structure in the Outpatient Treatment of Latency Age Children—*Gerald Schamess, M.S.S.*   29

Part III   The Use of Groups for Diagnostic Purposes

    Chapter 4   Diagnostic Play Groups for Children: Their Role in Assessment and Treatment Planning—*Jerome H. Liebowitz, M.D. and Paulina F. Kernberg, M.D.*   71

Part IV   Where, When, and How

    Chapter 5   Child Group Psychotherapy in Special Settings—*Beryce W. MacLennan, Ph.D.*   83

Chapter 6   Applications of Child Group
             Psychotherapy—*Thomas Gaines, Jr., Ph.D.*   103

Chapter 7   A Two-Stage Model for Group Therapy
             with Impulse-Ridden Latency Age
             Children—*Judy Crawford-Brobyn, C.C.W. and
             Andrea White, M.S.W.*   123

Part V   The Therapist

Chapter 8   Countertransference: In and Beyond Child
             Group Psychotherapy—*Fern J. Cramer Azima,
             Ph.D.*   139

Chapter 9   Training and Supervision in Child and
             Adolescent Group Psychotherapy—*Edward
             S. Soo, M.S.*   157

Chapter 10   Research on Child Group Therapy: Present
             Status and Future Directions—*Robert R. Dies,
             Ph.D. and Albert E. Riester, Ed.D.*   173

Part VI   Looking Forward on the Foundation of the Past

Chapter 11   Activity Group Therapy Revisited—*Mortimer
             Schiffer, M.S.*   223

Chapter 12   Innovative and Creative Approaches in
             Child Group Psychotherapy—*Irvin A. Kraft,
             M.D.*   263

Name Index   273
Subject Index   279

Acknowledgment

Saul Scheidlinger, Ph.D., was President of the American Group Psychotherapy Association when the organization decided to sponsor this exciting Monograph Series. His extensive knowledge of group psychotherapy theory and practice is internationally recognized. The dynamic ways that the group experience can help children with developmental and emotional problems has been a primary focus of his distinguished career. His lectures, books, journal articles, workshops, supervision, and clinical work have all served to teach the clinician to lead groups in accordance with the emotional and cognitive readiness of the child. For these reasons, the authors of this Monograph acknowledge Saul Scheidlinger by dedicating this book to him.

For those of us who struggle to understand the ways that the group can bring about change in children, Dr. Scheidlinger has been an inspiration and a person to emulate. He is the giant in our field because of his unique capacity to integrate behavioral science theory with practice. This special gift to the group psychotherapy movement gives child group psychotherapists the tools and understanding necessary to orchestrate group experiences so learning and healing can occur.

Albert E. Riester
Irvin A. Kraft

Contributors

Fern J. Cramer Azima, Ph.D., is Associate Professor of Psychology at McGill University and Codirector of the Therapy Day Centre, Royal Victoria Hospital, Montreal.

Judy Crawford-Brobyn, C.C.W., is Family and Group Therapist on the Etobicoke Team at Thistletown Regional Centre in Toronto.

Robert R. Dies, Ph.D., is Professor of Psychology at the University of Maryland and Editor of the *International Journal of Group Psychotherapy.*

Thomas Gaines, Jr., Ph.D., is Clinical Associate Professor of Psychiatry at the University of Texas Health Science Center at San Antonio, Director of School and Community Consultation at the Community Guidance Center, and in private practice.

Paulina F. Kernberg, M.D., is Associate Professor of Psychiatry and Director of Child and Adolescent Psychiatry at New York Hospital–Cornell University Medical Center in White Plains, New York.

Irvin A. Kraft, M.D., is Clinical Professor of Mental Health, University of Texas School of Public Health, Houston, and Clinical Professor of Psychiatry, Baylor College of Medicine, Houston. In addition to his teaching duties, Dr. Kraft also maintains an active private practice.

Jerome H. Liebowitz, M.D., is Assistant Professor of Psychiatry and Director, Child and Adolescent Outpatient Department, New York Hospital–Cornell Medical Center in White Plains, New York.

Beryce W. MacLennan, Ph.D., is Mental Health Advisor, GAO, Washington, D.C., Clinical Professor at the Medical and Behavioral Science Center, George Washington University, and in private practice.

Albert E. Riester, Ed.D., is Professor of Education at Trinity University, Clinical Professor of Psychiatry at the University of Texas Health Science Center at San Antonio, and Senior Consultant, San Antonio Children's Center.

Gerald Schamess, M.S.S., is Professor of Social Work and Chair of the Treatment Methods Sequence, Smith College School for Social Work and engaged in Group Consultation and Private Practice, Northampton, Massachusetts.

Mortimer Schiffer, M.S., is now essentially retired after more than forty years of practice, teaching, supervision, and writing in child group psychotherapy. He is one of the founders of children's group therapy.

S. R. Slavson (1890-1981), was an internationally recognized pioneer in developing theories and methods for the use of the group modality in the treatment and learning process. He was the founder of The American Group Psychotherapy Association and wrote prolifically on a variety of subjects such as education, parenting, recreation, social philosophy, analytic group psychotherapy, human growth and development, and activity group therapy for children.

Edward S. Soo, M.S., is Supervisor of Group Therapy, Jewish Board of Family and Children's Services, New York City.

Andrea White, M.S.W., is Clinical Coordinator on the Etobicoke Team at Thistletown Regional Centre in Toronto.

Foreword

The appearance of this comprehensive, finely balanced, and up-to-date volume on child group psychotherapy is long overdue. It must be left to the future historians of our field to explain the irony of why child group treatment, conceived in the early 1930s, did not until now produce a satisfactory text.

As it is, I welcome this book warmly from two perspectives: as AGPA President at the time it was proposed as part of our new monograph series; and as a teacher who will finally have a single volume for reference, instead of having to send students in search of widely scattered sources.

Since the editors and contributors to this volume constitute a veritable Who's Who in child group psychotherapy, it covers in exemplary fashion all of the topics and issues central to this field. It is bound to capture the attention of workers from all the varied disciplines engaged in the realm of child mental health, whatever treatment modality they prefer.

Congratulations are due to the editors, Drs. Irvin A. Kraft and Albert E. Riester, to the chapter authors, to Dr. Fern J. Cramer Azima, General Editor of the AGPA Monograph Series and, last but not least, to Marsha Block and her invaluable staff at the AGPA Office.

Saul Scheidlinger, Ph.D.

Consulting Editor's Introduction

It is fitting that the first clinical volume of the American Group Psychotherapy Monograph Series begins with the application of group psychotherapy to children. In fact, many of the early pioneers of group therapy referenced in this book, started their practice with children and mothers.

This book, so capably edited by Drs. Albert Riester and Irvin Kraft, begins with a republication of a seminal paper by Slavson, and proceeds to an overview of present day theoretical, technical, training, and research approaches in a wide area of child group psychotherapy in clinic, schools and in-patient settings. The editors have successfully drawn together a group of psychotherapists actively working in the field, who share their thinking and clinical expertise with us. The diversity and breadth of the approaches by the authors attest to the importance of group therapies in the treatment of children. The clinical vignettes by the various authors enrich the varying theoretical frameworks, and engage the reader in an appreciation of the leaders' skills and the adaptive capacities of young children to modify in the interaction with their peers.

I have had the unusual privilege of being involved in a consultative role to the editors and publishers, and as a contributor to the text. It is, therefore, particularly gratifying to introduce this Monograph that I have no doubt will be an invaluable resource for both the beginning and senior therapist, and make an important contribution to the advancement of group psychotherapy training and practice with children. Equally, the insights from child group theory provide the necessary basic constructs for the advancement of knowledge for the group theory and treatment of adolescents and adults.

Fern J. Cramer Azima, Ph.D.,
Consulting Editor, American Group
Psychotherapy Association
Monograph Series

Part I
The Context of Child Group Psychotherapy

Chapter 1
Past as Prologue to the Future in Child Group Psychotherapy Practice

IRVIN A. KRAFT, M.D.
ALBERT E. RIESTER, Ed.D.

We had the usual grandiose plans for this monograph: to depict the past succinctly and to predict the future more or less accurately. As our several outlines evolved into more realistic views of what we could do, the following set of themes and topics emerged. After a basic introduction to the field of group psychotherapy of children, we offer developmental and structural considerations, with particular emphasis on diagnosis. The book then moves to "nuts and bolts" issues: setting, times to apply group therapy, specific circumstances, and techniques. After delving into these basics, we turn to the therapist himself: his training, how he deals with transference and countertransference, and what research reveals about him and his work. A retrospect and prospect by Mortimer Schiffer is next, followed by a discussion of how to be innovative and creative in child group psychotherapy while remaining clinically sound.

In viewing this era in group psychotherapy, we find that an historical overview serves as a useful first step. Try to move yourself back in time over fifty years, to a United States gripped by the most severe depression it had ever known. In New York City, S. R. Slavson, trained as an engineer and working as an educator in a social agency, began work with children within a format he later termed *activity group therapy*. This procedure, as Slavson taught and developed it, laid the groundwork for further developments in the group psychotherapy of children and adolescents.

Underlying this technique were two major historical themes: the humanism that has pervaded Western thought beginning with the Renaissance, and the psychoanalytic conception of the development and functioning of personality. As an example of the former, note how Jean Jacques Rousseau's "case study" of Émile stresses the value of learning from direct experience and of understanding individual differences. Rousseau also stressed the importance of physical activity and good bodily health in the education of children, as well as the need for self-expression through art, music, and play. His historic contribution lies in his emphasis upon sensitivity to the child's level of development in designing learning experiences.

Johann Heinrich Pestalozzi, the eighteenth-century educator and disciple of Rousseau, merits special recognition for his view that learning begins with the simple elements of what the child has experienced. He expounded his views in a didactic novel, *Leonard and Gertrude,* in which children are taught to pay particular attention to what they see and hear: accurate observation through the senses comprises a basic first step toward real knowledge. Thus, differences within and among individuals and their common life experiences serve as bases for each developmental stage.

In a similar fashion, classical psychoanalytic theory and therapy underlie Slavson's work and such later developments as play group psychotherapy. In 1937 Bender reported using groups in the treatment of children in a hospital ward. These early efforts engaged children in learning through experience and activity as they engaged in arts, crafts, and games. The originators avoided judgmental confrontation and interpretation, thus following both the progressive education premise that children learn from here-and-now experience and the psychoanalytic assumption that experience and peer interactions can "work through" conflicts and self-barricades in a nonverbal medium.

Activity group therapy provided the foundation for further developments. In the 1940s various investigators devised methods which met the developmental considerations of the usual age groupings of children, especially latency and adolescence. Concomitantly, therapists and administrators realized that techniques were needed to match the exigencies of different settings, as group psychotherapy appeared useful for correctional institutions, public schools, hospitals, residential treatment facilities, and pediatric clinics. When the mid-1960s brought significant sociocultural changes, including the emergence of an adolescent counterculture, widespread drug abuse, changes in definitions of masculinity and femininity, and the "decloseting" of homosexuality, a number of "newer therapies" emerged as well. Groups for healing fitted into a spectrum from traditional group psychotherapy to human potential groups, consciousness-raising groups, and the self-help groups (AA, Synanon, Overeaters Anonymous, etc.). While few of the latter directly apply to work with children, derivatives have found their way into this area of group therapy.

Thus, throughout the brief history of child group psychotherapy we discern a common humanistic trend: the child as person was ever its focus. Following a developmental road map, at some point the child detours. Therapy and family involvement in a systems theory fashion aims at restoration of the child's mental pathway. Usually such a therapeutic journey corrects personality malformations and facilitates further development of interpersonal skills, for these are conspicuous by their absence or lack of development. These children may experience rejection by both groups and individuals, frequently resulting in a cyclic pattern of failure and frustration. They miss out on significant opportunities to learn cultural mores, social skills, ways of resolving interpersonal conflict, and basic coping skills and therefore do not attain the socialization and learning appropriate to each developmental stage. Subsequently these disturbed youngsters lack the knowledge necessary for successful social functioning, and this often leads to rejection and failure in early primary group experiences. Self-esteem, initially low, fails to thrive, scapegoat and failure roles providing additional negative experience.

The child's need for peer involvement finds gratification in the group process, often involving positive identifications with significant others, both in the group and in the larger environment—family, play groups, clubs, and teams. Anna Freud's work laid the theoretical foundation for this emphasis on the child's interactions with family and other groups.

Further practical issues involve funding this form of child therapy. Activity group therapy, as developed from Slavson's original design, requires space, which in these days of cost accounting may be available primarily in such institutions as child guidance and community health centers. The private practitioner tends to turn to other formats, the interview-activity model for example.

A child therapy group may be set up and run in many different ways, depending in large measure on the setting. In public service clinics and centers, there are often enough children available to put together several groups. Patient selection offers choices and options that frequently do not exist in a private practice setting, and therapists may construct modifications that are comfortable for them.

A group may begin with even two children; once it is started, others may be added. Using age and developmental levels as primary positive indicators, one then uses exclusionary criteria, such as the child's being sexually active, severely brain-damaged or retarded, or heavily sociopathic.

At least six methods, centering on verbalizations, lend themselves to productive sessions. The leader or leaders introduce activities congruent with developmental levels and abilities, communicate verbally through neutral objects (games, arts and crafts, etc.), promote a common experience for the entire group (e.g., a field trip), plan for less structured activities (such as refreshment time), model the verbalization of feelings and needs, and reinforce both verbal and nonverbal communication during the sessions. Note how a constant interweaving of activities and verbalizations occurs in these techniques, for activities stimulate verbal and nonverbal interactions among group members.

As one might predict from family systems theory, when children in the group begin to improve, their parents find reasons to interrupt therapy. The therapist must anticipate this if he is to maintain group membership. Parents require a clear understanding of group psychotherapy if they are to avoid this tendency to remove the child from treatment.

The training of group therapists for children includes classroom work in child development, the nature and development of substance abuse in children and adolescents, the psychodynamics of family systems, and the principles and practice of child group psychotherapy and family therapy. Practical experience includes participation as a patient in group psychotherapy and about 450 hours of supervised individual and group therapy with children.

In short, this specialized area of group psychotherapy challenges us, across a wide range of stratagems and tactics, to harness and to flow with the developmental forces of the children and their family systems. Therapist creativity constantly figures in the intricacies of group dynamics. Children respond rather readily and, as with other types of therapy, the leader may experience a great deal of satisfaction. We hope this volume intrigues the beginner and beguiles the experienced into further adventures in group psychotherapy of children.

Part II
Developmental Perspectives and the Change Process

Chapter 2
Differential Methods of Group Therapy in Relation to Age Levels

S. R. SLAVSON

> *Certainly any group within the community, educational or noneducational, has a right to initiate activities to meet special conditions which it recognizes. This in no way relieves the school or the community from the necessity of action in respect to the needs of all members of the community. If certain groups are being adequately cared for by individual private agencies, there is no reason why such programs should not be encouraged by every possible means short of the granting of public funds.*—1944 Yearbook of the National Education Association: Toward a New Curriculum.

Where there are no organic causes for it, psychologic problems stem from interference with the child's normal growth, from blockings of the natural trends to autonomy and self-reliance, or can be traced to emotional insecurity in the home and maladjustment in group living. The orderly growth of a child requires security as a biologic and psychologic entity. He must feel adequately protected from danger and must be certain of physical survival. But such security is not enough. His strivings to become independent as his powers evolve, and as he grows stronger, must be met as well. This involves sloughing off the authority and protection of parents and other adults who are ordinarily responsible for the child and who now must gradually transfer this responsibility to the child himself. If the child is to grow into a balanced adult, the natural movement from dependence needs to be encouraged and so canalized as to strengthen his character.

Reprinted with permission from *Nervous Child,* vol. 4 (1945), pp. 196–210.

Either denial of the trend to self-reliance and autonomy, or its acceleration, increases the child's anxiety and rebelliousness against those who frustrate him. In either case—that of retardation or of acceleration—there is implied rejection of personality as such. When he is unnecessarily inhibited, the child translates this as a rejection of himself. Restraint, while necessary in training, should be employed as a tool for helping growth rather than to arrest development. One who still cannot view relationships in a rational and objective manner interprets prohibition to mean rejection.

Where, on the other hand, the child's growth is accelerated in any direction through the zeal of parents and teachers, his psychomotor organization is strained and the development of the personality is unbalanced. Exaggerated strivings of this kind on the part of parents, teachers, and other adults set up psychologic concomitants. When adults desire a child to be different from what he is, they reject him as he is. The child is fully aware of it, even if he cannot formulate his awareness in words. He feels inadequate and undesirable. Such fixed conviction of inadequacy causes many psychologic dislocations and development of compensatory character traits and behavior.

Needs of growth and security are many and are expressed in numerous ways at various stages in the individual's growth. They also differ for different individuals. The basic and most universal of these are full acceptance by parents, certainty of their love, and a harmonious relationship between them. These foundational requirements are too commonly known to all who deal with children to require elaboration here. Progressive educators and other enlightened persons are also fully aware of the value of appropriate creative activity and psychomotor expression in the development of an integrated and balanced personality. Less common is a recognition of the importance of the family *as a group* in this connection; nor are other, extrafamilial groups stressed in discussions on education and therapy.

The overlooking of the group as it affects psychosocial and psychosexual development in our culture is a serious defect in education and therapy. It is at the root of many personality maladjustments and of much social pathology. It is becoming increasingly apparent that the individual cannot be understood or treated apart from his culture. The totality of the conditions of his life, the biosphere, affects and molds him; in a broad analysis, it is part and parcel of his personality. Even infants and young children are influenced by it via parents and nurses, as the latter are in turn affected by the socioeconomic and psychologic conditions of their lives. Just as a plant cannot escape the effect of sun rays and weather, man cannot escape the pressures and tensions of his social environment. The kernel of a democratic society is the group. The capacity for group action and the individual's adaptation to group living are the foundation of the democratic life pattern.

Association with groups must be recognized as a prime experience for life in our culture. The capacity to work with and become part of a group is an indication of a well-balanced person. One who isolates himself is as disturbed as one who pursues association too vehemently or one who consistently gets into difficulties with people. The values of groups to the individual are many. Clusters, colonies, schools, flocks, herds, and groups are universal in nature. They are essential means for biologic survival in lower animals and in man. They are essential to the latter for his psychologic and spiritual life as well. As a social phenomenon, the group is not an invention of man; it has its roots in nature. Man, however, consciously uses groups for enhancement of personality and for psychologic survival. Every healthy person in our culture strives to be well thought of, respected, and wanted. Perhaps these cravings have their origin in the family through dependence on parents and their surrogates, through sibling relations and rivalries. They are probably further enhanced through our cultural values, such as school grades and scores in recreation, and through community recognition. Despite the many conscious and tacit artifices for promoting social values, group life must be recognized as an extension of biologic life and as an integral part of nature.

Whatever the *raison d'être* is, an important fact to be recognized in dealing with people in education and therapy is that the craving for acceptance by and association with other persons is a primary one. One of the universal complaints of a neurotic is that people do not like him, and one of his common fears is the fear of group association, which, according to him, must result in failure. Though the neurotic's disturbance is intrapsychic, it manifests itself as a social maladjustment and his most ardent striving is to overcome this handicap. But social maladaptation is not confined to the neurotic alone. Patients with other difficulties are similarly afflicted. Whether an individual falls within the clinical category of neurosis, psychosis, behavior or character disorder, or psychopathic personality, his difficulties are in relation to people. It is therefore understandable why an effort should be made to explore the possibilities of employing the group as a corrective tool.

In the orderly growth of an individual in our culture, he comes in contact with eight types of groups. While all of them contribute to ego building and social adaptation in similar ways, each makes, in addition, specific contributions to the formation of character. The groups, in the order in which they become important to the individual, are listed in the accompanying table. It should not be assumed that these groups are disparate. Most of them are coextensive, and the individual comes under the simultaneous influence of several of them at any given time.

It may be helpful at this point to establish some orientation for the concept of orderly development and the various phases of growth as they relate to our topic. It will also be helpful at this time to define the role of the adult during the different phases of the child's development, as a reference for the various functions that the therapist has to assume in the treatment of children at different age levels.

Different phases in child development, as is well known, have been categorized by many students and writers. These classifications deal variously with biologic and organic growth, psychologic development, learning stages, and social development. Since in the present paper we are rather concerned with the psychologic dynamics, interference with which creates problems in personality, we shall classify the several phases as those of *nurture, discipline,* and *education.*

The period of nurture is early infancy, when the child lives a parasitic life, largely an extension of his intrauterine existence. During this period all his needs and wants are more or less instantaneously met and his peremptory demands, punctuated by crying and screaming, are immediately satisfied. At this period the child is a completely

Major Contributions of Successive Groups to Personality Development

Order	Group	Major Contribution
1	family	acceptance, unconditioned love
2	nursery or play	social experimentation (socialization)
3	school	creative-dynamic expression
4	one sex	identification (socialization), sexual reassurance
5	heterosexual	heteroesexual adjustment
6	occupational	social adequacy, economic security
7	adult voluntary	social acceptance (socialization)
8	family	mating, parenthood, self-perpetuation

For more detailed discussion of these groups, see Slavson, 1938, pp. 339–343; pp. 37–43.

dependent entity but at the same time autonomous. He does not need to submit to any external disciplines or routines or to the will of other people. The plan of his life is centered around his wants, needs, and impulses, which are unconditionally gratified. He is imperious, autocratic, and entirely self-centered, or, as it is sometimes described, autoerotic. However, as he grows older there appears a need for placing limitations upon his functioning. This usually begins in the area of eating, when the nipple is denied him and other means of feeding are substituted. The new feeding methods involve greater participation and effort on his part to gain the sustenance he needs. The baby is no longer completely indulged but is expected to exert himself in order to gain oral and gastrointestinal gratifications.

The next step in disciplining, or habit training, concerns itself with the anal-urethral activity of the child, when toilet training begins. In some ways these limitations are even more difficult for the child to accept, for here he has to give up part of himself to the will of the person who does the training—the nurse or the mother. Just as he rebelled against giving up the nipple and refused to eat from a spoon, he also refuses to submit to the training in the second stage, and it is only with great difficulty that he brings himself to do so.

Education starts later in life—in our culture, around the age of six years, when a definite regimen of acquiring skills, learning facts, and being trained in behavior begins. The present paper is not concerned with this latter stage and will confine itself to the first two stages, namely, nurture and discipline.

One of the common observations in young children with psychologic difficulties is that either nurture, namely, the stage of helplessness and self-indulgence, was extended beyond the normal time and into the phase of discipline, or discipline was begun too early, namely, it was substituted for nurture. Children in the first category, those in whom nurture has been extended into the period of discipline, are usually infantilized, pampered children, who present problems of maladjustment because of weak egos. They are the overprotected persons who either adopt patterns of withdrawal or are unreasonably demanding. Children who have been controlled and frustrated, and whose behavior was managed and directed too early in life, develop behavior disorders, become aggressive, and fall into social maladjustments of various kinds. These are usually children who are fundamentally rejected. The rejection may be either direct (as in the case of restricted children) or indirect (as in the case of overprotected, infantilized children). Parents who basically love their children may either pamper or discipline them, but it can be expected that the presenting problem will be milder than in cases in which either disciplining or pampering is an outcome of basic rejection.

Frequently children come to us for treatment manifesting intense anxieties of a neurotic nature, resulting from such pathologic situations as sleeping in the parental bedroom, being frightened by the dark, or having developed tyrannical superegos or obsessive fears and anxieties. Treatment therefore must be suited to the particular presenting problem, in which, as we shall presently see, the age factor is of major importance.

A child can be so deeply rejected in the family that he cannot satisfactorily relate himself to others. The anxiety aroused by human association is so great that his behavior presents a serious problem to groups and individuals: he disturbs the home atmosphere, the school class, and the play group. On the other hand, the child's aggressions may become inverted and result in withdrawal or schizoid personality, or may form a basis for a neurosis later in life. Still another type of client with whom we deal is the one with a character disorder as differentiated from a mere behavior problem. Here we are confronted with personality qualities that proceed from the adaptations that the child has had to make in order to survive and be accepted. A child who has not had the comfort and security of love and satisfying relations acts out his early infantile demands; satisfaction of these may cause a general improvement. But when, let us say, a child submits to the frustrations and denials of his early life, or when he is forced to make adaptations to pressures from parents and others at an early age, these patterns of behavior and feeling tones become characteristic of his personality as such, and they present themselves as character malformations.

Although we can assume that the sources of maladjustment reside within the personality itself, i.e., that they are intrapsychic, the contributory factors are outside of the individual personality and can be described as extraindividual. This is particularly true where the child's personality has suffered injury. Common to our culture are suppression of spontaneity, inhibition of autonomous trends, and faulty feeling relationships with the supportive individuals, such as parents, nurses, and siblings. Where such tensions have been intense, the organization of the libido and the ego becomes to varying degrees pathologic. The correction of the states that interfere with the individual's satisfactory functioning in his social milieu is the concern of psychotherapy.

Until comparatively recently, psychotherapy was confined to the individual interview (with or without insight giving), on the basis of a transference relation of varying degrees of intensity. Recently, however, it has been found that in specific disturbances, *experience* and *group situations* can correct behavior, overcome fixed early impressions of people, and, where the patient is helped to perceive himself and others in a less lugubrious light, remove psychologic distortions and blockings. In some instances, especially in young children, fundamental changes in the psychic structure can be effected by this method. A child who can be assured of his own worth may overcome the blockings of spontaneity and self-expression that have resulted from early repressive, frustrating, and fear-producing experiences. Some inhibited and frightened children can be helped to overcome their repressed aggression, and when they are thus helped to discharge hostility without fear of being destroyed, their natural impulses and drives are released. As a result, inner tensions are reduced or removed and the child's behavior grows more normal and acceptable. He is then in turn able to accept the regulations and restraints of reality.

It is understandable that a full-blown neurosis requires individual therapy, since the center of a neurosis lies in the early relations to the parents, which are tinged with sexuality. The transference relation with the therapist is central in the treatment here. The confusion of libidinal cravings in a neurotic can be corrected through a true transference only. Such a transference is not necessarily indicated in other types of problems; in such cases the relationship can be on a less deep level. We may say that in the treatment of a disorder of behavior we deal with peripheral personality, while in a neurosis we deal with its core. We have also found that, at least as far as children are concerned, actual experience in realistic situations can correct character malformations in which no deep neuroses are involved. Since the characteristic patterns of reaction are acquired through adaptation to situations, they can be corrected by living different and corrective situations. This is especially true where the neurotic anxieties are not very intense and the child is still young and in a formative state.

What has been said does not mean that transference to the therapist can be eliminated in any type of psychotherapy. The difference lies rather in the depth of the transference and the use that the therapist makes of it. Of necessity, the transference is less intense in group treatment than in individual psychotherapy, both because the types of clients that can be treated in groups need a less intense relation, and because it is greatly modified through the multilateral relations that exist among the members of the group.

The values of the group lie in the fact that it accelerates the initial steps in treatment, that transference to the therapist is facilitated, and that intermember transferences are established. Members of a group give one another support and security; each feels less threatened by the therapist and by the material produced. It is a matter of common observation that productivity is incomparably greater in groups than in individual treatment, and that patients reveal problems at a considerably greater rate. This is true of adults as well as children, in neuroses as well as in other types of personality problems. The fact that other persons have similar difficulties makes each one feel less unique and less stigmatized than he otherwise would. The group members act as emotional catalyzers and activate one another to discussion of their difficulties.

Group therapy is practiced on different levels and in discussing its functions in therapy it is necessary that these levels be kept in mind. While the objective in all psychotherapy is the same, namely, correction and improvement of personality and of social adjustment, it should be recognized that the processes by which these corrections can be achieved vary in different treatment situations. For the very young child, for example, prolonged experiencing of relationships and a favorable environment are adequate. An inhibited child whose growth has been blocked develops patterns of withdrawal and a general quality of unsatisfyingness in mood and character, which eventually will stamp his personality. When such a child is provided, while he is still very young, with opportunities for releasing spontaneous drives, and is encouraged to act out or play out his emotional preoccupations, he can be started well on the way to psychologic balance. This is especially so when the mother (and sometimes the father) can be treated as well. A therapeutic setting that provides the materials and opportunities for acting out feelings and impulses will tend to change the basic moroseness and withdrawal. There are, however, many instances in which deeply disturbed children require individual psychotherapy even at the age of four or five. Such children may need individual therapy solely or in combination with the influence of a group or a nursery class.

For a child who has been abused, frustrated, or punished, or whose parents and nurses have been cold, restricting persons, therapeutic groups provide the possibility of learning human relationships anew. Groups are especially valuable for children who have for various reasons withdrawn from contact with adults. Such children have the opportunity to relate themselves to persons of their own age and within range of their own emotional and social capacities. Through appropriate physical activity and creative work, it is possible for the child to discharge feelings and thus break the dams that block the flow of energy. Repressed resentment and hostility can be discharged with impunity. Egress of these removes inner tensions that have caused many forms of disturbance, such as fears, nightmares, and restlessness. The removal, in the group, of inhibition of self-expression, is equally important to older children, adolescents, and even adults. However, the methods of achieving this vary of necessity in accordance with age. What little children can gain through play and acting out, young children in their latency period and early adolescents achieve through manual activity, creative expression, play, and free interaction with one another. Older adolescents and adults require verbal expression and insight to gain the same benefits.

Children's early behavior in groups is very infantile. They rush about helter-skelter at times; they fight with one another, make demands, are provocative and unreasonable. As their basic problems are resolved, their behavior becomes controlled and mature. We have observed that the conversation in interview group therapy with adolescents and adults is also at first of a very infantile nature. They seem to throw off the customary restraints and freely speak of matters that are taboo in ordinary circumstances. While in young children unrestraint takes the form of hilarity and diffuse aggression, in adolescents and adults the same impulses are expressed in language. In both instances there is, however, a return to the infantile (preoedipal) level, on which the individual was free to act out and do whatever he wished. This is made possible by the accepting and tolerant attitude of the therapist (the good mother) and the assurance that each member receives from the others in the group.

In both activity and interview group therapy, however, the flow of energy gradually becomes canalized. More purposeful and more disciplined behavior emerges. Children begin to work on definite projects and their relations with one another show growth as well. The conversations of adolescents and adults point to their problems and difficulties. This is made possible by the changing attitudes of the patients toward one another, by the changing role of the therapist, and by the development of the transference dynamics. As the life of the group progresses, early antagonisms, dependencies, and ambivalence among the members of the group are transformed into more definite feelings of tolerance, acceptance, and cooperation. The worker's role is gradually changed from that of a neutral, passive, and accepting person. At different stages he becomes an active participant, an image of authority and restraint, and one who understands and interprets problems. The change in functions is determined by the growing maturity of the patients and their increased capacity to accept and cope with reality.

The very important differences in the ego structures of children of different ages make differential treatment imperative. The very young child of prenursery and nursery age has not yet fully repressed primitive impulses and strivings. The taboos and social amenities that come later in life are as yet either nonexistent or inadequately formed. The child is still able to act out his primitive nature and, when he is made afraid to do so, resorts to fantasy and substitute gratifications, usually of a pathologic nature.

We are agreed that problems in young children arise from lack of security and interference with primary biologic functions. It is therefore necessary in the therapy of very young children to supply them with materials through which they can act out problems around these functions and by means of which at the same time spontaneous drives to activity and association can be fulfilled. Water, clay and plasticine, water colors and finger paints, are primary requisites. Dollhouses, and dolls that represent mother, father, and babies, are used in working through fantasies associated with persons in the family, and toy bathroom fixtures help to discharge repressions and fears established in toilet training and to overcome rebellion against the parents associated with evacuation and voiding. Sometimes the child's association in relation to his play is elicited, and simple interpretation is given by the therapist. But when the disturbances relating to these areas have not assumed too great proportion, living over in play of the traumatic situations, under the guidance of a friendly and comforting adult, is sufficient in itself.

The infant or young child is very much a part of the mother, both from the point of view of his own feelings toward the mother and from that of the mother's feelings toward him. This relationship can be described as symbiotic, and whenever it is in any way pathogenic, treatment of both the infant and the mother *as a unit* is essential. The most effective results can be obtained where this procedure is followed. Since the child's personality is still weak, he cannot retain improvement against the pressures of his relationship with the mother. Treatment of mothers of young children is nearly always indicated, and in many instances treatment of the mother alone is adequate to correct whatever problems the infant may have. This is true in the treatment of children at all ages, but is especially in point where infants and young children are concerned.

The use of messy and plastic materials like clay, plasticine, and water has an effect of regulating the child's behavior because of anal satisfactions that he may receive from such play. It is therefore more valuable to set the stage so that he can redirect or sublimate his interests through creative effort. Sometimes direct suggestion for work with suitable materials is indicated.

Little is known as to what the values of a group to a child of three or four may be. The ordinary processes that one observes in groups of children of ten and eleven, for example, do not seem to operate. Very young children appear to act very much like isolates, but the tendency to isolation must be assumed as normal for babies and very young children. Organic immaturity, intensity of emotional dependence on the mother, and the natural fear of the unfamiliar cause the child to isolate himself in his own preoccupations and fantasies. Only occasionally does he break through the walls of his ivory tower of imagination to observe or speak to another child. We can assume, however, that these stray and occasional contacts have great value to the developing child, in normal growth or in therapy.

As the infant grows into childhood he has to give up his autism and narcissism, and his natural egocentricity must be transformed into the ability to make contact with other persons and later to share with them. Though we usually find little actual contact or cooperation among nursery children, there is great awareness of one another among them. This awareness is revealed by imitation, manifest suggestibility, occasional struggles for possession of tools and materials, rivalry for favor with the teacher or therapist. It is this awareness that is important, for through it the growing child breaks the confines of his encapsulation. This process can be characterized as *psycho-osmosis*, i.e., interpenetration of personalities without overt or observable action.

The skillful therapist is able to contrive situations in which some associations can take place. The most common of these occasions are the eating and cleaning-up periods and the outdoor playtime. But one cannot expect too much sociability from children at this age, though more of it appears at mealtime than at any other period. Contacts among such very young children are at best fleeting and perfunctory, for the egocentric (autistic) trends are at all times predominant.

The therapist's role here is not as permissive as it is in dealing with older children. We have seen that freedom is the primary condition for therapy, especially freedom to express aggression and hostility. But freedom and restraint have to be balanced in education and in therapy. The younger the child, the more restraint he needs. Self-restraint is learned when the child incorporates the restraints of adults whom he accepts and trusts. The young child emerging from a state of nurture, when all his wants and whims were unconditionally satisfied, needs time, strength, and maturity to incorporate these restraints. Discipline and authority acceptable to him, and graded in intensity, are necessary for the child's personality integration, but they have to be applied with discrimination and care. The frightened and withdrawn do not need such control; rather, they need release. The overactive and aggressive need restraint. Their diffuse aggressiveness and pugnacious trends have to be impeded. Since the child has not as yet established controls within himself, these must come from the outside, namely, from the adult. It is to a kind and acceptable but firm adult that the child will give up his egoistic and narcissistic characteristics.

In therapy groups, children between the ages of five and seven have a tendency to explosive behavior that may become violent at times. They tend to stimulate and reinforce one another and join together in rather extreme hilarity and destructiveness. There is little value, therapeutically speaking, in this explosive behavior.[1] In individual therapy the therapist can treat the causes of the aggression through release, play therapy, and interpretation, for behavior here is more often related to the central problem of the child than it is in groups. In groups, aggressiveness is suggested by one of the children and taken on by the others without its having special meaning to them,

---

[1] Such behavior is anal in nature and is in fact frequently accompanied by passing of flatus. It has been shown that passing of flatus and belching are used as aggression.

except that they "let off steam." In groups, therefore, explosive activity is not always related to the central problem of each member, and has no particular meaning in terms of therapy of basic difficulties. Release through aggression and hostility has value when it is related to the problem. When it becomes diffuse, it may have the opposite of therapeutic effect, namely, it may disorganize personality. It has the effect of preventing integration.

It must be expected that in the early stages of treatment, after the initial insecurity is thrown off, there will be considerable diffuse hilarity and "wild" behavior. These should be viewed, however, as a preliminary stage in acclimatization and testing of reality, especially testing of the therapist. In a sense this is the most trying period for the latter. He must convince the children of his basic acceptance of them and at the same time prevent too great disorganization of the group and of the children. Most often hilarity is suggested by activating materials (see Slavson, 1943a, pp. 191ff.), which should be removed before the next meeting. Shortening the treatment hour is a good device. Introducing food at a high point in hilarity, a walk outdoors, or a story can also be effective. When hyperactivity persists, it may be advisable to reexamine the personnel of the group. There may be one or more children not as yet ready for group treatment.

An example of the effect of activating material in group disorganization is offered in the following situation. Water in pails was made accessible to children from four and a half to five and a half years old. Because this gave them an opportunity to splash, pour the water back and forth, and throw it at one another, the group was soon in a state almost of panic. They threw paints, water colors, clay, and other materials into the water and onto the floor and trampled on the resulting mess, screaming at the top of their voices and pushing one another around. This was the result of the therapist's unwise procedure in encouraging these very young children to carry water in pails and pour it into basins. Because the children were physically not ready to do this satisfactorily, some water was spilled on the floor; this provoked their extreme behavior. The group became quite uncontrolled and the therapist was unable to check it except by extreme and arbitrary means, thus jeopardizing her role as therapist. It was therefore necessary to remove temporarily the opportunity of using water, and only a small pitcher of water for drinking purposes was placed in the room.

Had the group therapist planned the setting better and not encouraged the children to undertake a task beyond their strength and powers of coordination, she would not have activated disorganization in the group.

It was also discovered that the therapist had to help the children a great deal with their work because the tools were too advanced for them. Drills and saws were too difficult to manage and therefore the therapist had to help. This increased the children's dependence upon the adult. It also kept her very busy, which in turn made her tired and unconsciously irritable. As a result she was at times peremptory with the children as shouts for help came from all sides. Removal of these overdifficult materials and tools helped greatly in stabilizing the group. It was also found that a period of an hour and a half indoors was too long for children so young, and brief walks around the block or along the nearby river after about fifty minutes or an hour of activity reduced much of the tension. When the children became too hilarious, the therapist read to them, which quieted them down, and picture books that the children themselves could read were also helpful.

One therapist directed the children's activities into overmature channels. For example, she put together jigsaw puzzles, with the intention of interesting children of four and five in the same activity. This was evidently an overmature and overdifficult activity. The adult should work with materials that are within the children's capacity and interest range rather than initiate occupations that will require help and direction. It was easier for the children to take up the same activity as the adult when the worker played with blocks. The supervisor also suggested that materials and tools be laid out on the table, instead of being left in a closet difficult for the children to reach; this would also utilize visual suggestion. Among these materials were plasticine, blocks, a few simple tools, dolls, male and female ducks, a monkey marionette, crayons, and large sheets of paper. Because of the children's hyperactivity, paints were temporarily eliminated and large crayons easy for children to hold were provided instead.

Much has been said regarding the value of release of aggressive drives in children. Without going too far afield, it must be said that the release of aggression (abreaction) has therapeutic value when it is an extension of basic emotional and character disturbances of the patient. If there is no such relation, diffuse and uncontrolled hyperactivity serves to keep the child in a state of immaturity. Physical combat among preschool children is infrequent. It occurs most often among children between seven and twelve and is accompanied by intense anger, redness of the face, screaming, and tears. There is probably less fear than anger in the fights of very young children; this seems to be reversed in the case of older children. In the latter, a greater element of fear accompanies fighting. It is of comparatively little value for the ordinary child of three or four either to win in combat or to be vanquished, and the therapist should not permit continuance of the situation. It is advisable to stop fights between young children as soon as the conflict occurs. This does not apply as much in the case of the frightened and inhibited child who through the treatment situation has reached a stage at which he can mobilize power to fight. He should be encouraged to win a fight or two. Older children should be permitted to bring a struggle to a conclusion through their own or group efforts.

Restraint in therapy may be either active or passive. Passive restraint is derived from a situation or from behavior of the therapist as a result of which the child controls his own acts. In activity group therapy (see Slavson, 1940, 1943a, 1944) for children between the ages of nine and fifteen, restraint is almost entirely of a passive nature as far as the role of the therapist is concerned. The situation is so arranged that the materials and tools, as well as the group relations, exert a limiting influence upon the child. Only in rare situations does the therapist use direct control, inhibition, or restraint. In the case of particularly aggressive children with psychopathic trends, or of infantile, overpampered children, direct restraint may be employed. However, in the case of children with behavior disorders or neuroses, direct restraint is not used until the treatment has gone on for a long time, in fact, not until nearly the end of treatment. In the case of very young children, however, the restraint must be direct and early, because situational or passive restraint is not apparent to them.

As we move on in terms of age, we find that we must vary the materials, the equipment, and the role of the therapist. For some older children, between the ages of eight and fourteen, playing with fire is essential. With adequate precautions in setting and equipment, it is possible to supply children with this activity. The less hazardous fire equipment consists of electrical pyro pens with which the child can burn wood and paper and thus work through sexual aggressive trends. An electric stove should be added to the equipment, and cans of sterno placed on asbestos pads are very helpful. The resistivity of materials is also adjusted to suit age levels (Slavson, 1944).

With the older children, the therapist is more permissive than with little ones. Much freedom must be given to children between the ages of seven and twelve, so that they can find their own way in establishing relationships and evolving self-controls. We have found this procedure suitable because at this age there already exists a degree of awareness of good and bad behavior, of right and wrong. Having passed through the oedipal stage and having identified to a degree with parents, the child has taken on some of their mannerisms, values, and attitudes. We must therefore utilize for further growth whatever values the child has already incorporated. To gain most from a social situation, he has to experiment with it and experience reactions. Since he has already incorporated values of behavior, he can register the reactions of the other children and of the therapist, build restraints, and pattern his actions so as to become acceptable to the group. At some time during these years there appears in a child a need for association and play with other children. Although this need in some form has existed before, it now becomes intensified and a real necessity.

The road inward to the child's personality, in those patients who are chosen for group therapy, is the exploitation of this trend, which we describe as *social hunger*. During the years between the ages of seven and twelve, the egocentric trends are normally transformed into social trends. However, some of the group control at these ages, especially in the younger age range, must proceed from the therapist. Though the children are more ready to evolve group controls than they were in prenursery and nursery years, they cannot achieve this entirely on their own. The function of the worker therefore must be graded to the evolving personalities of the children and their readiness to form a group amalgam, as a result of which they develop controls for behavior. The younger the child, the greater the activity of the therapist.

Because the present paper is devoted to group therapy for children up to the age of twelve, variations in treatment of children beyond this age are omitted. However, for the sake of completeness, it must be said that children chosen for group therapy at age ten years and up must be such as are capable of adapting themselves to a group situation and ready to give up egocentricity and undesirable behavior in return for the acceptance of the group. If for any reason such social hunger is nonexistent, as is the case in psychopathic personalities, extreme neurotics, and psychotics, treatment in groups is counterindicated. When the appropriate choice of clientele is made, and the group is balanced in terms of aggressive, normal, and withdrawn children, therapy through the group can be effective. When, however, the combination of the group clientele is faulty, very little can be done for them either through manual activities or the activity of the therapist. The therapeutic medium lies within the group itself and not in extraneous appurtenances. A therapist in charge of an imbalanced group will be compelled to act in the role of the adults who originally contributed to the genesis of the problems of the children. He will be compelled to act as a repressive force and authority, instead of as the symbol of tolerance, acceptance, and goodness that the clients require.

In summary, the function of the group in the treatment of young children lies in three areas: (1) play and activity; (2) association with other children of the same age; (3) the role of the worker.

Materials must be planned to provide projection of aggression and hostility upon objects as substitutes for parents, siblings, and nurses. The materials in the case of very young children, especially, should afford substitution for inhibited activity on the biologic plane, such as oral, anal, and urethral functions. They should supply gratifications of the polymorphous trends of the child and give satisfaction to both his sexual and nonsexual cravings. Playing with water and fire have sexual meaning in the child's fantasy, while playing with clay and water satisfies his anal and oral drives. Shouting and receiving food from the worker assuage oral cravings. Materials should not be too varied or too difficult to understand or manipulate at a given age. The child has to see results of his efforts within a short period of time and should not be expected to postpone gratifications unduly. Materials of greatest value are those of graded resistivity and graded complexity. Materials for young children must be soft and pliable, such as clay, plasticine, paints, and water; but as the child grows older more difficult materials, such as wood and metals, should be introduced. This gradation aids in the development of power and self-regard.

The values of a group to children of different ages, as already indicated, vary greatly. In all instances, however, its major significance for therapy lies in the fact that it supplies a field in which the child may relate himself to others, thus helping him to break through isolation, withdrawal, and aggressive rejection of people. The natural craving for other people causes the individual to go out of himself, as it were, into the human environment, thus leading out from egocentricity and narcissism to object relationships. There is also opportunity for the child to test himself against others and to discover the boundaries of his ego. The presence of other children also offers the possibility of developing patterns of relationship with human beings of the same intellectual, emotional, and social development, in which the feeling of sameness and therefore of comfort and security is greatest. This is particularly of value to only children or to children with intense sibling rivalries. The child utilizes the group in accordance with his capacities, especially as they relate to age. Very young children's groups are less mobile than are groups of older children and require a more carefully set environment. The activities are less varied, repetition of occupations is not as irksome to very young children as it is to older ones, and relationships are on a less personal basis.

As the children grow older, their autonomous trends find expression also in the pattern of the group. They control the situation more, formulate codes, or develop tacit controls for behavior. Definite friendships make their appearance and generally there is greater interaction among the members. At this stage, therefore, the group can be used consciously as a tool in treatment, since the older child needs group association and acceptance more than the preschool child does.

The function of the worker also varies with age. His participation must of necessity be greater in the group of younger children, who are still dependent upon support from an adult. Much of the necessary authority must come from the therapist. The therapist here has to act as authority more frequently and in a more direct manner than he must where older children are concerned. Where authority can evolve from the group itself, the worker need not, in most cases, exercise it. The role of the worker is a constantly changing one, both in relation to the ages of the children and in relation to their evolving personalities. While he functions at first as a source of security and support, his role changes to one of guidance and authority.

REFERENCES

Ackerman, N. W. (1943), Group therapy from the viewpoint of a psychiatrist. *Amer. J. Orthopsychiat.*, 13:678–687.
——— (1944), Dynamic patterns in group psychotherapy. *Psychiat.*, 7:341–348.
Gabriel, B. (1939), An experiment in group treatment. *Amer. J. Orthopsychiat.*, 9:146–169.
Glauber, H. M. (1943), Group therapy from the viewpoint of a psychiatric case worker. *Amer. J. Orthopsychiat.*, 13:671–677.
Lucas, L. (1943–1944), Treatment of young children in a group. *Amer. Acad. Psychiat. Soc. Workers News Letter*, winter issue.

Miller, C., & Slavson, S. R. (1939), Integration of individual and group therapy in the treatment of a problem boy. *Amer. J. Orthopsychiat.*, 9: 792–797.

Slavson, S. R. (1938), The group in development and in therapy. *Proc. Nat. Conf. Soc. Work.*

——— (1939), *Character Education in a Democracy.* New York: New York Association Press.

——— (1940), Group therapy. *Ment. Hyg.*, 24:36–49.

——— (1943a), *An Introduction to Group Therapy.* New York: Commonwealth Fund.

——— (1943b), Principles and dynamics of group therapy. *Amer. J. Orthopsychiat.*, 13:650–659.

——— (1944), Some elements in activity group therapy. *Amer. J. Orthopsychiat.*, 14:578–588.

Chapter 3
Differential Diagnosis and Group Structure in the Outpatient Treatment of Latency Age Children

GERALD SCHAMESS, M.S.S.

Effective group treatment for latency age children is contingent on the therapist's capacity to formulate a group structure that addresses the phase-specific developmental needs of the individuals being treated. Differential diagnosis provides a conceptual framework for creating specific group structures that facilitate the emergence of a developmentally appropriate mode of communication in each model of intervention. Optimally, the mode of communication that emerges should be compatible with the defensive organization, as well as with the level of cognitive, social, and emotional development of individual members and the group as a whole. Under such conditions, group members can express primitive wishes, family conflicts, interpersonal difficulties, and idiosyncratic ways of thinking without being overwhelmed by painful affects and superego prohibitions. When this occurs, individual members form an intense attachment to the group at their phase-specific level of object relatedness. The therapist's ability to recognize the symbolic and developmental meanings of different modes of communication is essential to the treatment process.

The probability that treatment will be successful increases markedly if therapeutic interventions are primarily designed to promote progressive emotional, social, and cognitive development. This proposition is applicable to groups of children in all diagnostic categories. In groups where the participants have achieved a level of intrapsychic organization that permits them to integrate insight and where they demonstrate some motivation to understand themselves, interpretation is the intervention of choice because it best advances the developmental level of individual group members and the group as a whole. In groups where these conditions have not yet evolved, a corrective emotional experience directed toward mastering specific developmental tasks is more effective than interpretation. When treatment is successful, experiential groups tend to evolve into insight-oriented discussion groups.

These principles contrast sharply with the basic assumptions that define group therapy practice with adults. Psychodynamically oriented practitioners assume that adults in most diagnostic categories can be treated effectively in discussion groups, all of which share a common structure. While group size, therapeutic contract, and frequency of meeting may vary from group to group, clinical experience indicates that the therapist's differential use of self is the primary determinant of successful treatment, and that other structural elements usually play a minor role.

GROUP STRUCTURE

By structure I mean the following elements, which may vary considerably in different childrens' groups.

1. Size and location of the group therapy room.
2. Furniture and equipment (mirrors, sandboxes, sinks, climbing equipment, etc.).
3. Toys and craft materials (if any) and how they are located in the room.
4. Size of group, length and frequency of meetings.
5. Along a continuum from permissive to directive, the degree to which specific activities and interactions are planned and/or scheduled in specific time blocks.
6. Along a continuum from active to inactive, the degree to which the therapist:
    a. takes responsibility for maintaining the room, equipment, and supplies as part of the preparation for each session;
    b. provides a gratifying atmosphere for the group as a whole and gratifies particular children in accord with a specific treatment plan;
    c. directly or indirectly establishes limits;

    d. acts as an auxiliary ego for individual members and the group as a whole;
    e. acts in ways that make an object for positive identification;
    f. encourages or insists upon verbalization;
    g. explores, clarifies, and interprets.

The fourth, fifth, and sixth structural elements will be discussed throughout this paper in regard to specific diagnostic categories and models of treatment. The first three elements, while not usually considered very significant, are nonetheless crucial in establishing, maintaining, and managing cohesive childrens' groups. I will discuss them in some detail below.

The Physical Environment: The Room, Its Location and Furnishings

    Although such factors as the size, location, and furnishings of the group therapy room may not seem critical to the treatment process, children are profoundly influenced by their physical environment. It is an observable fact that a large, sparsely furnished room will encourage large muscle activity, even among relatively constricted children. Conversely, a small, densely furnished room will precipitate intense emotional and physical interaction while restricting motility. A damaged room (broken furniture and fixtures, toys with missing parts, etc.) will inspire destructiveness, and a dirty room will encourage messing.

    In rooms containing expensive furniture and carpeting intended for adult use, latency age children may feel they are expected to be on their best behavior. In such circumstances, group members typically express their discomfort by testing the therapist's reaction to breakage and messiness. If the room must be kept in pristine order, interpersonal conflict quickly arises between therapist and members. Extensive conflict of this kind frequently threatens the continued existence of the group and the employment of the therapist. For this reason, staff conference and board meeting rooms are not appropriate places in which to conduct children's groups.

    A related problem arises when the group therapy room is located in the center of a busy clinic setting. The noise, activity level, and curiosity of even the most sedate children's discussion group is likely to be disruptive to therapists conducting individual treatment in adjacent rooms. Unless one has a need to repeatedly explain the complexities of children's group therapy to an audience of disapproving colleagues, it is advantageous to find a room in which the group can meet in relative seclusion.

Equipment and Play Materials

Similar dynamics affect how play equipment is likely to be used by specific groups of children. Latency age children respond to their physical environment and its contents as if they have received an explicit message regarding the parameters of acceptable behavior. When there is a significant discrepancy between what the physical environment invites or prohibits and what the group leader expects, children react as if they have been given confused and conflicting instructions akin to a "double bind." Depending on the group's composition and the dynamics of individual members, specific groups react idiosyncratically to a confusing physical environment. Nonetheless, one can be certain that there will be a reaction, and that it will be problematic for everyone concerned, group members and therapist alike.

Ordinarily, in a "good enough" physical environment group members use whatever equipment is provided to express themselves through action, talk, or symbolic play in ways compatible with their level of development. Within limits, however, the therapist can shape the form of communication the group adopts by giving careful thought to the likely effects of physical surroundings on the core conflicts, expressive needs, interactive patterns, and psychosexual development of the group members. For example, the inclusion of a punching bag as part of a group's play equipment is likely to evoke high levels of aggression that will be expressed in real or "play" fights between group members. The therapist who provides such equipment should be prepared to deal with aggressive interactions, and should also have some conviction that the direct expression of aggressive impulses through fighting will be therapeutic for individual members and the group as a whole. Similarly, if there are clothed family dolls in the room, at least some group members will undress them, thereby focusing the group process on sexual curiosity, excitement, and the need for accurate information about gender differences and reproduction. Here again the therapist, presumably having made an informed choice as to play equipment, should be prepared to deal with sexual content, both symbolically and through direct discussion.

CONSTRUCTING A DEVELOPMENTALLY APPROPRIATE MEDIUM OF COMMUNICATION

Most latency age children do not talk readily to adults about their inner world or family problems. Although such reticence is developmentally appropriate and characterizes all children in this age group, it may also be the consequence of significant developmental pathology and should be considered in the context of a careful diagnostic assessment. I will discuss the normative issues first and then consider the communication problems that arise as a result of developmental arrests and character malformations.

Phase-Specific Issues

The psychoanalytic literature tends to view latency age children as normatively pliant, well behaved, and educable. Sarnoff (1976) discusses latency as the visible manifestation of a specific ego organization that allows children to cope with intense unconscious drive activity neither acknowledged nor accepted by Western industrial and postindustrial society. The specific defensive organization that emerges during latency is characterized by an expanding capacity to use fantasy, symbolism, and cognition to create and maintain a stable balance between drive activity and defense, thereby creating an impression of compliance and malleability. The capacity to use symbolism and cognition, both defensively and to achieve mastery, facilitates a gradual initiation into the expectations and role possibilities of society, thereby preparing the child for adult responsibilities and gratifications within a particular social context.

In many clinic settings, therapists do not have any real choices as to where the group therapy room is located, its size, or even how it is equipped. Under such circumstances it is particularly important to choose a treatment model appropriate not only to the developmental needs of the group members but also to the physical environment available. In this matter, I feel as much concern for the therapist as for the children. During fifteen years as a group therapy consultant, I have seen far too many talented therapists leave the field after excruciating experiences in which they attempted to use a treatment model that did not recognize the members' developmental needs, or was incompatible with the physical resources available. While some group failures are probably unavoidable, failures that result from the use of an inappropriate physical environment are not. Before starting a group, the therapist should consider whether the available room, equipment, and materials can facilitate the emergence of a developmentally appropriate medium of communication, and whether these elements will combine to form an appropriate holding environment for the children being treated. If the physical environment is not suitable and cannot be modified, it is frequently possible to correct the deficiencies by selecting different children, adjusting the group balance, or changing other structural elements. If none of these measures seem likely to be successful, it is far better to delay or abandon the project than to subject both therapist and children to a therapeutic failure.

In my opinion, Sarnoff's viewpoint is accurate but incomplete, in that it does not systematically consider how latency age children are affected by close friendships and unstructured group situations. Although Sarnoff clearly acknowledges the intensity of covert drive activity during latency, I think he does not fully recognize the degree to which latency age children are able to gratify a range of pregenital impulses, particularly sexual curiosity, in private interactions with peers. Such activities provide a partial explanation for the intensity with which latency age children conceal their "passions" from the adult world. Even when direct gratification is not attempted, latency age children give expression to drive derivatives, intense affects, and conflictual family dramas, through physical activity, fantasy play, dramatic play, and competitive games. These modes of expression allow the child to explore a range of socially structured and approved ways of vicariously gratifying particular impulses, without risking rejection from a libidinal object, or the shame, guilt, anxiety, and fear of punishment connected with being discovered by an adult while engaged in forbidden activities.

The forms in which these real and fantasized explorations are symbolized constitute an age-specific mode of communication in which latency age children are fluent. While adults typically have difficulty understanding the unconscious meaning of such play, children recognize it almost immediately. It is such an explicit form of communication in latency that groups of children create elaborate collective play activities without recourse to speech, except for the few words necessary to establish the common theme that is being developed. Erikson (1977) captures both the intensity of passion and the richness of symbolic nonverbal communication in his discussion of the games that children begin to play in latency:

> symbolic acts can be committed, symbolic emotions experienced,

and alternations of symbolic doom and triumph accepted which in 'real life' might mean the absolute dominance or total defeat of one or the other side, with all the inhumanities and reality distortions attending the reciprocity of mortal enmity among different species. It is in gamesmanship that man is most human in the sense of an acceptance of his adversary as equally human: as one side enjoys unambiguous victory with usurpation, and clear-cut defeat without annihilation, an equilibrium of skill and chance is maintained. [p. 72]

If we acknowledge that latency is characterized by the growing conviction that it is necessary to conceal sexual and aggressive longings, not only from oneself (through repression and displacement) but also from the prying eyes of parents and other adults, we can begin to understand the quiet, covert warfare that normatively characterizes certain relationships between adults and children. During the latency years, adults try to educate and socialize children, who alternate between compliance and resistance. When inclined to resist, they do so through reticence, fantasies, and networks of peer friendships and activities hidden from the coercive power of adult authority. Consider the plight of any substitute teacher who takes over a fourth or fifth grade class: warfare is openly declared, and the children take overt pleasure in the tricks and humiliations they inflict on an authority whose rule is temporary and insecure. Although adults find this phenomenon disconcerting (as children intend it to be), it seems clear that both reticence and covert warfare are in the service of progressive development for children in this society.

As group therapists, then, we would be well advised to respect these phase-specific characteristics. By making provision for nonverbal modes of communication that permit group members symbolically to test our understanding and acceptance, we create conditions that will eventually make it possible for them to talk openly about their feelings and problems. Because we as therapists are fluent in verbal communication, we tend to assume that discussion groups will be easier to manage, or will produce deeper insights. In making this assumption, we forget that talk does not necessarily help us enter the inner world of the child, nor does insight directly address the developmental needs of children with serious deficiencies in ego development.

Developmental Pathology

When we consider developmental pathology, communication issues become extremely significant. The capacity to talk in a meaningful way about inner experiences and interpersonal relationships comes about as the result of maturational processes linked to the development of a coherent sense of personal identity, the establishment of object constancy, and the evolution of a defensive organization based primarily on repression, isolation, and intellectualization (Blanck and Blanck, 1974, pp. 114–115). Verbal communication implies that the individual can delay gratification, tolerate considerable amounts of frustration and maintain substantive control over motility. From a psychosexual perspective, these accomplishments are seen in children who have reached the phallic stage of development and whose functioning reflects a neurotic or "almost neurotic" level of structural organization.

The simple fact is that most of the children treated in therapeutic groups do not even approach that level of organization. Asking children with significant developmental delays to use speech as their primary medium of communication is akin to demanding that they cure themselves as a prerequisite to entering treatment. Most developmental and character problems evolve as part of a defensive effort to deal with unmastered maturational tasks and to compensate for inadequately developed ego capacities. While speech is certainly present in most children with developmental arrests or character malformations, it is not a reliable indicator of what such children know or feel, nor is it used by them primarily as a mode of interpersonal communication. Successful treatment of these disorders is based on an effort to help the child with ego and superego capacities that are distorted, absent, or only partly developed. "Compensatory" models of treatment therefore differ markedly from the more traditional psychoanalytic models, in which the primary therapeutic goal is to analyze defenses and resistances for the purpose of uncovering unconscious wishes and anxieties.

Traditionally, most models of children's group therapy have provided significant opportunities for compensatory ego development by offering an accepting physical and emotional environment in which children are initially encouraged to express themselves in ways compatible with their level of psychosexual development (usually through some combination of activity, games, fantasy play, and conversation). In these group models, maturation and trust are measured by a growing capacity to talk openly about affectively charged issues. For children with serious developmental pathology, the capacity to engage in meaningful discussion with peers and an adult therapist indicates the completion of a compensatory therapeutic process in which missing ego and superego functions have gradually been established as integral parts of the child's intrapsychic organization. For most children treated in groups, this accomplishment is the culmination, not the starting point, of effective treatment.

DIAGNOSES AND MODELS

The rest of this chapter will address differential treatment approaches with children in three major diagnostic categories: characterological or developmental disturbances, psychosis, and neurosis. In discussing these categories I will refer to both psychoanalytic formulations and the DSM III typology. A careful use of diagnosis increases the likelihood that different clinicians will reach some level of consensus in categorizing children with roughly the same presenting problem and personality structure. However, it should be understood that any diagnostic assessment of a latency age child is of necessity tentative. During latency, intrapsychic structure is only provisionally established and children are still quite open to environmental and interpersonal influences. While problematic character patterns arise in nascent form as part of the child's adaptive effort to deal with environmental stress and pathogenic object relationships, these patterns do not take on the rigidity of adult character pathology until well into adolescence. The therapist who diagnoses latency age children should therefore be prepared to see uneven and shifting patterns of internal structure and symptomatology. Differential diagnosis is difficult, and at best can only approximate the configuration of shifting internal structures.

All of the treatment models described in this chapter are designed to bring about substantial personality ("structural") change over time. While symptom alleviation is an important treatment goal, these methodologies are fundamentally designed to help children change major adaptive patterns, modify self-concept, and reorganize internal structure. Accordingly, treatment is most effective when children continue with the same group and therapist for relatively long periods of time (one to three years). From a psychoanalytic viewpoint, the degree of personality change that takes place in these groups is noteworthy, as most of the models are essentially experiential or "compensatory" in nature, and do not attempt to promote insight through the use of interpretation.

Since the prototypical group methodologies for children (Slavson, 1943; Axline, 1947; Ginott, 1961; Schiffer, 1969) are most effective in treating an intermediate level of characterological or developmental pathology, I will begin by discussing that diagnostic category and in the process will briefly indicate how various models originated and evolved over time. Subsequently I will consider group models for borderline levels of organization, psychosis, and neurosis.

THE INTERMEDIATE LEVEL OF CHARACTER PATHOLOGY AND DEVELOPMENTAL DEVIATION

This level comprises children with less than neurotic intrapsychic structure who are fixated at, or have regressed to, preoedipal levels of organization. These children are well described by the typology proposed by Kernberg (1970) for adult patients. In patients with an intermediate level of character pathology, ego and superego functions are not yet fully differentiated. As a consequence, intense wishes for love, power, and admiration coexist with contradictory and relatively primitive demands for perfection and goodness. Clinically, one sees "disassociated expressions of unacceptable sexual and/or aggressive needs. . . , a structured impulsiveness. . . , decreased capacity for experiencing guilt. . . , and the contradictory demands of sadistic, prohibitive superego nuclei, on the one hand, and rather primitive (magical, overidealized) forms of the ego ideal, on the other hand" (pp. 806–807). Ego defenses are organized primarily around repression, although reaction formation, regression, acting out, dissociation, splitting, denial, and projection may all be present to varying degrees. Object relations are stable for the most part and there is some capacity for tolerating ambivalence and interpersonal conflict.

DSM III describes these children in several different categories, including:

314.01 and 314.00: attention deficit disorder with and without hyperactivity.
312.21: conduct disorder, socialized, nonaggressive.
312.00: conduct disorder, undersocialized, nonaggressive.
312.23: conduct disorder, socialized, aggressive (mild to moderate in severity).
312.21: avoidant disorder of childhood.
313.81: oppositional disorder.

307.60: functional neurosis.
302.60: gender identity disorder of childhood.
401.60: dependent personality disorder.

Children in these categories account for a very high percentage of all children evaluated for treatment in clinical settings. When such children are considered for individual treatment, they should routinely be evaluated for group. My clinical experience indicates that approximately 50 percent of characterologically disturbed children treated privately, in clinics, or in school settings could benefit from either exclusive group therapy or a combination of individual and group treatment. When such children are asked to express a preference, a remarkably large percentage choose a play-oriented group rather than individual treatment. The fact that so few children are treated in therapeutic groups does not reflect on the modality nearly as much as it does on the limited opportunities for group treatment that exist in most clinical settings, and on the resistance that most psychodynamically oriented individual therapists have to treating children in groups.

Models, Structures, and Modes of Communication

Activity group therapy and the nondirective play group. The major models of group treatment for children with an intermediate level of character pathology have evolved from the pioneering work of Virginia Axline (1947) and S. R. Slavson (1943). They are fully described by their originators and constitute a set of variations on a central theme. The basic theme involves the creation of a balanced, "permissive" (Slavson), or "nondirective" (Axline) single-sex group meeting in a large, well-equipped playroom designed to provide a safe physical environment for the group members. "Neutral" arts and crafts materials that can be used either for guided regressive play or to promote mastery (Slavson, 1943) are provided in the activity group therapy model. Evocative toys that encourage fantasy play and memories of pathogenic family interactions (Axline, 1947) are provided in the nondirective play group. Both types of play equipment evoke wishes, memories, and fears that are then expressed in the group setting. Because a wide range of play or craft materials is freely available during each meeting, individual group members can choose the mode of communication best suited to their level of cognitive and emotional development. The group process itself serves as a medium through which pathological family roles can be replicated and modified. In both models the therapist organizes and maintains the physical environment and the play equipment, thus creating an emotionally safe and gratifying atmosphere in which the children can express themselves freely. In activity group therapy, the therapist establishes situational limits through nonverbal interactions with individual children and with the group as a whole, while also serving as a model for positive identification. In the nondirective play group, the therapist acts as a verbal mirror reflecting back what each child is saying, doing, and feeling, thus encouraging group members to think and talk about the fantasies or problematic interactional patterns they are expressing through their play.

The modified nondirective play group and the therapeutic play group. Ginott (1961) and Schiffer (1969) modify the two basic models in ways that minimize the differences between them. They recommend (1) the use of a smaller room to control motility; (2) inclusion of both craft materials and evocative toys to increase the range of expressive and communicative modes; and (3) a more active, limit-setting role for the therapist with the aim of reducing the level of intensity of behavioral regression, while maintaining the fundamental principles of permissiveness and acceptance on which each model is based.

Among other things, these changes in structure encourage group members to talk with one another. While Schiffer and Ginott value and encourage the increased verbal interaction, they agree with Slavson that for latency age children "insight is frequently derivative and non-verbal and [is] attained without the aid of interpretations and explanations.... Self-knowledge is developed through experience with many different relationships" (Ginott, 1961, p. 10; see also Schiffer, 1969, pp. 95–96).

By modifying group structure in ways that constrain behavorial regression while encouraging fantasy play and discussion, Ginott and Schiffer make it possible for clinicians to use the activity-play group methodology in a number of clinical settings where noise, mess, and physical activity create problems (schools, private practice offices, clinics without a special group therapy room, etc.). In addition, these changes expand the group's capacity to provide effective treatment for children who approach the neurotic range of intrapsychic structure and who therefore need an opportunity to verbalize their conflicts. At the lower end of the diagnostic spectrum, properly balanced groups can accommodate some impulse-ridden children, who need clear behavioral limits and benefit from the opportunity to identify with a strong and active therapist.

While these changes in group structure and therapeutic role generate new treatment opportunities, some benefits of the original methodologies are attenuated because of the changes. The revised models are somewhat less effective in addressing the developmental needs of children with gender identity, avoidant, oppositional, and dependent personality disorders (DSM III: 302.60; 312.21; 313.81; 301.60). Children with these symptom constellations derive particular benefit from a group experience in which they can become aware of and express hostile feelings through openly defiant behavior that opposes the ordinary expectations of parental authority. The original activity-play group models provide unequalled opportunity for constricted and superego-bound children to act defiantly without creating real problems for themselves or others, and without being overwhelmed by the guilt and anxiety that originally constricted their character development.

Activity-interview groups and interpretive group psychotherapy. In spite of the modifications that Ginott and Schiffer initiate, they remain committed to an essentially experiential and compensatory form of treatment. Kraft (1967) and Sugar (1974) further modify the basic models, with the intent of using interpretation as a significant instrument of change. Kraft (1967) describes an "activity-interview group" methodology in which "the therapist actively interprets to the children their actions and verbalizations as they involve themselves with the usual materials used in play therapy and activity therapy"; he adds that older latency age children (nine to eleven) will readily accept an interview format "with little toy play and no use of tools or arts and crafts" (p. 1464). The transition to an interview format is facilitated by including children of both sexes in the same group. In a personal communication Kraft (1983) notes that "girls tend to act as a quieting influence on the boys . . . [allowing us to] devote at least 20–30 minutes of the session to 'problem talk.'" Summing up, Kraft (1967) states: "In this type of group therapy, as with pubertal and adolescent groups, the children verbalize in a problem-oriented manner with the awareness that problems brought them together and that the group aims to change them. They report dreams, fantasies, day-dreams, traumatic and unpleasant experiences. These and their group behavior undergo open discussion" (p. 1464).

Sugar (1974) describes a model involving "unstructured" single-sex groups in which considerable use is made of evocative play equipment and craft material. During the initial stage of the group process, the therapist acts to keep the group together and to help group members address their feelings and needs to one another, rather than to the therapist. This is accomplished through "defaulting" techniques in which the therapist refers comments and questions to the group as a whole, thereby making it clear that he will neither meet the group's dependency needs nor provide an authoritarian structure. Once cohesion has developed, the therapist actively interprets, basing his interpretations on the symbolic themes that emerge as individuals, dyads, and the group as a whole play with various pieces of equipment. Interpretations may deal with thoughts, feelings, and attitudes, as well as with family dynamics, interpersonal patterns, and transference phenomena.

In this format, play materials clearly serve as a significant medium of expressive communication. Sugar emphasizes that the therapist must be sensitively attuned to whether specific play equipment is having a constructive or a disorganizing effect on individual children and on the group as a whole. When particular equipment stimulates "overwhelming" sexual or aggressive impulses, it is necessary to remove either the child from the equipment or the equipment from the group. A particularly interesting aspect of this model is that Sugar routinely includes mildly retarded and physically disabled children in the group, thereby creating a group culture in which children are expected to accept differences and disabilities that are both real and symbolic in nature.

Overview. The introduction of interpretation as a major therapeutic intervention makes it necessary to reevaluate the ways in which these models are conceptualized. It is difficult to determine whether interpretation is viable in these modified group models because Kraft and Sugar are so skillful in their use of it, or whether it works because they are treating a large proportion of children whom Slavson, Axline, Ginott, and Schiffer would diagnose as essentially neurotic. Because the DSM III classification focuses on observable behavior, it provides a useful instrument with which to compare cases treated in interpretative group therapy with those treated in essentially experiential groups. Such a comparison could clarify this particular issue if practitioners were willing to present case material in greater detail.

A second, more complicated problem arises in attempting to determine what effect interpretation has on the group process and individual change in the treatment of characterologically disturbed children. The work that Kraft and Sugar report indicates that within the context of positive individual and group transferences, latency age children do not necessarily view interpretation as an assault on their self-esteem and ego integrity. This is a significant finding, given the degree to which characterologically disturbed children ordinarily anticipate disapproval from adult authorities. Although this finding seems valid, I remain dubious about the proposition that latency age children in this diagnostic category are able to emotionally "metabolize" interpretation in ways that promote structural change. My own clinical experience, both as therapist and consultant, indicates that these children tend to view interpretation in one of three ways: at best it is seen as an expression of the therapist's interest, positive feelings, and wish to be helpful; at worst it is experienced as a criticism or humiliation and an expression of the therapist's dislike; usually it is simply ignored because the child (defensively) feels it is irrelevant and uninteresting.

Interpretation in this type of group treatment is of therapeutic value when the child views it as a sign of the therapist's positive interest and affection. Children with significant characterological disturbances do not ordinarily feel loved or understood, and are quite uncertain about whether they are even marginally acceptable. In an illuminating example, Sugar (1974) describes making a rather elegant transference interpretation to a child in one of his groups. He connects the child's statement that "I can always play alone," with an earlier request to go to the bathroom and the child's unhappiness about his upcoming vacation. He interprets that the child may be indicating a desire to play alone in the bathroom with his penis. The child responds with "mock shock" followed by laughter and then the exclamation, "Oh, Dr. Sugar!" (p. 663). While we could debate the dynamic effects of this interpretation, what seems evident is the child's pleasure in Sugar's acceptance of his masturbatory wish.

While at this time it seems unlikely that different practitioners will agree as to the importance and function of interpretation in these group models, there is substantial agreement regarding some of the other curative factors. All of these groups offer a safe physical and emotional environment in which children can act out or symbolize a wide range of sexual and aggressive impulses that have arisen as a result of pathogenic family relationships. This occurs in the presence of an adult transference figure who is able to accept these impulses, while also containing any acting out that is likely to be self-destructive or result in serious social and interpersonal consequences. The group as a whole becomes not only a protective environment, but also a gratifying one. Winnicott (1965) makes the point that the characterologically disturbed child's "maladjustment" is always the result of "a failure of the environment to adjust to the child's absolute needs at a time of relative dependence"—a "failure of nurture." He notes further that the child (and later the adult) never completely loses the hope that "the environment may acknowledge and make up for the specific failure that did the damage" (p. 207). The combination of permissiveness, gratification, and safety in these group models provides the "special management" or, in Winnicott's terms, the compensatory "spoiling" that allows group members (1) to reexperience the original "failure in nurturance" and (2) to restructure both object representations and real relationships in ways that reflect greater trust as well as a more positive internal balance between aggressive and libidinal impulses.

The group's effectiveness is also derived from the changes in primitive and sadistic superego prohibitions that result as the therapist and other group members gradually come to represent behavioral expectations and ideals that are more realistic, reasonable, and humane. As these new expectations are internalized and the child experiences increasing success in meeting them, self-representations shift in a more positive direction. The child begins to demonstrate real confidence in his or her capacity to exercise appropriate ego control over unacceptable libidinal and aggressive impulses. This is accompanied by a marked reduction in anxiety as well as by a newly acquired capacity to acknowledge problems and talk about them in an emotionally meaningful way. When these changes have taken place, the child has reached a neurotic level of functioning, and in most instances is able to resume progressive emotional development without further treatment.

THE LOWER LEVEL OF CHARACTER PATHOLOGY: BORDERLINE AND PREPSYCHOTIC CONDITIONS

In describing the lower level of character pathology in adults, Kernberg (1970) emphasizes the following structural phenomena.

There is a minimal level of superego integration, accompanied by severe impairment in the capacity to experience guilt or concern for others. The delimitation between ego and superego is not well established and the synthetic function of the ego is severely impaired. The ego's defensive organization is based on extensive use of splitting, projective identification, idealization, and devaluation. Under ordinary circumstances these mechanisms are adequate to prevent psychotic decompensation and to maintain homeostasis in spite of a preponderance of pregenital aggression. Aggressive identifications are seen in both ego and superego functioning. They emerge in the form of "sadistically infiltrated polymorphous perverse infantile drive derivatives which contaminate all the internalized and external object relations. . . ." Object relations are experienced as either need-gratifying or threatening, in the absence of both object constancy and an integrated self-concept. Kernberg includes infantile personalities, antisocial personalities, impulse-ridden characters, inadequate personalities, and most narcissistic personality disorders in this diagnostic category, which in his view constitutes the "field of borderline disorders" (pp. 807–810).

Pine (1974) observes that borderline states in children arise as a consequence of arrested or aberrant development that interferes with the establishment of basic ego functions and appropriate levels of object relatedness. These deficits reflect primary developmental failures rather than secondary regressions. Pine argues that clinicians should consider borderline pathology along a continuum that emphasizes "aspects of pathological phenomena" rather than diagnostic entities. Accordingly, he distinguishes between several different levels of borderline adaptation, including chronic ego deviance, shifting levels of ego organization, internal disorganization in response to external disorganization, incomplete internalization of psychosis, and severe stunting of ego development. Although Pine's formulation is not markedly different from Kernberg's, it is noteworthy because he does not include case examples of impulse-ridden children in his typology.

While I accept Kernberg's contention that the impulse-ridden character is a specific symptomatic manifestation of borderline organization, in developing effective methods of group intervention for "borderline" children there are compelling reasons to identify at least two distinct symptom configurations. Clinical evidence indicates that aggressive acting out, whatever its aim, is typically directed against the perceived "bad object," with the intent of alleviating states of intolerable tension while protecting a precarious internalized representation of the "good object." For this reason it seems likely that splitting is an underlying mechanism in determining the object against whom aggressive acting out is directed. However, even if splitting is an intrinsic component of aggressive acting out, there is ample evidence to demonstrate that acting out is neither a necessary component nor a consequence of splitting. Children who exhibit bizarre mannerisms and peculiar ways of thinking, who are anxiety-ridden and lost in fantasy, who are withdrawn and isolated, or pathetically needy and dependent, present behavior patterns and management problems quite different from those presented in impulse-ridden children. While it is sometimes therapeutically indicated to add one or two impulse-ridden children to groups consisting of five or more withdrawn and anxiety-ridden children, such decisions should be based on a careful assessment of (1) the degree to which the aggressive child will need to dominate and sadistically exploit weaker and more vulnerable children, and (2) the child's capacity to respond positively to external limits. For all of these reasons, impulse-ridden children frequently have a better prognosis (and are less problematic to the group as a whole) when they are treated in relatively homogeneous groups. On the basis of these considerations, I will divide the borderline diagnostic category into two sections, one focused on group treatment with homogeneous groups of impulse-ridden children, the other on group methodologies with ego-damaged children whose developmental deficits manifest themselves through peculiarities in thinking, withdrawal, and panic states, but not through chronic failures in impulse control.

Models, Structure, and Modes of Communication for Work with Impulse-Ridden Children

DSM III categories:
312.00: conduct disorder, undersocialized, aggressive.
312.23: conduct disorder, socialized, aggressive (severe).

The Small Room Technique. In a previous review of differential group models (Schamess, 1976), I included the Small Room Technique (Anthony, 1957) as a specific methodology for the treatment of impulse-ridden children. After considerable discussion with other practitioners, I have decided not to review that methodology here.

While the model is conceptually clear and ideologically appealing, particularly to psychodynamically oriented clinicians, it is so deeply rooted in Anthony's formidable skill as a diagnostician and practitioner that it is extremely difficult for other practitioners to replicate. The degree of noise, physical activity, fighting, and peer intimidation that is likely to occur in these groups makes them impracticable for most clinic settings and impossible for the inexperienced therapist. Even well-trained group therapists find it difficult to formulate interpretations that effectively limit acting out with groups of impulse-ridden children who literally have "no exit" from the group room. For all of these reasons I think the methodology can best be considered a *tour de force*, to be attempted only by the confident and experienced practitioner. As such, it does not seem readily applicable as a therapeutic model.

The "Common-Sense Club." Epstein and Altman (1972) discuss the evolution of a discussion group model called the Common-Sense Club. The participants are told that the group is a place for them to talk about their difficulties and that its main purpose is "to help the members learn how to use their heads to stay out of trouble." Snacks are served but no equipment is provided. Interpretation of underlying meaning is not attempted. The therapist establishes physical and verbal limits, actively disapproving of acting out and encouraging group censure of "babyish" or antisocial behavior. If the therapist is able to maintain his "power position" in the group the children become eager to please him in order to win his praise. To accomplish this they gradually modify their delinquent behavior in accord with his expectations and learn to criticize and denigrate antisocial behavior as reported or acted out by group members. The act of propitiating the therapist is viewed not as mere submission but "as a normal developmental phenomena for this age group" (p. 99). As the group members achieve better impulse control, discussion about realistic life goals and problems in interpersonal relationships become increasingly significant in the group process.

Parents are invited to attend one children's group session monthly. This provides an opportunity for the group and the therapist to learn about "distortions and blatant fabrications" (p. 98). According to the authors, the confrontations that occur in these meetings open meaningful avenues for communication between parent and child.

Intermediary group treatment. Ganter, Yeakel, and Polansky (1967) report on the procedures and results of a study in which 47 children, ages five to twelve, were treated in a series of experimental outpatient groups. More than half of them had been referred for residential treatment and another quarter had been recommended for removal from their homes. All of them were hyperactive and aggressive or showed other indications of serious ego damage. Thorough clinical evaluation indicated that they were "inaccessible" to outpatient treatment.

The groups met twice weekly for two-hour sessions over a period of six months. Each group had a membership of six children. When possible the groups were coeducational, though boys outnumbered girls in the study four to one. Male and female cotherapists were used consistently. Parent group meetings were held on a weekly basis.

The group methodology was designed specifically to increase each child's capacity for verbal self-observation and to help define and strengthen ego boundaries ("organizational unity"), particularly in regard to impulse control and perception of reality. To achieve the latter goal, each group session was planned to provide a repetitive, limiting structure of carefully graded activities the children could successfully complete in very limited periods of time. A typical meeting would provide regular periods of craft activity, large-muscle game activity, painting, rhythm activity, and feeding. The therapists helped children move from one activity to another with minimal disorganization, offering recognition for accomplishments, and encouraging problem solving by helping individual children establish priorities and complete activities. Children who were unable to maintain impulse control were removed from the group for brief individual interviews during which they were encouraged to discuss their feelings.

Attempts to increase the child's capacity for verbal self-awareness developed out of the painting and rhythm activities. The therapist would verbally associate colors, visual forms, and rhythmic patterns with human experiences and emotions. As the children played, the therapists would use the already established labels ("red is anger," etc.) to comment on the child's activity. These comments frequently evoked verbal responses that reflected the child's emotional state and attitude. A tape recorder provided opportunities for the children to listen to themselves and each other. Recordings were made frequently, particularly when a child was angry or upset. While the child talked into the recorder, the therapist would interject reflective comments or clarifications of what the child was saying. Tapes were available for the children to listen to on request.

The therapists in this project were extremely careful not to be drawn into transference situations that would replicate the original pathogenic family relationships. Initially they ignored provocative behavior and refused to become involved in any type of struggle except when a child had to be removed from the room. Later in treatment, they confronted some types of provocative or impulsive behavior within the group, emphasizing their repetitive, nonadaptive aspects.

Given the extent of pathology, the results of this project were impressive. Sixty percent of the children in the original population were able to complete successfully a trial period in individual treatment after six months of group. Two-thirds of the children, who had originally been referred for residential treatment, were able to continue in the community. Nine of the eleven children who had been suspended from school at the beginning of the study were attending school regularly at the time of a follow-up study two years later. Although the methodology is unconventional in terms of group therapy models, the results indicate that the technique deserves replication and careful evaluation. Unfortunately, in spite of its success, no replication has been attempted since the original trial in 1967. In several personal communications, the authors state their conviction that the methodology is viable if practitioners are given adequate administrative and supervisory support.

Modified activity group. Frank (1983) describes a methodology for the treatment of "ego-impoverished" impulse-ridden girls. Starting with the physical environment and craft equipment that characterize activity group therapy, Frank modified the therapist's function in the group and added role playing as a significant medium of communication. The resulting methodology was designed to address the developmental needs of children who lack "self-awareness, an understanding of the relationship between feelings and behavior, and any sense of the effects their actions might have on the feelings of others" (p. 150).

Frank proposes that "children who do not have the equipment to curb or sublimate their impulsive behavior need not only the safety of protective limits, but simultaneously, active tutoring in ego capacities. If the group members cannot carry the main role of 'teacher' then the therapist must initially, and often, for a period of time" (p. 149). By suggesting a number of possible solutions to interpersonal conflicts, all of which represent higher levels of ego functioning than the group members have attained, the therapist attempts to interest the group in different ways of dealing with primitive impulses, intense feelings of deprivation, and sibling rivalry. At first the group responds to this initiative by choosing the most structured and obsessive of the options offered. Over time, however, a preference for talking solutions gradually emerges, thereby introducing group discussion as a significant part of the ongoing therapeutic process.

In this model the therapist initiates role playing both as a non-threatening, ego supportive medium of communication and as a way of moderating the level of intensely aggressive interaction that seems normative for these children. Initially, the typical role playing involves an infuriated student locked in verbal conflict with an unempathetic and punitive teacher. The therapist acts as an alter ego, attempting to give voice to the student's underlying fearfulness and desire for approval from the adult authority. During this stage of treatment, the group members typically insist that they never have any such feelings or wishes. Over time, however, they are able to acknowledge how frightened they are of being afraid, and how difficult it is for them to express any need for approval or affection. "The role-playing provided them with distance, action and the opportunity to learn about themselves. . . . Eventually they could understand the teacher's feelings, and finally, the interaction between student and teacher" (p. 151). It is interesting to note that Holland and Nagler (1981) also comment on the usefulness of dramatic play in working with small inpatient groups of impulse-ridden and withdrawn borderline children.

Overview. Although there is little discussion of attendance patterns in these groups, it seems likely that in at least two of the models (Common Sense Club and intermediary group) the individual child's regular participation is ensured through the efforts of the parents, who are themselves participants in parent groups. These two models are structured so that group members are faced with real expectations and/or frustrations that precipitate feelings of anxiety, helplessness, and hostility. Since regular attendance is mandated by parental authority, the child cannot readily flee the group, but must instead either struggle against the frustrating authority or ally with it through identification. Each model provides some acceptable mode through which hostility can be expressed without provoking punishment or other retaliation. As a result, the child is strongly motivated to identify with whatever authority the group exerts, whether it is implicit in the structure (intermediary group), or explicit in the therapist's role (Common Sense Club).

The tendency to identify with authority (i.e., the aggressor) was established decades ago, in the child's identification with the depriving or rejecting parent. The group situation promotes a repetition of this process, but attempts to alter the introject by providing a healthier, more gratifying, more reality-oriented, and more powerful new object for identification. It is interesting to note that these treatment methodologies tend to support Aichhorn's observation (1935) that internalization of a new, healthier, and more powerful object is the essential component in successful treatment of acting-out children and adolescents.

In the intermediary groups, which are oriented toward helping the impulse-ridden child achieve mastery of specific developmental tasks, the new introject is in the image of a compulsive parent who is accepting of feelings but who has strong and clear-cut expectations about orderliness, organization, constructive activity, and the development of new skills and interests. These expectations help the child neutralize and sublimate aggressive impulses in the service of ego mastery. The Common Sense Club is more problematic. It presents an image of the therapist as master manipulator of group interaction. By encouraging peer confrontation of deviant members, as well as peer competition for adult praise and approval, the therapist is able to apply maximum pressure for change on individual group members. While the model may be effective in changing undesirable behavior patterns, I am doubtful about the long-term benefits of the child's new identification with a therapist who uses power to humiliate and control people in a weaker position. Nor can I agree with Epstein and Altman's contention (1972) that "propitiation" of the therapist is developmentally normal or desirable for latency age children.

The modified activity group is quite different in that it encourages identification with a gratifying object who exemplifies the mediating and integrating functions that characterize a mature and well-organized ego. This attempt to encourage identification with particular ego attributes is predicated on the therapist's success in helping the group control and modify excessively aggressive patterns of interaction. Frank's use of "teaching" and role-playing techniques to achieve these goals is promising and deserves further study.

It should be noted that two of these three models require a particular physical environment as well as a distinctive medium of communication. In both the intermediary group and the modified activity group, specific procedures are used to help the group members develop the capacity to recognize, acknowledge, and verbalize thoughts and feelings that are causally connected to their behavioral difficulties.

Models, Structure, and Modes of Communication for Work with Withdrawn and Anxiety-Ridden "Borderline" Children

DSM III categories:
313.22: schizoid disorders of childhood.
299.90: childhood onset, pervasive developmental disorder.
312.00: conduct disorder, undersocialized, nonaggressive (some).

The modified experiential group. In addition to their problems in ego development and integration, the children Scheidlinger (1960, 1965) describes have also experienced the chronic dislocations and environmental inconsistencies that accompany family disintegration and extreme poverty. In the DSM III typology they would be coded as having experienced a high level of psychosocial stressors, on Axis IV. Although the prognosis for these children is guarded, Scheidlinger has demonstrated that an effective method of group treatment can be devised for them. The model used is a modification of the activity group therapy format. The groups have a membership of approximately eight children, three or four of whom may be seriously ego-damaged. The physical environment is designed so that the children may use craft materials to either act out their conflicts or to develop age-appropriate skills. Corrective peer interaction is emphasized and real gratifications (food, projects, etc.) are provided at a level compatible with the developmental needs of the group members.

Because these children have experienced such serious inconsistency and deprivation in their early object relationships, the therapist makes every effort to provide a safe, consistent, predictable, and gratifying environment. This involves giving up the nonintervening, nonverbal role that the therapist traditionally assumes in activity groups. Ego-damaged children do not perceive such neutrality as an indication of positive interest. They feel enormously threatened by their own impulses and by what they perceive to be the hostile intent of other group members toward them. Accordingly, the therapist becomes actively involved in offering protection, setting indirect limits, clarifying reality, and making sure that each child receives a fair share of the food and materials. A high level of real gratification is maintained during the beginning and middle stages of the group's existence.

After the initial stage of "guided gratification," during which time the purchase, preparation, and serving of food plays a predominant role, the group goes through a period of regression similar to that ordinarily occurring in activity groups. This is followed by a period of "guided upbringing and socialization" (Scheidlinger, 1965) during which the therapist begins to establish expectations related to frustration tolerance, impulse control, and age-appropriate socialization. These maturational expectations are gradually accepted and internalized within the context of the gratifying and protective group environment.

These groups are specifically designed to provide corrective object relationships that will strengthen the child's capacity for basic trust and object constancy. As the therapist is able to provide an atmosphere of protection and consistency, the child's anxiety decreases to a point where he can begin to distinguish between fantasy and reality. As his sense of having been gratified increases, he is gradually able to accept the reality demands implicit in his play with peers and materials. Once this level of maturity has been attained, the child progresses in much the same way a less disturbed child does in an activity group setting.

These groups have not proved successful with ego-damaged children who are extremely provocative and aggressive. Such children tend to disrupt the group because of their high level of stimulation and their unresponsiveness to limits. They usually have to be removed from this group so that other children can develop the trust and security necessary to use the experience constructively.

CHILDHOOD PSYCHOSIS: AUTISTIC AND SYMBIOTIC

Mahler, Pine, and Bergman (1975) define autistic child psychosis as a "fixation or regression to the autistic phase of earliest infancy, that is, the mother does not seem to be perceived at all by the child as representative of the outside world. There is a frozen wall between the autistic child and the human environment. Psychotic autism constitutes an attempt to achieve dedifferentiation and deanimation; it serves to counteract the multitudinous complexities of external stimuli and inner excitations which threaten the rudimentary ego of the autistic child with annihilation" (p. 289). The same authors state that in symbiotic child psychosis:

> The symbiotic developmental phase, although grossly distorted, has been reached; the child treats the mother as if she were part of the self, that is, not external to the self but fused with it. He is unable to integrate an image of mother as a distinct and whole external object, but instead seems to maintain fragmented good and bad part images (introjects) of the object. . . . There is, without therapy, insurmountable interference with any progress toward separation-individuation. . . . Restitution mechanisms which create the varied symptomatology are attempts to restore and perpetuate the delusional omnipotent mother-child symbiotic unity. . . . [p. 293]

Models, Structure, and Modes of Communication

DSM III categories:
299.00: Infantile autism.
299.01: Infantile autism, residual state.
299.90: Childhood onset, pervasive developmental disorder.

Very few therapists have attempted to treat psychotic children in homogeneous groups. For that reason it is startling to discover that the major projects reported during the last twenty years have all been notably successful in reducing autistic withdrawal and promoting progressive ego development. Because the children treated are so severely disturbed, these methodologies all emphasize specific structural elements that reduce the use of autistic defenses, contain panic, limit aggression, and promote interaction both between peers and between individual group members and the therapists. Activity, sometimes at an extremely primitive level, is the primary medium of communication until the group members develop a capacity for symbolic play and verbal expression, usually after a year or two of treatment.

Group therapy. The first systematic attempt to treat psychotic children together in a group was made by Speers and Lansing (1965). Their first group was composed of one autistic and three symbiotic children, ranging in age from three years, three months to four years, ten months. They later added five additional children, for a total of nine. Sessions were held twice weekly, lasting for three hours on Tuesdays and one and a half hours on Fridays. A mothers' group that met for one and one half hours a week was initiated concurrently with the start of the children's group, and, as the family pathology became more evident, a fathers' group was organized.

The children's group met in a room approximately 280 feet square, which provided a safe physical environment. All furniture was removed except for a table with a phonograph.

> The original play equipment included two rubber balls the size of basketballs, an inflated clown four feet tall (the kind that bobs up when you knock it down), several stuffed animals, and a dozen 1 1/2 inch sponge blocks. The first phonograph records we used were children's stories, but we soon learned the children disliked these. When we substituted records with catchy, strongly rhythmic tunes, with or without words, they were obviously pleased and seemed calmer and less aggressive. Loud marching tunes, to which the therapists beat time with hands or feet, were most effective in alleviating group tensions and anxieties. [Speers and Lansing, 1965, p. 63]

A large observation mirror covered most of one wall and became an important focus of play and self-observation. Cotherapists were present during every session. When regression was particularly intense, other therapists joined the group to provide both individual attention and limits.

The authors contend that autism is a defensive attitude used to preserve infantile omnipotence. "Early in group therapy, the autistic defense fails, either due to the enhanced anxiety resulting from the new and unfamiliar situation, or because of the active penetration of the defense by the other children in the group" (p. 63). Penetration of this defense leads initially to panic accompanied by intensely aggressive behavior. The therapists managed aggression through firm but gentle physical restraint, which frequently involved holding individual children for long periods. During episodes of panic or rage, the mirror was purposefully used to control and modify affective states. "We took the child to the mirror, touched and named him the various parts of his body. Each person in the room was also named and pointed out in the mirror. We often noted that when anxiety threatened to overwhelm a child, he would get as close to the mirror as possible, as though to correlate touch and sight and thus maintain identity" (pp. 64–65). Once the "rage-like" behavior had been controlled, group members progressed to less extreme forms of aggression. For the most part these acts were directed toward other children, and seemed to signal a wish for interpersonal contact.

As the group progressed, eating and toilet training became significant activities. In addition, group members expressed their sexual impulses quite directly. Undressing, masturbation, urination, and active attempts to explore the anatomical differences between boys and girls occurred frequently. These actions were understood and accepted as expressions of anxiety or sexual curiosity that could not be expressed in words or symbolic play. The therapists intervened by verbalizing feelings, providing accurate information about anatomical differences, and interpreting the underlying anxiety. Such interventions seem to reduce anxiety, and the group members had achieved, by the second year of treatment, at least a tentative sense of personal and sexual identity.

Initially the group members used whatever toys were available, either for purposes of autistic withdrawal or to aggressively drive away "intruders" or "intrusive reality." Over time, with considerable encouragement from the therapists, interactive play gradually developed and more expressive toys were introduced. In the third year of treatment, a formal educational program and a scheduled outdoor play period were incorporated into the group structure. The authors note that the group members had severe problems with speech and communication when they started treatment, even though all of them could "unmistakably" communicate with each other nonverbally. After two years in the group, verbal interchanges were common, especially among the four children who had started the group together. After four years of treatment, verbal communication was well established and the eight children who remained in the group were all able to function successfully in public school or comparable educational facilities.

In the fourth year of treatment, the thirty-minute "preschool" program, which had been incorporated into each group session a year earlier, became the focus for a resurgence of sexual activity. During this stage of treatment, sexual acts with distinctly phallic-exhibitionistic aims (undressing, attempting to urinate on one another, etc.), were initiated by the male group members, in a manner that totally disrupted the school activities. During this anxiety-provoking regression, themes of dominance and humiliation were prominent, and castration fears were explicitly acted out. Neither exploration nor interpretation were effective in containing this behavior, which apparently reflected transferential as well as developmental issues. Speers and Lansing observe that when the group as a whole was given responsibility for determining when the educational program would begin and end, and how long it would last during each group meeting, the boys were gradually able to gain control over their phallic impulses. This led to the formation of a "group superego," as evidenced by the gradual incorporation of rules and procedures that helped individual members and the group as a whole exercise reasonable self-restraint in subsequent sessions.

Early in the treatment process, the authors note, learning had been contingent on the children's capacity to invest intense affect in human relationships: "at first inanimate objects were strongly invested with affects displaced from people and the therapy was largely directed toward 'depersonalizing' these fetishistic objects. Once this had been achieved and the affects redirected toward people ... then learning about inanimate reality became possible" (p. 157). At this later point in treatment, the authors speculate, learning was dependent on the children expressing their sexual impulses to the point of "exhaustion." It seems possible, however, that the boys' need to disrupt the educational program was dynamically related to an oedipally tinged power struggle; by asserting their dominance over each other, the female group members, and, ultimately, the therapists, the male group members tested how the male cotherapists would respond to an overt challenge to their leadership. When the group leaders indicated that they were not threatened by this behavior, and had confidence in the group's ability to deal with the problem, there was a rapid reduction not only of castration anxiety, but also of the underlying psychotic anxiety, related to control and annihilation.

Speers and Lansing comment that while at the end of the study mothers and children continued "to share ego boundaries in certain specific areas" (p. 180), the children were for the most part able to limit their psychotic behavior to the group. At home and at school their functioning was observed to be "schizoid" but not psychotic. Even in the group there was a vigorous level of peer interaction accompanied by considerable group solidarity and a strong commitment to learning. Some positive changes were also noted in the parents' marital relationships and in the mothers' capacity to deal with their own narcissistic needs. This is an impressive outcome, particularly for children whose prognosis is universally considered to be very poor.

Relationship group therapy. Lifton and Smolen (1966) reported on a project with schizophrenic children and their parents, in which intensive outpatient group therapy for the children was the major treatment modality. Their groups comprised children, four to twelve years old, who had been diagnosed by "independent evaluators" as autistic or schizophrenic. Symptomatology included "bizarreness; delusions; intensely provocative, aggressive, or self-punishing behavior; and physical attack. Grouping was based on [compatibility in] level of ego organization, ego strengths and weakness, and specific pathology. Groups met for two hour sessions three or four times a week" (p. 26). Group size averaged six members, and the groups were led by co-therapy teams. The parents were also treated in groups, but the marital dyad was separated and each parent was seen in a different parents' group. In a personal communication, Lifton (1984) commented that this innovation was particularly successful in modifying pathogenic parent-child interactions.

The methodology is based on the premise that the "schizophrenias of childhood" result from early disturbances of relationship which interfere with all aspects of ego development, but most particularly with object relations and the establishment of a secure, individuated sense of self. The major goal of treatment is to help each child develop a relationship with the therapist and with other children in the group, as a prerequisite to reestablishing the capacity for progressive ego development.

The physical environment was purposefully designed to provide an atmosphere of cheerfulness and warmth. Materials were used with the specific aim of strengthening ego functioning: "for example, mirrors, solid wooden manikins that cannot be pulled apart, and coloring books that have outline drawings are provided" (pp. 25–26) to aid in the development of an integrated body image. Toys and other materials that evoke fantasy or regressive play (finger paints, clay, etc.) were generally excluded, but could be provided for specific children who demonstrated a capacity to use such materials therapeutically. When an individual was given special play materials, the therapist explained to the other group members why these materials had been provided for a particular child but not for the group as a whole. Soft, malleable craft materials were avoided because they often precipitated intense anxiety. Lifton and Smolen (1966) make the interesting observation that "the children respond best to materials that have a definite shape and are easier to control" (p. 26). For this reason marking pens, hard pencils, and crayons were considered preferable to pastels or watercolors. Over time, as the group progressed, evocative toys and craft equipment were introduced to encourage higher levels of symbolic communication.

This methodology combined play, activities, and discussion. "Free play" was rarely permitted because of the authors' conviction that it promotes "confusion, withdrawal and panic." Children were not encouraged to fantasize or express unconscious wishes directly in their play. Lifton and Smollen agree with Scheidlinger's statement that limits and structure alleviate anxiety for the ego-damaged child. Like Speers and Lansing, they suggest the use of physical as well as verbal "restraints."

In these groups the therapist explores, verbalizes, and interprets the behavior of individual group members and the group as a whole, concentrating on "here and now" interactions and the reality situation within the group. All behavior is viewed as an attempt at communication. The therapist actively works to promote group discussion and to sensitize other group members to the themes and interactive patterns that are significant for each individual member. Having demonstrated that he is trustworthy, the therapist attempts to promote progressive ego development by placing "those demands and pressures on the child, . . . which the child can tolerate and which (the therapist believes) will produce growth" (Lifton and Smolen, 1966, p. 34). Aggressive or negativistic behavior is evaluated and controlled by the therapist in terms of how much expression can be mastered by individual children and by the group as a whole, without promoting panic, withdrawal, and decompensation.

The authors comment that group therapy may be the "treatment of choice" in childhood schizophrenia, since it "offers the most effective way of promoting socialization . . . shortens the time required to build relationships . . . and gives the child more stimuli than can be afforded in individual treatment sessions. . . . As one child unhappily remarked when he wanted to withdraw from the group, 'I can't ignore them' " (p. 35). In addition, the more positive aspects of group pressure (the "group superego") tend to motivate individual children to move to higher levels of ego functioning. This treatment model was very successful in keeping these children in the community and facilitating their adjustment to "normal" school settings.

Group treatment with primitively fixated children. Trafimow and Pattak (1981, 1982) describe an evolving group methodology for "post-symbiotic" children whose clinical diagnoses range from schizophrenia to borderline personality organization. From the authors' viewpoint, these children are fixated at an "early-object" (need-gratifying or transitional) stage of personality organization, and therefore have not yet achieved object constancy and "true object" relations. Successful groups have been established on inpatient and outpatient units, as well as in day hospital settings. Selection is guided by the basic principle that all members must have achieved some significant development beyond the symbiotic stage. "Children are . . . grouped to form a balanced network of functional capacities and defensive styles . . . and a variety of developmental deviations that maximize the range of the objectal array" (1982, p. 448). Because more boys than girls in this diagnostic category are referred for group treatment, the groups are of boys only or may be coeducational. Optimal size is four members; if coeducational, it should be comprised of two boys and two girls. All groups are led by a cotherapy team, and generally meet for forty-five minutes once a week.

In this model, the physical environment is viewed as an important treatment variable that can be organized to "support and enhance internal functioning" (1982, p. 448). Room size, for example, is determined by the personality organization of the individual members and by the group goals—to reduce physical and emotional isolation, promote maximum peer interaction, and minimize engulfment anxiety. Equipment and furniture are chosen using the same principles. In addition to a round wooden table and chairs, the room is furnished with large wooden cubes with one open side, bulky enough so that two or more children must cooperate in order to move them. The need to collaborate physically encourages interpersonal contact and leads to the development of shared fantasies which gradually become part of the group process. The table and chairs are used during structured "table-talk" periods at the beginning and end of each session. At these times, children and therapists sit down together around the table to talk with one another in as reality-oriented a way as they can. These discussions are not intended to encourage affective expression or promote insight. They have a calming and organizing effect, thereby helping the group members manage the intense anxiety and regressive impulses that erupt during beginnings, endings, and other transitional periods. "The very firmness and unchangeable nature of the table and the chairs strengthened each child's body boundaries and helped define physical limits. Further, eye contact encouraged and promoted cognitive recognition of the others present" (1982, p. 452).

The authors identify three major curative elements in their methodology. The first and most crucial of these is the presence of other children, who offer each individual child a range of "objectal alternatives." Since postsymbiotic children tend to be less anxious with peers than with adults, they are better able to express their developmental needs in interactions with peers. Repeated interactions over time eventually promote imitation of, or identification with, the more adaptive personal characteristics and coping strategies that other group members have achieved.

The second element is the cotherapy team. The two therapists function as "auxiliary group egos" providing whatever "aspect of ego functioning is missing in the group at . . . [a particular] time. However, . . . [the therapists' goal] is always to return the group to the children: To enhance or support the workings of the group, to reinstate enough equilibrium for the group members themselves to take over again" (1981, p. 196). In this methodology, the therapists may choose to establish behavioral limits through physical restraint, or to explore, confront, and interpret. It is interesting to note that most of the therapeutic interventions reported in these papers focus on encouraging peer interaction, identifying the effect that a particular child's behavior is having on the other group members, acknowledging and verbalizing a child's affective state, and providing nonverbal signals (touching, smiling) that convey "regard" or comfort.

The third curative element is the group as a therapeutic entity. Because the members consistently view the group in affectively positive terms, they can not only tolerate the frustrations, peer conflicts, therapist absences, and changes in membership that are an inherent part of group life, but can also gradually master the potentially disorganizing internal sequelae of these conflictual interpersonal events. Trafimow and Pattak cite the work of Scheidlinger (1974) on the "mother group," and of Kauff (1977) on the group as a "transitional object," to account for this effect. They note that in this model the group as a whole appears to serve the role of "symbiotic mother," thus sustaining and protecting the individual members until they are ready to differentiate and function more autonomously.

Overview. Although these authors use a variety of conceptual frameworks, there is remarkable consensus in their recommendations about group structure, modes of communication, the value of peer interaction, the nature of the therapeutic role, and the curative effect of the group as a whole. All the models make use of a carefully planned physical environment, both to ensure safety and to promote a high level of peer interaction. Carefully selected play materials (mirrors, phonograph records, art supplies that encourage self-control and reinforce interpersonal boundaries, etc.) are used to reduce annihilation anxiety, affirm body integrity, and promote more realistic contact with the object world. Limit-setting through physical restraint, as well as more traditional verbal interventions involving exploration, confrontation, and interpretation are all considered essential parts of the therapeutic role. Cotherapists are used to maintain structure and facilitate the development of ego capacities that are lacking in individual group members and in the group as a whole. Peer interaction and the group's capacity to serve as a benign holding environment are viewed as crucial elements in limiting withdrawal and dissolving autistic defenses.

The models differ in two significant respects: (1) the degree to which primitive, primary process behavior is sanctioned as a necessary part of the therapeutic process; and (2) the optimal focus for interpretation. Speers and Lansing (1965) implicitly assume that acting out will take place in the group and that it is an essential part of the drive-taming process. They directly interpret impulses, wishes, and primitive fears, as well as defenses and pathological patterns of object relatedness. Lifton and Smolen (1966) limit acting out and ignore both hallucinatory and delusional productions. They positively reinforce socially appropriate behavior and attempt to extinguish socially inappropriate symptomatology by not responding to it. Their interpretations are typically designed to promote awareness of underlying affect (anger, jealousy, sadness, etc.) which, in their view, is defended against by pervasive patterns of psychotic withdrawing or attack. Trafimow and Pattak (1981) implicitly assume that even though acting out may at times be unavoidable, it is not a prerequisite for intrapsychic reorganization. Aggression and sexual acting out are for the most part contained by the group structure. In this model, interpretation is directed toward the interpersonal consequences of behavior, and toward the painful feelings that negative peer responses evoke in the individual. The need to withdraw and fantasize is scrupulously respected until the individual demonstrates a willingness to interact.

The group as a whole is viewed as the primary impetus and support for growth.

It is interesting to note that all of these authors agree that the group as a whole is the primary factor in promoting progressive development. In attempting to explain the group's healing effect, they propose a variety of formulations including "group ego," "group superego," "mother group," "group as a transitional object," and "group as symbiotic mother." While these concepts usefully remind us of individual developmental processes, they do not adequately describe the group's particular effectiveness in modifying developmental pathology at a psychotic level of organization. Concepts of the group as a symbolic family or as a self-regulating system need to be studied more carefully as we attempt to understand the benefits that these very disturbed children derive from their participation in group life.

NEUROSIS AND THE HIGHER LEVEL OF ORGANIZATION OF CHARACTER PATHOLOGY

Neurotic organization

Pine defines neurosis as a "focal drive conflict" in the context of more or less normal ego and superego development—a "relatively healthy" state of intrapsychic organization (Pine, 1974, p. 345). Object constancy and identity have been established, object relations are relatively mature, and repression is the major defense mechanism. Psychological dysfunction is for the most part limited to symptomatic forms of expression that include phobias, anxiety states, hysterical conversions, and obsessive-compulsive actions, all of which are ego alien.

The Higher Level of Character Pathology

Kernberg (1970) notes that at this level of organization, genital primacy has been achieved, the superego is relatively well integrated (but excessively severe), and repression is the central mechanism of defense. Object relations are stable, self-concept is well established, and the person is capable of experiencing intense affects including guilt and mourning. Personality dysfunction is expressed in inhibitions and defensive character traits, which usually are experienced as ego alien. Kernberg includes "most hysterical characters . . . obsessive compulsive characters . . . and depressive-masochistic characters" in this category (p. 806). Since both of these diagnostic categories require interpretive forms of treatment and both are characterized by ego alien symptomatology, I have included them together as "neurotic" disturbances. While I appreciate Kernberg's distinction, I prefer the older concept of "neurotic character," particularly in describing childhood psychopathology.

Models, Structures, and Modes of Communication

DSM III categories:
300.02: generalized anxiety disorder.
300.29: simple phobia.
300.20: obsessive compulsive disorder.
309.21: separation anxiety disorder (some).
313.00: overanxious disorder (some).
300.40: dysthymic disorder.
309.00: adjustment disorder with depressed mood.
309.24: adjustment disorder with anxious mood.
309.25: adjustment disorder with mixed emotional features.
309.23: adjustment disorder with academic inhibition.

In general, group therapy has not been considered the treatment of choice for neurotic latency age children, except as an adjunct to individual psychotherapy. In recent years, however, a number of clinicians, including Anthony, Kraft, Slavson, Schiffer, and Sugar, have all recommended variant forms of interview group therapy as a specific intervention for children who are neurotic, or whose functioning reflects the higher levels of organization of character pathology.

Anthony (1957), for example, states that neurotic children are quite willing and able to talk in groups if they are given the opportunity to do so: "Gossip is their strong point. They enjoy discussing personalities and group relationships. They are shy about their symptoms . . . and dread losing face. In later stages, the preoccupation of the pre-pubertal members with such topics as sex differences, sex roles . . . problems of birth and death, and the fears of calamitous happenings at home is very much in evidence" (p. 197).

The models in this category are quite similar in technique. Usually a few simple craft materials are provided, mostly as "props." These give the children something to do while talking, and at times facilitate symbolic expression of unconscious feelings. Heterogeneity in group membership is preferable. The therapist stops destructive and physically dangerous activity if it occurs. In some groups food is served and discussions take place around a table. In Anthony's groups, "props" are not used and the children wander about the room, sitting on tables and window ledges while talking to one another.

Even though Gabriel's groups (1939) included some children with more serious pathology, her group records indicate that there was discussion of issues such as birth, sex, masturbation, defecation, and attitudes toward parents and siblings. Anthony's group records confirm Gabriel's observations and also document the expression of transference feelings toward the therapist and other group members, as well as discussions of dreams and family mysteries such as illegitimacy.

Anthony recommends that the therapist explore and interpret material, avoiding only interpretations that reflect on the individual child-therapist relationship. Gabriel explores or interprets and usually limits her comments to situations in which the children specifically ask her for some assistance. It is interesting to note that the issues discussed in her group records are very similar to those Anthony reports, in spite of the marked differences in therapeutic technique. Kraft (1967) and Sugar (1974) interpret freely, with no particular limitations. Slavson and Schiffer (1975) recommend that interpretations be conceptually simple, brief, direct, and "devoid of complex elaboration" (p. 303). They also note that it is preferable to phrase interpretations in the same language the child uses to express conflicts. In their view, questions, simple explanations, and the use of language to describe what the child is attempting to express, behaviorally or in play, may be as effective as interpretation in promoting insight and structural change.

Schiffer suggests that coeducational therapeutic play groups (see also Kraft, 1983) with male and female cotherapists can be helpful to latency age children in working through oedipal problems. "The behavior of the therapeutic 'parents' reduces the inordinate pressures of guilt and anxiety which are attendant to the oedipal conflict. The eventual therapeutic outcome is the development of a healthier superego structure and effective sublimations" (Schiffer, 1969, p. 113).

The issues and techniques involved in treating neurotic children have been discussed so frequently and in such detail that further elaboration seems unnecessary. It is clear that neurotic latency age children talk freely in groups and that peer interaction actively stimulates meaningful self-revelation. The material summarized here indicates that an interview model of group therapy, with or without simple activities, is an effective form of insight-oriented treatment for many neurotic children, particularly as they approach puberty.

CONCLUSION

This analysis of the literature supports the premise that group treatment is an effective modality for children in all the major psychoanalytic and DSM III diagnostic categories. In the models reviewed, differential treatment is organized around group structures that allow the participants to symbolize and work through specific developmental deficits. Developmentally oriented group structures share certain elements in common. These include (1) a safe physical environment that supports but does not demand peer interaction; (2) furniture, equipment, and play materials that facilitate emotionally meaningful communication at a level compatible with intrapsychic organization; (3) the planned use of time, equipment, and play materials either to promote internal organization or to encourage controlled regression and reintegration; and (4) a clearly defined therapeutic role directed toward helping individual members and the group as a whole master specific developmental tasks. Groups for more seriously disturbed children tend to be compensatory rather than insight-oriented in their aims and methodology.

Group structure is least important in treating children who function at the higher levels of intrapsychic organization. Such children make good use of any model that encourages affective expression and promotes insight. Structure is critical in the treatment of impulse-ridden, borderline (the lowest level of organization of character pathology), and psychotic children. These children need a carefully constructed holding environment in which they can feel emotionally safe while they gradually develop the ego functions they lack. The organizing effect of specific group structures makes it possible for the group members to internalize new self- and object representations and to reorganize pathological patterns of defense. Children at an intermediate level of character pathology benefit from a relatively permissive group structure in which there are opportunities for controlled regression, reorganization, and symbolization. A carefully structured lack of structure provides the active impetus for change in these models, by making it possible for the participants to covertly defy the group therapist, whom they transferentially perceive as depriving, critical, and demeaning. The therapist's ability to maintain an accepting, gratifying, and safe group climate in the face of hostility and rebelliousness makes it possible for the members to modify superego structures in ways that promote autonomy, self-control, and self-esteem.

It has been noted that some borderline and psychotic children benefit from participation in well-balanced, heterogeneous groups designed to meet the developmental needs of children at an intermediate level of character pathology (King, 1959). These beneficial results occur in situations where the group as a whole is relatively cohesive and individual members have achieved enough internal structure to provide the organizing experiences and external controls that seriously disturbed children need in order to mature. Nonetheless, such children can be so disruptive to a group process that, typically, only one can safely be included in a well-functioning group of five or more. In settings which serve large numbers of borderline and psychotic children, groups are of necessity relatively homogeneous. Accordingly, successful treatment in most settings depends on the creation of specific group structures that will encourage higher levels of object relatedness while facilitating compensatory ego development.

REFERENCES

Aichhorn, A. (1935), *Wayward Youth*. New York: Viking.
Anthony, E. J. (1957), Group analytic psychotherapy with children and adolescents. In: *Group Psychotherapy*, ed. S. H. Foulkes & E. J. Anthony. Baltimore: Penguin.
Axline, V. (1947), *Play Therapy*. Boston: Houghton Mifflin.
Blanck, G., & Blanck, R. (1974), *Ego Psychology: Theory and Practice*. New York: Columbia University Press.
Epstein, N., & Altman, S. (1972), Experiences in converting an activity group into verbal group therapy. *Internat. J. Group Psychother.*, 22:93–100.
Erikson, E. (1977), *Toys and Reason*. New York: Norton.
Frank, M. (1983), Modified activity group therapy with ego impoverished children. In: *Ego and Self Psychology*, ed. E.S. Buchholz & J.M. Mishne. New York: Aronson, pp. 145–156.
Gabriel, B. (1939), An experiment in group treatment. *Amer. J. Orthopsychiat.*, 9:146.
Ganter, G., Yeakel, M., & Polansky, N. (1967), *Retrieval from Limbo*. New York: Child Welfare League of America.
Ginott, H. (1961), *Group Psychotherapy with Children*. New York: McGraw-Hill.
Grossbard, H. (1962), Ego deficiency in delinquents. In: *New Approaches to the Treatment of Delinquency*. New York: Family Service Association of America.
Holland, H., & Nagler, S. (1981), Out of chaos: Group therapy at children's psychiatric emergency services. In: *Reaping from the Field: From Practice to Principles. Proceedings of Social Group Work III*, Vol. 1, ed. N. Goroff, pp. 413–426.
Kauff, P. (1977), The termination process: Its relationship to the separation-individuation phase of development. *Internat. J. Group Psychother.*, 27:3–18.
Kernberg, O. (1970), A psychoanalytic classification of character pathology. *J. Amer. Psychoanal. Assn.*, 18:800–821.

King, C. (1959), Activity group therapy with some schizophrenics. *Internat. J. Group Psychother.*, 9:184.
Kraft, I. (1967), Group therapy. In: *The Comprehensive Textbook of Psychiatry*, ed. A. Freedman & H.I. Kaplan. Baltimore: Williams & Wilkins, pp. 1463–1468.
—— (1983), Personal communication.
Lifton, N. (1984), Personal communication.
—— Smolen, E. (1966), Group psychotherapy with schizophrenic children. *Internat. J. Group Psychother.*, 16:23–41.
MacLennan, B. (1977), Modifications of activity group therapy for children. *Internat. J. Group Psychother.*, 27:85–96.
Mahler, M., Pine, F., & Bergman, A. (1975), *The Psychological Birth of the Human Infant.* New York: Basic Books.
Pine, F. (1974), On the concept "borderline" in children: A clinical essay. *The Psychoanalytic Study of the Child*, 29:341–368. New Haven, CT: Yale University Press.
Rank, B. (1952), Treatment of young children with atypical development by psychoanalytic technique. In: *Specialized Techniques in Psychotherapy*, ed. G. Bychowski et al. New York: Basic Books.
Redl, F., & Wineman, D. (1951), *Children Who Hate.* Glencoe, IL: Free Press.
Rosenthal, L. (1977), Qualifications and tasks of the group therapist with children. *Clin. Soc. Work J.*, 5:191–199.
Sarnoff, C. (1976), *Latency.* New York: Aronson.
Schamess, G. (1976), Group treatment modalities for latency-age children. *Internat. J. Group Psychother.*, 26:455–473.
Scheidlinger, S. (1960), Experiential group treatment of severely deprived latency-age children. *Amer. J. Orthopsychiat.*, 30:356–368.
—— (1965), Three approaches with socially deprived latency-age children. *Internat. J. Group Psychother.*, 15:434–445.
—— (1974), On the concept of the "mother-group." *Internat. J. Group Psychother.*, 24:417–428.
Schiffer, M. (1969), *The Therapeutic Play Group.* New York: Grune & Stratton.
Slavson, S. R. (1943), *An Introduction to Group Therapy.* New York: International Universities Press.
—— Schiffer, M. (1975), *Group Psychotherapies for Children.* New York: International Universities Press.
Soo, E. (1974), The impact of activity group therapy upon a highly constricted child. *Internat. J. Group Psychother.*, 24:207–216.
Speers, R., & Lansing, C. (1965), *Group Therapy in Childhood Psychoses.* Chapel Hill: University of North Carolina Press.
Sugar, M. (1974), Interpretive group psychotherapy with latency age children. *J. Amer. Acad. Child Psychiat.*, 13:648–666.
Trafimow, E., & Pattak, S. (1981), Group psychotherapy and objectal development in children. *Internat. J. Group Psychother.*, 31:193–204.
—— —— (1982), Group treatment of primitively fixated children. *Internat. J. Group Psychother.*, 32:445–452.
Weill, A.P. (1953), Certain severe disturbances of ego development in childhood. *The Psychoanalytic Study of the Child*, 8:271–286. New York: International Universities Press.
Winnicott, D.W. (1965), Psychotherapy of character disorders. In: *The Maturational Processes and the Facilitating Environment.* New York: International Universities Press, pp. 203–216.

Part III
*The Use of Groups
for Diagnostic Purposes*

Chapter 4
Diagnostic Play Groups for Children: Their Role in Assessment and Treatment Planning

JEROME H. LIEBOWITZ, M.D.
PAULINA F. KERNBERG, M.D.

Diagnostic and therapeutic work with children in groups, where the focus and goal is psychotherapy, dates back over forty years to the pioneering work of S. R. Slavson (1943) and Fritz Redl (1944). Both used for therapeutic purposes "the predilection of latency-age children for group experiences" (Scheidlinger, 1982, p. 131). With his therapeutic approach for late-latency youths, "activity group therapy," Slavson was the first to emphasize and develop the therapeutic use of *peer group phenomena* and to point to the diagnostic possibilities of the group.

Redl (1944) used "diagnostic groups" in an "attempt at developing a new instrument of diagnosis" (p. 57). He combined the elements of activity and play with discussion and interpretations by the therapist, approximating what Slavson (1952) later described as "activity interview groups." Redl, noting that "neither the idea nor the arrangement of diagnostic groups [was] entirely new" (p. 54), found the use of such groups necessary because of the exigencies of the time, when psychiatric services were severely cut and the limited remaining clinical resources had to be used for treatment and supervision of only the most disturbed cases. Because agencies could not afford "thorough and time-consuming interviews for diagnostic aims with lighter cases" (p. 54), groups were formed to supplement the often very insufficient diagnostic information with "group-originated diagnostic materials." Slavson's and Redl's focus on peer group phenomena and the individual child's relation to the peer group is at the heart of our use of such groups diagnostically—especially since peer relationships are a major area in the assessment of health or sickness in children.

E. James Anthony (1957), another major pathfinder in group psychotherapy, reintroduced the idea of the group as a diagnostic instrument and added the idea of using brief, time-limited diagnostic groups as part of every diagnostic evaluation to aid in treatment planning. In one simple but eloquent paragraph, added almost as an afterthought to his chapter on group-analytic psychotherapy with children and adolescents, Anthony says:

> The psychiatrist, in his diagnostic interview, has the opportunity of seeing two children, the one child looking even physically different from the other—the clinic child and the group child. Unfortunately, he does not always avail himself of the group interview, and may carry away the impression of a pale, sad, inhibited child, looking somewhat 'dead,' and with very little to say for himself. Should he, by chance, place the child in a children's group for a period long enough to let him 'warm up' after his clinic experience, he will observe him opening out like a japanese flower in water, suddenly full of colour and spontaneity. A remark often heard in a child guidance clinic is that such-and-such a mother had painted her child as a lion, and when he walked into the clinic, he was just a little lamb. Half an hour in a diagnostic group would convince the psychiatrist that a mother knows a lion when she meets one. [p. 232]

Despite this long history of diagnostic group work with children, only a few therapists have described the diagnostic use of groups in outpatient settings:

Scheidlinger (1960) described how he originally used groups "for observation of children on whom there were inadequate diagnostic data. In the course of this observation the striking pathology of these children emerged readily enough to view" (p. 358).

Field (1966) noted how activity groups provide an exploring, role-taking, and testing medium whose main contribution "may be *the accumulation of behavioral data* for the psychiatric social worker who guides and focuses the therapeutic effort at home and at school" (p. 49, italics ours).

Smolen and Lifton (1966) demonstrated diagnostic as well as therapeutic group work with severely disturbed young children preparatory to their total hospitalization. They commented on several children who improved and had their clinical diagnoses altered by observation of their response to the group situation.

King (1970) saw children for four sessions in diagnostic activity groups as an integral part of the intake study and planning process in a family service agency. King reports that certain aspects of the children's developmental levels and functioning emerged more than others in their diagnostic group experience. Each child's current ego functioning was most clearly demonstrated, especially in regard to object constancy and relationships, reality testing and judgment, impulse control, frustration tolerance, and characteristic defenses. There also emerged much useful data pertaining to level of psychosocial development, aspects of the self-concept, and sexual identification. The groups also offered an opportunity to observe the degree and quality of energy expressed in motor activity, outward-directed interests, and curiosity. Short attention span and inability to concentrate, used as indicators of withdrawal and excessive fantasy, were also available for observation.

Gratton and Pope (1972), in a school setting, saw five to six children in a diagnostic group one hour a week for three weeks and also conducted time-limited weekly group psychotherapy for twelve weeks. They focused on the time-saving use of such groups in processing or screening a large number of children.

Paulina Kernberg (1978) reported on her innovative use of diagnostic groups in the training of child psychiatrists.

Based on those experiences, we added, in early 1980, a diagnostic peer group to the evaluation of latency age children consisting of two group diagnostic sessions. The child is seen by one therapist (or two cotherapists) with several other children being evaluated in the Child Outpatient Department. The sessions take place in a large playroom equipped with a table, chairs, a variety of toys and games appropriate for school age children, and materials such as paper, crayons, clay, blocks, balloons, ropes, and a blackboard with chalk. The children do not know each other and are told by their evaluator that they will participate in two meetings to see how they play and relate to other children. The groups are mixed in terms of diagnosis, sex, and age (although at times we are able to be more homogeneous with regard to the last). This mixing has raised some concern among colleagues, but as Anthony (1957), writing about treatment, notes:

> Some types of disturbed children . . . do better in mixed diag-

nostic groups, some with groups in which there are mixed sexes, and some in settings where the age range has been stretched a little to include both younger and older children. Again, some children are more responsive when confronted with a group occupation, whereas others will create their own interests and activities or restrict themselves for long periods to purely verbal interchanges. Some of these differences are related to the age and sex of the child, but temperament, personality, and diagnosis also play a considerable part. Having male and female therapists and cotherapists also available serves to expand the spectrum of treatment still further. Although such provisions aim at obtaining the right type of group for the right patient, it is well to remember that selection criteria are, at best, only approximately effective in this respect, and that it may be of more therapeutic worth to allow the individual to adjust himself to the requirements of the group than to find a group that is ideally adjusted to his idiosyncrasies. [p. 186]

How the child adjusts to the group and the group process is a major focus of our two diagnostic group sessions. The attempts of the group to resolve disturbing differences and/or the disturbances associated with differences is, as Anthony points out, "a crucial therapeutic function of the group." When in doubt, therefore, Anthony advises that "it is still worth trying him out in a group when age, sex, and diagnostic considerations do not appear altogether promising" (pp. 186–187).

Since 1981 these sessions have taken place in front of a one-way screen, and the evaluators of the children—and any other interested trainees and clinicians—have been able to observe the groups live.

CLINICAL EXAMPLE

Following is a vignette of one such group session. The members, together for the first time, presented as follows:

Lisa, nine and a half, was referred by her school psychologist because of anxiety possibly interfering with school adjustment. Her parents wanted to know the advisability of transferring Lisa to a private school. They felt that she does not adjust well to peers and is lonely at times, and wondered if she were able to do better academically or if she had a learning disability. They complained that "it takes her forever" to do something. On school days, Lisa frequently had physical ailments and complaints. She also wet the bed occasionally. The initial clinical impression was that of a probable neurotic personality disorder, avoidant type, with more schizoid pathology or severe separation anxiety of a borderline nature pretty well ruled out. Her mild school phobia was felt to be secondary to her avoidant personality and anxiety in the school situation. Psychological testing revealed a mild learning disability contributing to this. We hoped that the diagnostic group would help give us a clearer, "live" sense of the peer problems that she herself discussed, since she did have friends and could relate episodes in which she got along fairly well with peers.

Rachel, seven and a half, was referred because of lack of interest in school work and some school refusal. She was described as primarily interested in playing, with some excessive aggressivity with peers. There was also some defiance of her mother. The initial clinical impression was that of an anxious child. A question of sexual identity concerns was raised, as it was felt that Rachel showed no evidence of feminine identification in her individual sessions.

Adam, also seven and a half, was referred because of poor school performance in spite of what seemed to be above-average intelligence. He had no friends and engaged in virtually no peer play. The initial clinical impression was that of a bright, verbal, but very anxious boy, with concerns about sexual identity.

Tom, a boy of ten, was referred because of encopresis, lying, and stealing. The initial clinical impression was that of an intelligent, neurotically conflicted boy who expresses his aggression regressively in the symptom of encopresis and in purposeful lying and stealing.

Michael, also ten, was referred because of very aggressive behavior, fighting in school, hyperactivity, and poor school performance with evidence of learning disability.

The group session. The group begins with Rachel's insisting that her mother stay in the room. One of the two leaders, both male, explains that the group will meet twice, an hour each time, and that they are here primarily to play so that we might learn how they play and deal with each other. Early on, he establishes that each of the children is seeing a therapist.

Michael and Tom are up and about from the start, motorically active, throwing a ball and banging into things. Lisa stands by herself at a table, playing aimlessly with items on the table and watching the boys' activity with some interest. Adam remains "parked" at his position, too, but is apparently oblivious to what is going on in the room. Rachel sits with her mother on the sidelines.

The beginning phase of the group is relatively quiet. We learn that Rachel had been afraid to enter the room and that one of the leaders had had to spend time with her before she would enter, and then only with her mother. She eventually gets up and moves about the room with a broom, sweeping into a dustpan, like a tidy housewife. After 17 minutes, she lets her mother leave.

Michael is the first to violate boundaries and continues to do so. He goes to Lisa's table—the first of several invasions of her space made by one or another of the children. Lisa ignores these intrusions as if a glass wall had been erected around her, even during one period of mayhem. Even when everyone else in the room is engaged in some kind of play (12 minutes into the session), she continues to play aimlessly, remaining a watcher and showing some pleasure observing what's going on with the others.

A more active middle phase follows, with several questions regarding limits. The group as a whole accepts verbal limits, although Tom, extremely motorically active from the start, requires some physical limit-setting. During this middle phase, he goes into a flexible toy tunnel and stays in there much of the time, refusing to come out. Michael tries to provoke Tom and announces to the group, "Tom is a bum." Adam remains silently preoccupied with his own play.

Lisa builds a "wall" by positioning herself with her back to others while she works assiduously on a drawing. When asked how she can concentrate with all this wild play in the room, she shrugs. Later, when she shows her drawing to one of the leaders, we see her interest, expressed in body language, in being with and being appealing (perhaps seductively) to an adult.

Tom and Michael crash in on Lisa, who hands Michael the ball. (She had seen Adam do this earlier and repeats it now in an apparent attempt to defend herself against further involvement.) Both boys remain active and agree they "never run out of gas."

After 36 minutes have passed, Lisa moves from her table to the other side of the room, gets a large ball, and actively bounces it around. She negotiates with Rachel, verbally at first and then physically, to play baseball. Tom and Michael, in the tunnel, fall into the middle of the baseball game. Michael finally gets Adam involved in a wrestling match, and Lisa bounces the large ball on Michael's back.

The three boys return to playing with the tunnel—Tom inside, Michael punching him from without, and Adam sitting on the other end. Lisa peeks into the tunnel, curious about the silence in there. Tom says to Michael, "You're a savage."

Lisa and Rachel continue with their baseball game, and the boys join in as the game becomes more organized and bases are established. Michael gets hit by the baseball, but Lisa intervenes with the other, aggressive children as a limit-setter, taking on a superego role in the group.

Michael taunts Tom about being a girl and then gets on the real telephone (another boundary violated). More aggression follows, involving a large cardboard box the boys find. Tom gets into this, too, and has it shoved under a table (stuck in a cavity again).

By the end of the session, Lisa is able to walk around the room freely, cleaning up and orderly packing away all the items.

Diagnostically, this and the subsequent group session were helpful in several ways:

Lisa is much more inhibited in group than in individual sessions. She engages more with adults and is slow to warm. Although a "watcher" with a definite guardedness about her, she is able to show a lively, libidinal interest in others. The change in her use of space—from a position of being glued to her table with little sallies back and forth to the freedom she shows by the end of the session—is noteworthy, pointing to flexibility in her character style. The superego function she took on with the other children, modeled after adults, reflects her identification with her parents. Her sense of humor, evident immediately in individual sessions, did not come through until the second session, when she commented that it was "like World War II last time." Diagnostically, we confirmed our impression of an avoidant disorder rather than a schizoid or borderline picture.

Rachel, on the other hand, who showed more fear of the group initially, was able to become more physically active. In the second session her play was even more stereotypically feminine, even though she did end up in aggressive encounters with the boys, actually spitting at one of them. Except for the initial anxiety, she seemed more action-oriented and aggressive.

Adam spent almost all of the time by himself in quiet withdrawal; even when he finally wrestled with Michael, he remained silent. His use of space was quite limited and his initial lack of peer play was confirmed and seemed to emanate from him—that is, others tried to get him involved but were generally unsuccessful and eventually gave up.

Tom showed an extreme degree of aggressivity throughout, the only child in the group to require physical limit-setting. (The leaders, who deliberately assumed a "laid back" attitude, at times felt that they were right on the brink of personal danger.) Tom's tunnel play, later repeated in the carton, suggests a neurotic dynamic to his encopresis and some masochistic concerns.

Michael, whose history pointed to even more aggressivity than Tom's, was instead much better able to modulate his behavior, even after being sadistic. His marching about the room freely from the start as if it were his, his free use of the materials, and his engageability with the other children, as well as the leaders, suggested group therapy as an excellent treatment modality for him.

For the most part, the diagnostic groups have confirmed the impression of the best and most concerned reporter—usually the teacher. In this way the group affords a good opportunity to confirm the problem picture presented by the school. It has also been helpful in resolving a number of conflicting presentations. We have found the groups especially helpful in five ways:

1. Certain aspects of the child's personality structure are seen more easily and clearly through group observation than through other diagnostic means. Especially when viewing the child's relation to peers, materials, and the two cotherapists, "all areas [are] simultaneously available for observation and understanding" (Kernberg, 1978, p. 102). In addition, the way a child relates to an adult when other children are present may be very different from the way he relates when seen alone in an office. As Slavson (1943) observes, "The behavior of . . . children (and often the interview material they produce) in individual therapy is quite different from what it is in a group. In a group situation, the child sooner or later reveals his real character" (p. 107).

2. In such a natural setting (more natural, at least, than the therapist's office), the group free-play situation allows children to demonstrate their peer relation difficulties, fears of authority, inability to share, low frustration tolerance, and poor impulse control (this list comprises most of the chief complaints of referrals to our Children's Outpatient Department).

3. Certain kinds of data—relating especially to level and use of activity and aggression, motoric aspects of behavior, degree of inhibition and passivity, and degree of isolation or withdrawal—are more readily obtained from observation of the child in a group setting. By focusing our attention on specific aspects—as much on strengths as on weaknesses or deficits—the diagnostic group can shorten the time spent evaluating a child.

4. The groups also provide an interesting scale of comparison of the child relative to others in the group—for example, Lisa's real but much milder withdrawal as compared to Adam's almost total isolation, or Michael's more easily controlled and better modulated aggression as compared to Tom's. When we see a child in the office, all too often we tend either to overemphasize pathology or to minimize it (especially if the child is very appealing), not having as a yardstick other children of the same age; the group forces us to keep this in mind.

5. Lastly, such groups facilitate the Child Outpatient Department service function—aiding in the planful selection of children for group treatment (often the only treatment available when trainees' caseloads are full).

We concur with E. J. Anthony (1957), who wistfully commented, "Perhaps the day will come when no child in any clinic anywhere in the world will be placed in psychotherapy without a diagnostic evaluation . . . in the peer group" (p. 232).

REFERENCES

Anthony, E. J. (1957), Group-analytic psychotherapy with children and adolescents. In: *Group Psychotherapy*, ed. S. H. Foulkes & E. J. Anthony. Baltimore: Penguin, 1965, pp. 186–232.
Field, L. W. (1966), An ego-programmed group treatment approach with emotionally disturbed boys. *Psychol. Rep.*, 18:47–50.
Gratton, L. & Pope, L. (1972), Group diagnosis and therapy for young school children. *Hosp. Comm. Psychiat.*, 23:188–190.
Kernberg, P. F. (1978), Use of latency-age groups in the training of child psychiatrists. *Internat. J. Group. Psychother.*, 28:95–108.
King, B. L. (1970), Diagnostic activity groups for latency age children. In: *Dynamic Approaches to Serving Families*. New York: Community Service Society.
Redl, F. (1944), Diagnostic group work. *Amer. J. Orthopsychiat.*, 14:53–67.
Scheidlinger, S. (1960), Experiential group treatment of severely deprived latency-age children. *Amer. J. Orthopsychiat.*, 30:356–368.
——— (1982), *Focus on Group Psychotherapy*. New York: International Universities Press.
Slavson, S. R. (1943), *An Introduction to Group Therapy*. New York: International Universities Press.
——— (1952), *Child Psychotherapy*. New York: Columbia University Press.
Smolen, E. M., & Lifton, N. (1966), A special treatment program for schizophrenic children in a child guidance clinic. *Amer. J. Orthopsychiat.*, 36:736–742.

Part IV
Where, When, and How

Chapter 5
Child Group Psychotherapy in Special Settings

BERYCE W. MACLENNAN, Ph.D.

Different settings, that is, different types of agencies and services, influence the approaches which may be undertaken in group therapy of children. The types of children and their availability vary greatly between settings. The priorities and constraints placed on group therapy in different settings and even in institutions of the same type may vary widely. Children stay for longer or shorter periods, and their problems differ. Physical facilities for holding groups may vary in suitability. Programs are financed in many different ways, and funding may be easy or difficult to obtain.

This chapter discusses the types of groups which can be held in outpatient, private practice, inpatient, and school settings. Outpatient agencies include psychiatric facilities, family service programs, child guidance units, pediatric clinics, and day treatment programs. Inpatient settings include acute psychiatric units, general hospital wards, long- and short-term residential programs, and juvenile training schools. In schools, groups meet under several different auspices: in guidance departments, in special education, in therapeutic recreation, and in the regular classroom. Groups may be led by mental health professionals, guidance counselors, or specialty leaders. Leaders generally divide children's groups by age: preschool, latency age children, and children entering puberty. However, in some groups, where children have a common, narrow range of problems adjusting to a new school or to the divorce of parents, age may be less important.

In each setting the types of children to be found in the setting will be discussed and the groups that are appropriate for them described. We shall consider the general advantages and constraints of each setting and the ways in which it affects the management of the group program. Issues will be illustrated by different types of groups. The discussion will focus on the organization of group programs rather than on the illustration of specific methods and techniques.

Although many children's group psychotherapists mention prerequisites for their particular therapy groups, almost no literature exists which deals in any comprehensive way with the concrete and process issues involved in the conduct of different types of childrens' group psychotherapy programs. Slavson has been the exception, for he has described in detail the organizational and administrative requirements for children's group psychotherapy. In his early books, such as *The Practice of Group Therapy* (1947), he details the organization of activity group therapy, the methods he developed for selecting and inducting children into these groups, and the management of the relationships between the groups and their sponsoring institution. In his last book, *Group Psychotherapies for Children* (Slavson and Schiffer, 1975), he describes four methods in detail: activity group therapy, activity-interview group therapy, play group therapy, and therapeutic group treatment in the schools.

Slavson stresses the relationship between the group setting and the institutional environment, and the effect of the group room—its location, appearance, and appurtenances—on the climate and development of the group. Slavson and Schiffer implicitly consider spatial relationship theory (Hall, 1959) in their discussions of the size and appearance of the room as it is affected by the age of the children and the nature of the therapy. For instance, they describe the regressive aspects of messiness carried over from one meeting to another, the effects of color harmony or disharmony, the symbolism of cracks in the floor, and the challenge of locked doors. Slavson also emphasizes the relationship between the institution and the group, the different ways in which authority can be divided, and the presentation of the group to the children invited to attend.

INTERGROUP DYNAMICS

A knowledge of intergroup dynamics as well as small group process is necessary for the sound development of group psychotherapy programs for children. Intergroup relations vary in different settings and some important questions must be considered. Is group therapy perceived as an accepted activity within the institutional setting? Is it a major therapeutic alternative or a marginal activity considered peripheral to the mainstream of the organization? The latter may well be the case in hospitals, schools, correctional institutions, or clinics dedicated to training students in individual therapy. Whose clients are these—the institutions or the therapists? Who guards the entry gates to treatment? Are these individuals favorable to group psychotherapy? Is the climate of the group antithetical to the philosophy of the institution as a whole? How is authority distributed between the therapist and the institution? Are the different care providers and their functions in the institution integrated to provide a harmonious environment for treatment, or are they polarized and rivalrous, working to defeat each other with the client as the pawn in their games? Issues of power, control, authority, and boundaries all come into play so that systems theory and intergroup dynamic theory are both very relevant.

The understanding of group process and dynamics are important for the conduct of therapy groups in any setting. However, intergroup relations become especially important when group therapy per se is not the primary function of the institution, or when it is one of several treatments. For instance, in inpatient programs, group psychotherapy is one of a range of interventions and must be consistent with the others. The support of the nurses is particularly important. In outpatient programs group therapy cannot succeed if it is regarded as a second-best treatment to which patients no one else wants are assigned. The support of the institution is particularly important when, as in activity group therapy, the authority is divided, benign authority resting with the therapy and the institution maintaining overall control.

OUTPATIENT PROGRAMS

Outpatient programs for children, whether in psychiatric or child guidance facilities, community mental health or hospital clinics, or in family service agencies, originally offered individual treatment for children and their parents. The organization, facilities, and training of staff and students were all geared toward treating the individual. Gradually, with staff trained and influenced by Slavson and his disciples, activity group therapy was adopted in a number of clinics, particularly those treating a large number of latency age boys. Slavson and others such as Durkin (1965) also introduced parent guidance groups as companion to the treatment of the children. Play therapy, designed by Ginott (1961) and behavior modification groups (Brunning and Stover, 1971) were developed to a much smaller extent. In recent years, family therapy has become popular as an alternate treatment. Even today, however, unless trainees specialize in the treatment of children, most mental health professionals do not have any opportunity to lead children's groups during their basic disciplinary training, and many clinics still emphasize individual treatment.

Certain conditions are essential for managing an effective group therapy program. It is very difficult to fulfill these conditions if group therapy is not recognized as a primary treatment method. Group therapy must be considered a primary method at intake, so that sufficient numbers of children are available to achieve satisfactory grouping, and so that children and parents are properly prepared and not prejudiced against the method. Space must be adequate and supplies available as needed. The ratio of child to parent therapists must be considered so that the introduction of children's or parents' groups will not throw the organization out of balance. All staff must be prepared for groups and accepting of the program, and therapists must be trained and supervised.

When individual treatment is the primary method or when there are students who require individual cases, it frequently happens that these are selected first from the available pool of patients. The remainder of the children are then considered for group therapy, which often makes it impossible to select well-balanced, well-planned groups, and management of the group becomes very difficult.

When establishing a group program in an agency, it is important to scrutinize the total caseload and the actual and potential intake. Introducing group therapy into an agency program allows for an expansion of caseload, but staff balance and patient flow must be considered. All staff should be given introductory training and there must be a clear understanding that group therapy will be considered the treatment of choice for many children. Case-finding may become necessary if there are not enough children of a particular age or sex. If there are not sufficient children in the existing caseload, improved connections with local schools, juvenile courts, and churches are in order. The development of regular consultation with elementary school principals and their staffs can improve the referral flow of children from school to clinic, prevent inappropriate referrals, and obviate the kind of bottleneck where the clinic cannot fill its groups and the school cannot obtain treatment for disturbed and maladjusted children (MacLennan, 1975).

With good consultation, extensive intake procedures may not be necessary. Because many latency age children who are not psychotic respond well to activity group therapy, intake procedures have sometimes been modified to include one intensive interview with child and parents together and parents and child separately and a behaviorally oriented questionnaire and history, filled out by either the parent or the referral source. In group-oriented agencies, short-term diagnostic groups have also been developed. MacLennan (1982) describes a two-hour diagnostic group session, and Ganter and Polansky (1964), Churchill (1965), and King (1970) each describe four-session diagnostic groups.

Children who are treated in group therapy may be seen also in individual treatment. However, most maladjusted children with neurotic or behavior problems which are acted out will not require such treatment unless there is symptomatology which cannot be reached through the group experience. Most parents will also be treated in individual, family, or group therapy or in parent group guidance. Some clinics will not see any children without involving the parents or guardians in treatment. However, some children with immaturity problems, or who have lived through traumatic experiences or situational crises, may well respond to group treatment even though the parents are not included. This decision will depend on the extent to which parents are part of the problem and whether they will act destructively or supportively as the child responds to treatment.

The development of a group therapy program in a child guidance agency may change the required ratio of parent to child therapists. Placement of large numbers of children in groups will require fewer child therapists to serve the same caseload. Unless parents are also placed in groups and the program expanded, the agency will no longer need all its child therapists. This can cause resistance to the program if the problem is not addressed. A similar situation is created if parents are placed in group therapy and children are not. In one agency where this latter situation occurred, no parent groups were successful until the problem was identified, articulated, and dealt with.

Many clinics today design their facilities to include one or more large playrooms to serve as children's group therapy rooms. The room must be large enough for children to run about (20 by 30 feet) and is best self-contained, with its own toilet and separate entrance. Ideally, the room should not be used for other purposes, because the children and therapist should not be unduly constrained by thoughts of neatness and cleanliness. Closet space should be available so that each group can keep its own special supplies and products from one meeting to the next. If a clinic does not possess such space, it is possible to hold groups in recreation centers, church basements, or wherever space is available. This may place some constraints on the therapy because of the demands of the accommodating institution or the feelings of the children about the place.

In adult group psychotherapy, it has been customary to use therapy as a useful training method, pairing a trainee with an experienced therapist. A major concern in activity group therapy is that there not be an inappropriate ratio of therapists to children. The children must learn to run their own groups. Consequently, it is preferable to initiate training for therapists by observation through a one-way screen and/or analysis of video tapes or process records. Once the trainee has an understanding of the treatment method, he or she should be allowed to run a group alone under close supervision. Crisis and problem-oriented groups are more content-focused, and there a second therapist is more easily accepted. Groups for seriously disturbed children are quite different. In these situations, two or more therapists may well be needed to assist in stimulating interaction, keeping the children in contact, and counteracting the anxieties of individual children (Speers and Lansing, 1965; Gratton and Rizzo, 1973).

Group therapy for children in day treatment has many of the same characteristics of groups in long-term residential treatment, and the discussion in that section can be considered relevant. However, the parents are almost always involved in the treatment in day programs, and transportation is an issue, just as in outpatient clinics.

PRIVATE PRACTICE

A relatively small number of child therapists in private practice hold children's groups, as reported in two surveys of therapy groups conducted for AGPA (Waxenberg and Wiedemann, 1971: Waxenberg, Fidler and Wiedemann, 1976). In 1971 only 2 percent of all groups reported by members included children, and the authors stated that while 47 percent of all groups were held in private practice, children's groups were underrepresented in this category. In 1976 only 1 percent of all groups were conducted for children (66 such groups), and of these only 10 were conducted in private practice. Of the other children's groups, 25 were held in clinics, 17 in schools, 3 in hospitals, 3 in community mental health centers, 3 in day centers, and 5 in miscellaneous settings.

There are a number of reasons for the lack of groups in private practice. First of all, it may be difficult to bring together a sufficient number of suitable children. Children's groups are limited not only by problem and treatment need but also by age and sometimes by sex. A therapist must have a large practice or a wide referral network in order to run children's groups, unless they form part of a group practice. Some therapists serve as consultants to other social agencies and obtain referrals in that way. In one or two places, therapists have joined together systematically to organize referrals, but private practitioners, particularly at the start, find it difficult to establish children's groups.

Secondly, child therapists in private practice may not have a large enough playroom. Groups require two or three times the amount of space that individual treatment requires. Therapists working out of their own homes may be able to set up suitable space in a basement. Therapists in group practice may share a facility, or the therapist may follow the practice of some clinics and rent space nearby.

A third problem may be the transportation of the children and the treatment of the parents. Some therapists work in tandem, one seeing the children groups and the other the parent groups at the same time. This may result in some difficulty if either child or parent is temporarily in resistance and neither comes. In cities or towns with good transportation, the children may come on their own. If distances are not too great, the parent can just drop the child off and return at the end of the group. However, parents may become bored and resistive if several have to wait one and a half or two hours for their children and no provision is made for some program for them.

Financial considerations may also pose a problem in the establishment of children's groups in private practice. Reimbursement or payment for the full amount of time involved in running children's groups, plus the necessary collateral work, may be difficult to obtain. The groups may not be as financially profitable as seeing the children individually.

A special problem faces private practitioners who run activity therapy groups. It is difficult to split the benign and restricting authority; having no institutional structure, the therapist must be both rule interpreter and rule enforcer. Consequently, the therapist may have to bear the full brunt of negative transferences. This is in contrast to normal activity therapy groups, where the institution attracts the negative feelings and the therapist can remain in a more neutral position as a benign authority who clarifies reality.

INPATIENT SETTINGS

There is a variety of inpatient settings in which children's therapy groups may be conducted. Children with acute psychiatric breakdowns may be admitted to psychiatric units in children's or general hospitals or to children's units in specialized psychiatric hospitals. If no other facilities are available, they may enter state or county mental hospitals. In acute settings, stays for children may be rather short and turnover will be high. Consequently, therapy groups tend to be open-ended, child- rather than group-focused, and with relatively little opportunity for selection. In such settings, the majority of the children may be psychotic or very seriously disturbed, exhibiting withdrawn or extremely aggressive behavior, and may be out of contact part of the time. For these reasons it is usual to have two or more therapists participating in the groups; one manages the group, while others contain individual children or encourage their participation.

In general hospitals there may be a shortage of play space. Nonetheless, it is important to arrange for a private room. Room size may not be especially important because the number of children is usually small. Also, many therapists with very disturbed children use puppets, role playing, art, or doll play to help the children live out and learn how to cope with their problems, and these activities do not require a great deal of space. However, some therapists use dance, music, and rhythms to enhance body perceptions and may require a larger room.

Group sessions are usually quite short, anywhere from 15 to 45 minutes, because of the difficulty in retaining the children's attention. For instance, Williams, Lewis, Copeland, Tucker, and Feegan (1978) run groups for seriously disturbed children for 15 minutes at a time. Two therapists work with four or five children using puppets, art, drama, and music.

In both acute hospitalization and in long-term residential treatment, the need to synchronize the 24-hour milieu, the educational program, and individual and group therapy is more obvious than in outpatient treatment, where the three components are divided among family, school, and clinic respectively. Group therapy must be viewed and planned for as part of the overall treatment. Very often, two of the treatment team members, perhaps a nurse and a psychiatrist or psychologist, will run the group together. The relationships between team members are critical for the progress of the children. Special prerelease groups may be run, in which transitions back into the community and the home are worked out. Sometimes parents and outpatient therapists are included in these groups.

In general medicine, therapy groups may be run in either inpatient or clinic settings to deal with the emotional reactions of children with general medical and surgical problems. Groups are particularly useful for children with chronic problems, who may have to learn to accept long-term handicaps and to maintain a therapeutic way of life. Many such groups are problem-oriented, focusing on feelings about the children's handicaps, diet, exercise, and limitations. They examine the conflicts in interpersonal relationships which arise out of their handicaps, so that the age and sex of the children matter less than the commonality of their problems. However, it is still important to consider the makeup of the group and the potential for multiple negative transference reactions.

A particular problem in all inpatient and medically related groups is to determine who serves as the primary therapist and to what extent the group therapists have autonomy over what happens in the group. While the overall directions of therapy may be decided at team meetings or by a medical director, what happens in the group should be the responsibility of the group therapists and the children.

Long-term residential placements are often far from home, and it may be difficult for therapists to work concurrently with children and parents. Sometimes it is possible to run parent or multiple family groups if parents make monthly visits. Sometimes there is collaboration between the community agency at home and the residential treatment staff, the former working with the parents and the latter with the children. In all cases groups can be useful in working through transitions back into the home.

In the best residential and day treatment programs, group therapy is included consistently as part of a unified treatment plan with other interventions. The staff see themselves as a team in which each has an important function to play for each child and for the entire population. In such a setting, there may be several different types of groups: (1) a large group as a whole focused on the life of the community and its day-to-day problems; (2) therapeutic activity groups in which the children learn to interact with each other; and (3) the classroom group, where learning is more than just acquiring cognitive skills. Therapy groups are organized where children and their parents, separately or together, learn about underlying problems which affect their feelings and behavior. They experience how to cope with their emotions and how to interact with others.

In some programs the climate of the institution is such that disciplines compete with each other. Unit staff and therapists may be antagonistic and rivalrous, or a staff may be grief-ridden over the loss of a leader. When the staff are disturbed, it is not possible for the program to be therapeutic. The children are torn between competing factions and are filled with anxiety, confusion and guilt. It is likely that they will act out the conflicts of the staff in and out of the group or avoid the group altogether.

SCHOOL SETTINGS

There are many advantages and disadvantages to the schools as the place to run therapy groups. For most children between the ages of five and fourteen, the school is the primary institution, other than the family, with which they have contact. The school staff know the children well (at least in most elementary schools). Unless the children are truants, they are at school already and do not have to be transported to treatment.

On the other hand, therapy is not the school's primary function. In most schools children must have a pass to come to group, and a teacher may not always be willing to release the child, placing greater priority on academic learning. Children may also have to be escorted to group and no one may be available. In some unfortunate situations, space may be at a premium. Groups have been run in cafeterias, gymnasiums, sometimes even in corridors. It is usually not possible to have one room used exclusively for group therapy. Sometimes groups have had to be moved several times during a semester because some other activity is given higher priority. These conditions preclude the establishment of an effective group therapy program and should not be condoned.

It is not possible to keep secret that a child attends group therapy. Some children may have strong feelings about other children knowing they need treatment. The reputation the group therapy program develops in the school will be critical for the success of the groups. If the groups are respected, the program will undoubtedly garner a number of self-referrals. If the reverse is true, many children will avoid the group or refuse to attend, and children who do come may be teased or shunned by peers. The first group in the school will be extremely important and must be carefully planned.

It goes without saying, therefore, that the relationships between the therapist and the principal, teachers, and guidance personnel must be well worked out and positive so that everyone understands what the groups are about and that the authority of the school is behind them. The value system and tone of the school will limit what kinds of groups are possible there. A principal who is very strict and orderly may have difficulty tolerating an unstructured activity group in his domain. School rules may create problems. For instance, defiant children often seek to pit teachers against therapists. They may come to group without a pass, smoke cigarettes in restricted areas, or attempt to test out confidentiality.

The feelings of the children about the institution may influence their attendance and what can be achieved. For instance, if children are not happy in school and are truant, it will be difficult for them to come to group regularly. Habitual truants are best treated outside the school.

Groups usually have to be run within school hours and within the span of the semester, when the children are available. As a result, therapists tend to favor relatively short, time-limited groups which do not have an open enrollment. That is, they run for a specific period with a closed membership, end, and regroup if they start again.

As in groups in residential settings, the children have predetermined roles and relationships with each other which will precondition group interaction. Depending on the group method, the therapist may gather together a natural group and work with already established relationships or may group the children differently so that they will have to deal with a different set. For instance, a child who is a bully may be placed with older children, or a timid child with a group of children where there is a chance to lead or at least share fears.

Depending on the type, the group may be led by teachers with special training, guidance counselors, or mental health specialists who may or may not be part of the regular staff of the school. Unless there is a large child guidance department attached to the school system, therapists are often trained and supervised by a professional from outside the school system, a mental health consultant who has specialized in group psychotherapy. This consultant must be well accepted by the principal and the teachers, as well as the therapists supervised. Before the start of a group therapy program, it is useful to conduct some orientation for all the staff as to the nature of group therapy and what can be expected from it.

Because the schools are primarily concerned with children, parents may be less frequently involved in treatment than in mental health clinics. However, they must be involved at the referral stage, even though the referral comes from the child or the teacher, and permission for treatment must be obtained. Some guidance departments have successfully involved children and their parents in multiple-family therapy groups, particularly with older children.

In elementary schools, many of the children are drawn from the same neighborhoods, and children and parents may know each other outside the school. As family secrets revealed in the group may therefore become an issue, rules regarding confidentiality must be worked out at the start of the program and discussed with both children and parents.

Apart from the normal treatment groups for disturbed and maladjusted children, which may be conducted in several different settings, schools lend themselves particularly to short-term groups centered around crises and changes. Effron (1980) led short-term groups for elementary school children following the divorce of their parents. She used role playing, affective educational techniques, and creative writing to help them deal with the trauma. In schools with many military children or others from mobile families, who enter school at all times of the year, induction groups may be led. Role playing groups were run in many schools to prepare for school desegregation. Landgarten, Junge, Tasem, and Watson (1976) used art therapy and discussion in the classroom for crisis intervention following a neighborhood shoot-out.

CRISIS GROUPS IN DIFFERENT SETTINGS

A number of short-term children's groups dealing with crisis situations and held in unusual settings have been reported in the recent literature. Some of these include groups following natural disasters such as earthquakes or floods. Very soon after the event, the children with or without their parents are brought together to abreact some of the psychic trauma, fear, and guilt aroused by the disaster. These groups may be held in churches, town halls, or schools, wherever the survivors have been assembled. Naturally, there is little or no opportunity to be selective, and the groups may be quite large. Many of these groups discuss the disaster, the children's emotional reactions to it, and the everyday problems which have arisen. In the Omaha tornado crisis (Omaha Tornado Project, 1976), special coloring books were prepared to portray the event. Some leaders use psychodrama. Leaders of these groups are usually specially trained professionals, but they may be assisted by counselors who have trained with them as part of a disaster team.

Crisis group therapy may also be used to work with children in emergency shelters for domestic violence victims. Small groups may be formed to help the children understand and cope with what has been happening to them and to their parents. The groups in such a setting are likely to be relatively small, and there will be little opportunity for selection. Sometimes younger and older children will be placed together, in which case the groups may use puppets, fantasy-stimulating games, or just discussion. Groups for younger children tend to concentrate on play. The groups are held at the center and are usually open-ended, as children come and go. The children attend the groups as long as they live in the shelter.

All crisis groups are time-limited and focused on particular emotional and real-life problems. They are often conducted in settings which attempt to be supportive, and form part of a program which supplies physical necessities, warmth, rest, nourishment, and safety.

FAMILY OR PARENT GROUP PSYCHOTHERAPY IN DIFFERENT SETTINGS

Both the nature of the setting and the philosophy of the institution or therapist will affect how parents and families of children in group therapy are involved. Most child guidance clinics and mental health centers believe it is important to treat parents as well as children. If the children are placed in group therapy, the parents may be seen individually, in parent groups, or together with their children from time to time. Some parents may be involved as patients in individual or group psychotherapy.

In school systems, treatment is much more likely to be focused on the child. While some systems include guidance departments with staff trained to work with multiple-family or parent groups, most do not. It is much more likely that parents will be seen at the beginning for diagnostic purposes and to obtain permission for treatment. They may come together from time to time for conferences with the therapist, teacher, and child, and at termination to evaluate the program of treatment. Sometimes parents may be referred to a clinic or to a private therapist. When children are in special education or therapeutic day programs, there is more likelihood that parents will be brought together in guidance groups. These groups not only help parents manage their children but also help them work through their feelings about having a damaged or defective child.

There are now several programs throughout the country which have been established after a model developed in Nashville, Tennessee. Parents are trained in groups to work with their children, who are severely disturbed, autistic, or retarded. They come together with their children to the clinic and learn methods to modify behavior. Experienced parents help the others and form a crisis network. This has proved an effective system for treating very disturbed children at home. Similar programs start by admitting children to inpatient units for initial diagnosis and treatment planning, and then train the parents (Samit, 1982).

GROUP THERAPY FACTORS AFFECTED BY DIFFERENT SETTINGS

As illustrated in our discussions of group therapy for children in different settings, a number of factors are affected by the setting: space; transportation; time; integration of group therapy into the overall program; and financing.

Space. Space requirements vary with the ages and sizes of the children, their diagnostic problems, and the type of therapy planned. The availability of suitable space is of course affected by the setting.

Boundaries are important in all therapies. Cafeterias, large gymnasiums, or limitless space outdoors are generally unsuitable for group therapy because they lead to group fragmentation and provide insufficient structural support. On the other hand, if the room is too small, the child's personal space may be violated and he may become anxious. If there is insufficient room to "let off steam," disturbed children may become more aggressive and violent.

Activity group therapy requires space for the children to play actively, pursue crafts, and take refreshments (a room or yard about 20 by 30 feet), whereas play group therapy with small children, using fantasy toys, art, or drama, may be much smaller (perhaps 14 by 16). Discussion groups naturally require less space.

The shape of therapy rooms is also important. Long narrow rooms, rooms with nooks and odd angles, or those with too many doors do not promote good feelings, a sense of security, and easy communication. The group members should be able to have privacy and a sense of ownership of the room, even if only for the meeting time. Conditions are usually more easily met in settings where therapy is the primary activity. The room should be insulated from other institutional activities so that noise and the outflow of children from the room do not disturb others. In clinics, children should have their own entrance to the group room.

Needs for furnishings and materials vary greatly with different types of therapy and children. Slavson and Schiffer (1975) describe very precisely the types and numbers of tables, chairs, and other equipment required for activity group therapy. In play therapy, some therapists use sand and water and other regressive materials to stimulate fantasy. These may make a considerable mess and are contraindicated in some settings (Ginott, 1961). If a school has all its chairs and tables bolted to the floor in rows, the rooms cannot be used for group therapy. Glass in doors and windows must be protected if the children are likely to be rowdy or aggressive, or if they play ball. If therapists in private practice have only a multipurpose office-playroom, they will be limited in the kinds of groups they can hold.

Therapists working with seriously disturbed, psychotic children will be particularly concerned about the kind of supportive structure the setting can provide. Some therapists prefer a bare room with few toys or none at all, particularly if they use fantasy games such as the magic shop as a major therapeutic tool. Others like Speers and Lansing (1965) require that there be mirrors on the walls so that children may become more familiar with their body image. Trafimow and Pattak (1982) used both a rug for the children, so that they could be close and intimate, and small chairs, so that they could distance themselves when they felt anxious.

Transportation. In outpatient settings and in private practice, transportation and its management can affect attendance and the success of treatment. Transportation for trips may cause insurance difficulties.

Time. Temporal factors are conditioned not only by the problems of the children and the nature of the therapy but also by the institutional setting. For instance, in the treatment of psychotic children in acute hospitals, while the duration of each session will probably be short (15–50 minutes) because of the difficulty these children experience in maintaining attention, the group is also likely to be open-ended and the children will attend only a few sessions. On the other hand, the groups in residential settings are likely to last over a considerable period and there will be little change in group membership. In the school, short-term group therapy is likely to be the norm, as treatment is influenced by the semester. The duration of sessions will be conditioned by the length of class periods. The session will usually last either one or two periods. In private practice and outpatient clinics, there are fewer extraneous factors of this nature to affect treatment decisions, although availability of insurance benefits may affect length of treatment.

Integration into the overall program. As mentioned earlier, therapy groups cannot function independently of the rest of the program, with the exception of private practice and some outpatient clinics. Group therapy must be an integral part of both the overall program and each individual treatment plan. Group therapists should be included in the treatment and educational therapeutic teams. Roles and functions need to be defined so that territorial disputes over programs, groups, and children do not arise or can be speedily mediated.

Financing. Group psychotherapy for children conducted by licensed independent practitioners or in accredited health or mental health settings may be paid for by parents or third-party reimbursement. In a sample of 100 insurance plans, an American Psychiatric Association Task Force (Biegel, 1982) found that 84 percent of the plans would reimburse physicians for group therapy, 47 percent for psychologists, and 31 percent for social workers who practiced independently. Group therapy in schools, family agencies, and some residential settings may not meet eligibility qualifications. However, many community agencies receive funds from community chests or other charitable sources so that costs may be defrayed. In schools, group therapy may be paid for as a necessary treatment for severely handicapped children under PL 94–142, or it may be included in the school budget. Many schools provide group therapy as a service through their guidance departments and there is no separate charge. Similarly, some residential treatment programs and inpatient hospitals include group therapy in the residential charge. However, in medical settings groups may be reimbursable under Medicaid or insurance.

Special Settings

There are wide differences in fees for group psychotherapy. Some programs charge the same fee for group as for individual psychotherapy; others charge one-half or two-thirds the rate. Some practitioners charge by the session; others, particularly for short-term problem-oriented treatment, for the entire series. Some therapists prefer to charge by the month.

Financing of children's groups may be seen as unrewarding for the private practitioner as well as difficult to establish. Children's activity groups often have a membership of only four to six patients and may last two hours. There are supplies and refreshments to buy and there may also be collateral work with schools or social agencies as well as with parents. Consequently, as the return is relatively low, not too many child psychotherapists in private practice undertake children's groups. For these reasons, the trend is to establish family therapy or multiple-family groups rather than children's groups, although with latency age children group therapy may be the treatment of choice.

THE FUTURE

Two perceptible trends affect the directions of group psychotherapy with children. The first is a growing tendency to identify well-defined problems for which specific short-term group treatments are designed, and the second is an increase in family therapy. Short-term groups include post-disaster play groups; groups dealing with specific losses, grief reactions, and life transitions such as moving or divorce; groups for children suffering from particular illnesses or concerned with substance abuse; and groups for developing specific coping skills. It is likely that most of these groups will continue to be developed in the appropriate institutional setting rather than in private practice. There groups for children will continue to be the exception rather than the rule.

Family therapy is likely to increase in popularity, and more therapists will work with multiple family groups. As family therapy groups are relatively easy to organize and do not require the amount of space needed for children's activity groups, they will probably increase in popularity with private practitioners.

Third-party reimbursement mechanisms today reinforce the movement to short-term treatment and toward group rather than individual therapy in private practice in organized settings. We need to work for the recognition as independent practitioners of those mental health professionals who are licensed in their discipline and who are well trained as group psychotherapists, as well as toward the specific inclusion of group psychotherapy as a bona fide treatment modality in all insurance plans. There is also a need to define the family as a treatment unit and to establish parameters for the reimbursement of individual and group family therapy.

REFERENCES

Adams, M. A. (1976), A hospital play program. *Amer. J. Orthopsychiat.*, 46:416–424.
Biegel, A. (1982), Analysis of one hundred insurance plans. Washington, D.C.: American Psychiatric Association Task Force on Insurance.
Brunning, R.M., & Stover, D. (1971), *Behavior Modification in Child Treatment*. New York: Aldine.
Churchill, S. (1965), Social group work: A diagnostic tool in child guidance. *Amer. J. Orthopsychiat.*, 34:581–588.
Daniels, C. R. (1965), Play group therapy with children. *Acta Psychother.*, 12:45–48.
Durkin, H. (1965), *The Group in Depth*. New York: International Universities Press.
Effron, A. K. (1980), Children and divorce: Help from an elementary school. *Soc. Casework*, 61:305–316.
Ganter, G., & Polansky, N. (1964), Predicting a child's accessibility to individual treatment from diagnostic groups. *J. of Social Work*, 9:56–63.
Ginott, H. G. (1961), *Group Psychotherapy with Children: The Theory and Practice of Play Therapy*. New York: McGraw-Hill.
Gratton, L., & Rizzo, A.E. (1973), Group therapy with young psychotic children. *Internat. J. Group Psychother.*, 23:54–68.
Hall, E. T. (1959), *The Silent Language*. New York: Doubleday.
King, B. L. (1970), *Diagnostic Activity Groups for Latency Age Children*. New York: Community Service Society.
Landgarten, H., Junge, M., Tasem, M., & Watson, M. (1976), Art therapy as a modality for crisis intervention. *Clin. Soc. Work J.*, 26:475–486.
Lovasdal, S. (1976), A multiple therapy approach in work with children. *Internat. J. Group Psychother.*, 26:475–486.
Lemoncelli, J. (1977), Groups to combat reaction to flood disaster. Personal communication.
MacLennan, B. W. (1975), Program development and gaining access in community mental health consultation to the schools. In: *The Practice of Mental Health Consultation*, ed. F.V. Mannino, B.W. MacLennan, & M.F. Shore. Washington, D.C.: HEW, pp. 74–112.
——— (1977), Modifications of activity group therapy for children. *Internat. J. Group Psychother.*, 27:85–96.
——— (1982), An activity group for pre-adolescent boys. In: *Handbook of Short-term Therapy Groups*, ed. M. Rosenbaum. New York: McGraw-Hill.
Perry, E. (1955), The treatment of aggressive juvenile delinquents in family group therapy. *Internat. J. Group Psychother.*, 5:131–149.

Omaha Tornado Project (1976), Final Report to the Federal Disaster Administration. Omaha Eastern Nebraska Human Services Agency.

Rhodes, S. L. (1973), Short term groups of latency age children in a school setting. *Internat. J. Group Psychother.*, 23:204–216.

Samit, C. J. (1982), A group for parents of autistic children. In: *Handbook of Short-Term Therapy Groups*, ed. M. Rosenbaum. New York: McGraw-Hill.

Slavson, S. R. (1947), *The Practice of Group Therapy*. New York: International Universities Press.

—— Schiffer, M. (1975), *Group Psychotherapies for Children*. New York: International Universities Press.

Speers, R. W., & Lansing, C. (1965), *Group Therapy in Childhood Psychoses*. Chapel Hill: University of North Carolina Press.

Trafimow, E., & Pattak, S.I. (1982), Group treatment of primitively fixated children. *Internat. J. Group Psychother.*, 32:445–452.

Waxenberg, S., & Wiedemann, C. (1971), *Survey of Group Therapy by Members of AGPA*. New York: American Group Psychotherapy Association.

—— Fidler, J., & Wiedemann, C. (1976), *Survey of Group Therapy by Members of AGPA*. New York: American Group Psychotherapy Association.

Williams, J., Lewis, C., Copeland, F., Tucker, L., & Feegan, L. (1978), A model for short-term group therapy on a children's inpatient unit. *Clin. Soc. Work J.*, 6:21–32.

Chapter 6
Applications of Child Group Psychotherapy

THOMAS GAINES, JR., Ph.D.

Since its inception, child group psychotherapy has undergone developmental processes of differentiation and specialization. From Slavson's pioneering activity group therapy in 1934, the models of child group therapy have multiplied to include play group therapy (Ginott, 1961), group behavior therapy (Rose, 1973), activity group guidance (Hillman, Penczar, and Barr, 1975), and activity-interview group therapy (Schiffer, 1977). Specialized applications have also multiplied to include group treatment for parents, for socially deficient children, for children experiencing parental divorce, and for abused children. This chapter will explore these applications of child group psychotherapy.

GROUP TREATMENT FOR PARENTS

Slavson (1956) began conducting parent guidance groups shortly after he initiated activity group therapy for children, and reported such groups to be "more effective and efficient than individual guidance" for parents. The efficacy of group treatment for parents has been generally supported in the literature, despite the wide range of treatment formats and approaches that have been employed (Westman, Kansky, Erikson, Arthur, and Vroom, 1963; Green and Fuller, 1973; Patterson, 1974; Hoffman, Byrne, Belnap, and Steward, 1981; Cunningham and Matthews, 1982; Pevsner, 1982).

Westman et al. (1963) were among the first to describe "parallel group psychotherapy" as a method for treating both parents and children at the same time. Mothers, fathers, and children were seen separately in long-term, psychoanalytically oriented groups, with periodic joint sessions between mothers and fathers. This format has also been used by Speers and Lansing (1964) in working with parents of autistic children, and by Green and Fuller (1973) in working with parents of effeminate boys. Pasnau, Meyer, Davis, Lloyd, and Kline (1976) modified the format so that mothers and fathers were seen together in a single group.

There are many common elements in clinicians' descriptions of parent groups (Westman et al., 1963; Green and Fuller, 1973; Pasnau et al., 1976; Hock, 1977; Hoffman et al., 1981; Cunningham and Matthews, 1982). The parents are characterized as suffering from low self-esteem, shame and guilt, and social isolation. They usually have difficulty setting consistent limits and are dissatisfied with the child's failure to live up to unrealistic expectations. Many are conflicted about confronting the child with their dissatisfaction. They often assume passive and permissive roles in managing inappropriate behaviors, fearing the loss of their child's love if they confront such behaviors assertively. Their passivity is frequently punctuated by emotional outbursts toward the child when they can no longer control their frustration. Marital problems are common, with unresolved parental conflicts being displaced upon the symptomatic child. Despite their discomfort and dissatisfaction, these parents commonly find it difficult to admit that they have problems. Resistant to becoming involved in psychotherapy for themselves, they agree to enter a parents' group for their child's sake, especially if this is a requirement for placement in a children's group.

The initial focus of the parent's group is on the children's behavior. Parents show considerable curiosity about each other's children, and "story-telling" about the children abounds. Some parents will minimize the problems they encounter, while others will more readily admit to feelings of guilt and failure concerning their child's behavior. The initial sharing of children's problems helps reduce the sense of uniqueness parents feel about their child's difficulties; parents find they are not alone in being unable to cope. The description of children's problems elicits support and advice from other group members. Parents find it easier to express solutions for other parents' problems than for their own. Such common themes as playmates, chores, and schoolwork develop. While still child-focused, the support, advice, development of common themes, and reduction of isolation help the group develop cohesiveness which will later enable it to confront members' distortions and maladaptive responses to family situations. Group cohesiveness is also a prerequisite for parents to begin exploring their personal and marital problems.

The initial step in the shift from a child focus to a parent focus usually begins when parents begin discussing how they respond to their children's problems. Parents' responses to the same type of problem will vary, and the reasons for this variation should be explored. Atypical reactions involving unmet needs or unresolved conflicts in parents will attract attention from other group members. Group attention will also be focused upon parents who resist the group's suggestions for dealing with their child's problems. Encouraged by the therapist, the group will begin to explore the reasons for, and the consequences of, parents' maladaptive responses. A personal crisis experienced by a group member often precipitates group discussion of adult problems. Once the barrier against discussing personal problems is broken, the parent group has entered the working phase of treatment. Members are then free to deal with their difficulties on all levels: parent-child, parent-parent, and intrapsychic.

Parent groups involve dynamics of both group psychotherapy and family psychotherapy. The group dynamics of pairing, scapegoating, monopolizing, dependence and counterdependence upon the therapist, and intimacy are typical of parent groups. The initial resistance of parents, their displacing the focus of the family problem onto the child, their later willingness to deal with marital and personal issues and displacement of projections from their child to the group, and transfer of symptoms from one family member to the next—these are some of the family therapy dynamics often found in parent groups.

The advantages of parallel parent group psychotherapy have been described as follows:

1. Responsibility for resolving presenting problems is placed upon both parents and children, rather than upon the child "identified patient" alone (Westman et al., 1963).

2. Parental involvement in treatment encourages more regular and sustained attendance in both parents' and children's groups (Soo, 1979).

3. The sharing of problematic experiences reduces parents' sense of isolation and encourages them to try resolving the problem (Hoffman et al., 1981).

4. The group offers permission for expression of thoughts and feelings, and thereby helps parents become aware of their feelings of

guilt, shame, resentment, and failure concerning their children (Pasnau et al., 1976).

5. Parents are helped to recognize how they contribute to their child's problems and how they can modify this contribution (Pasnau et al., 1976).

6. The group offers a reality base to help parents correct distorted perceptions and unrealistic expectations (Cunningham and Matthews, 1982).

7. A better understanding of the nature of the child's problems replaces the myth of the child being "sick" with hereditary, irreversible defects (Cunningham and Matthews, 1982).

8. Parents are given emotional support as well as an opportunity to explore their unmet needs (Speers and Lansing, 1964).

The major disadvantage of separate parent and child groups has been the lack of actual interaction between parents and children. This has led to the establishment of joint parent-child groups. Hoffman et al. (1981) established a "semi-permeable" group in which mothers and sons met in one room with a monitored boundary between the two groups. Early in treatment the boys frequently intruded upon the mothers' group process. Since these intrusions also occurred at home, they became a central therapeutic issue. The therapist helped the mothers define the limits they wished to establish and then encouraged them to set these limits in a direct, positive manner. The actual interaction between mothers and sons enhanced the opportunities for developing better parenting skills and clearer communication between parents and children. It also allowed a more adequate reality base in the parents' group, as both therapist and members could see and hear actual parent-child interactions rather than relying upon parents' reports. However, the presence of the children appeared to inhibit the parents' ability to shift to personal and intrapsychic issues.

Cunningham and Matthews (1982) described a parallel group format in which parents and children met together once a month and separately the other three weeks. In this author's experience with both parallel and multiple-family groups, periodic joint and separate sessions provide an optimal general model for parallel group treatment. The joint sessions offer opportunities to review progress and set goals. The reality base that joint group sessions offer is important to both therapists and group members. Child group therapists become more familiar with their members' parents, and parent group therapists with the children. During joint sessions, the therapists can obtain more reliable information about parents' and children's progress at home, school, and with peers. The joint sessions also offer the therapists the opportunity to work on actual parent-child interaction.

One of the interesting phenomena observed during joint sessions, especially at the beginning of group treatment, is the reluctance of parents to initiate and direct group interaction. Through their inhibition and passivity, parents generally allow their children (or the therapists) to set the tone of the meeting. They then react to either their children's behavior or to the therapists' questions. This probably parallels the parents' reactive roles at home. To put parents at ease and thereby elicit their active involvement, I have found it useful to hold the initial joint sessions in the parents' therapy room and to follow the parents' verbal discussion format. Later on, the parents may be more conducive to joining the children in their room and in the activity-discussion format.

Separate sessions are also important, as they allow the parent and child groups to explore their respective issues with less inhibition. Parents need separate sessions to discuss personal issues, while children will not fully exhibit peer behavior in their parents' presence.

GROUP TREATMENT FOR CHILDREN WITH PEER RELATION PROBLEMS

Poor peer relations are a common reason for referring children to group psychotherapy. Socially unpopular children exhibit a variety of behavior problems which can be clustered into three general categories (Allen, Safer, Heaton, Ward, and Barrell, 1975). The first category includes shy and withdrawn children who are anxious in social interactions. These children have been found deficient in such social behaviors as making eye contact, initiating social interactions with peers, responding to peers' initiations, knowing how to make friends, and overall verbal output (Gottman, Gonso, and Rasmussen, 1975; Bornstein, Bellack, and Hersen, 1977; Ladd, 1981).

The second category includes aggressive and impulsive children who, by interrupting others, arguing and fighting, calling attention to themselves, and acting noncooperatively with group activity, reduce their chances of gaining entry into social groups (Putallaz and Gottman, 1981).

The third category includes attention-deficient children who have difficulty paying attention, following instructions, and staying with the group activity. Although motorically active, they often show deficits in motor skill performance, which also interferes with social popularity in latency age children (Broekhoff, 1977).

Children lacking social competence and popularity with peers have been found to become academic underachievers and delinquents (Roff, Sells, and Golden, 1972). Their social isolation reinforces low self-esteem and dependence upon family. Not surprisingly, they are several times more likely to be referred for mental health services than are their peers (Cowen, Pederson, Babigian, Izzo, and Trost, 1973; Allen et al., 1975).

Group psychotherapy provides a tolerant, supportive environment for learning social skills. As soon as children become comfortable with the group, they exhibit their socially deficient behaviors. Encouraged by the therapist, the group directly confronts these behaviors and suggests more appropriate alternatives. Through observing others and engaging in trial-and-error experimentation, children are able to learn new skills at their own pace. These new skills include awareness of social rules and expectations, ability to express needs and feelings, listening to others, and negotiating and compromising with others. Exhibiting new skills tends to be immediately reinforced by both therapist and group members (Coolidge and Grunebaum, 1964; Frey and Kolodny, 1966; Soo, 1974; Lovasdal, 1976; Weisselberger, 1977).

The development of social skills is a primary focus of all child group psychotherapy models. Groups using behavior modification principles offer specific strategies for teaching social skills. These strategies include contingency management, modeling, and coaching. Contingency management involves the selective rewarding of positive behaviors targeted to replace existing negative behaviors. Modeling involves the live or videotaped demonstration of target behaviors. Coaching involves direct instruction and demonstration of the targeted behavior, having the child practice it through rehearsal and role playing, and providing corrective feedback regarding the child's performance. A good behavioral program contains elements of all three of these strategies (no one of which has been shown to be superior) so that small, gradual changes in behavior are learned and reinforced (Hops, 1982, 1983; McFall, 1982).

A typical behavioral group begins with the assessment of inappropriate behaviors and targeting of new behaviors. This assessment is based upon reviewing the child's history, discussing current behavior with parents and teachers, and observing the child in a natural peer setting or during an initial group session (Allen et al., 1975; Johnson, 1975). Target behaviors for shy, withdrawn children include "playing with others" and "talking with others." Target behaviors for impulsive, aggressive children include "waiting your turn" and "keeping your hands to yourself." Children with attention deficits would be given the target behaviors of "listening to directions" and "staying with the group activity" (Durlak, 1977).

The target behaviors are discussed with each child, resulting in a behavior contract between therapist and child (Johnson, 1975). The child's progress toward fulfulling the contract can be graphed on charts placed in the meeting room (Durlak, 1977). Target behaviors for the whole group can also be formulated. These would include adherence to such group norms as listening quietly to the person speaking and talking to the group as a whole (Kelly and Matthews, 1971).

During initial sessions, the therapist explains the group rules and reinforcement system. Members are told they will receive chips for making progress toward fulfilling their contracts. The chips can be used at the end of each meeting to buy candy, small toys, or trinkets from the group "store." Chips are liberally given each time the child evinces a desirable behavior. Along with the chip, the child receives verbal praise from the therapist, as well as an explanation of how the child has earned the chip. The therapist also uses prompting to ensure that each child earns a minimum number of chips and is thereby able to sample the reinforcers (Stedman, Peterson, and Cardarelle, 1971; Johnson, 1975; Durlak, 1977).

During the beginning stage of treatment, therapist attention is focused upon identifying inappropriate behavior, rewarding desirable behavior, and reiterating the behavior contracts. At the beginning of each session, the therapist summarizes the discussion and homework assignments of the previous sessions. Members are rewarded for the successful completion of their assignments, and other outside experiences are discussed. The therapist maintains the group focus on topics relevant to problem areas, redirecting the group to relevant topics when it strays off course. Structured activities such as role playing followed by discussion may also be used. At the end of the meeting, the members' progress is reviewed and homework assignments are made for the next session (Johnson, 1975).

As therapy progresses, reinforcement is limited to performance of more advanced behaviors. For example, in Clement and Milne's group of withdrawn children (1967), members were initially rewarded for making eye contact or uttering single words. Later they had to both make eye contact and speak short phrases to get a chip. The frequency of reinforcement decreases in the middle stage of treatment, and homework assignments become more difficult. Durlak (1977) decreased his intermittent reinforcement from 50 percent of desirable behaviors in session 3 to 20 percent in session 7. In Leone and Gumaer's assertiveness training group (1979), members contracted to perform specific assertive behaviors with specified persons (e.g., asking parents' permission for a privilege, asking a teacher for help with schoolwork, asking a classmate to play) and to have the person sign the contract when its terms were fulfilled. Before being sent out with the assignments, the children thoroughly practiced the behaviors in role playing to maximize their chance of success.

During the middle phase of treatment, activities become less structured and more imaginative. Group members gradually assume responsibility for initiating group discussion. They introduce their own topics and problems to role play and discuss. As the group approaches termination, maintaining changed behavior and transferring it to external situations (response generalization) becomes the key therapeutic issue (Johnson, 1975). Members experiencing success outside the group receive verbal reinforcement from other members; those offering excuses usually encounter the group's disappointment. Once target behaviors are established, individual reinforcement may be discontinued. In its place the therapist may offer group rewards for encouraging and supporting behavior changes in each group member (Clement, 1973).

Variations of this basic model have been reported. Clement (1973) designated one child as chief for a given session. He then prompted the chief to bestow tokens and praise on other members when appropriate. In helping children with behavior problems similar to his own, the chief more readily learned appropriate behaviors. In addition to target behaviors, Allen et al. (1975) reinforced positive spontaneous behaviors above the level expected for the child, such as inviting an isolated child into group activity. Leone and Gumaer (1979) used guided fantasy and videotape to help children become comfortable talking in a group. After watching videotaped models of unassertive and assertive behavior, the children videotaped their own role playing for comparison. Reinforcement, behavior rehearsal, and homework assignments have also been successfully integrated into more traditional child group psychotherapy models (Bardill, 1972; Kern and Hankins, 1977; Clifford and Cross, 1980). The results of programs using behavioral techniques have been encouraging. Allen et al. (1975) found 75 percent of socially withdrawn children in their groups to be rated by peers as being more popular after participating in behavioral group counseling. Prior to the group experience these children had played by themselves for a majority of the time during school recesses; afterward, they rarely played by themselves. Significant achievement of target behaviors has also been reported by Clement and Milne (1967), Stedman et al. (1971), Bardill (1972), Durlak (1977), and Leone and Gumaer (1979). These results indicate that achievement of specific social skills leads to a general improvement in social competence and popularity (Putallaz and Gottman, 1981; Hops, 1983).

GROUP TREATMENT FOR CHILDREN OF DIVORCE

The mushrooming rate of divorce over the past twenty years has led clinicians and researchers to evaluate more carefully the dynamic effects of marital disruption upon children. Beginning with an acute crisis at the time of parental separation, the divorce process typically involves several years of family disequilibrium involving a variety of major adjustments. Wallerstein (1983) identifies six major psychological tasks facing the child whose parents divorce: (1) acknowledging the reality of the marital rupture; (2) disengaging from parental conflict and distress to resume customary pursuits; (3) resolving the multiple losses experienced in divorce; (4) resolving anger and shame concerning the divorce; (5) accepting the permanence of the divorce; and (6) achieving realistic hope regarding relationships.

To master these tasks, a child needs considerable attention and support. However, the process of divorce usually reduces the level of assistance offered to the child. Parents are often emotionally unavailable, as they are overwhelmed by financial and psychological pressures. Relatives usually play insignificant roles due to geographical separation, shame concerning the divorce, or fear of intrusion. Probably as a result of an ineffective support system, many children continue to exhibit maladaptive symptoms several years after the divorce (Wallerstein and Kelly, 1980).

Although many social institutions are involved in the divorce process, schools have taken the lead in developing programs to help children cope. Most of the group treatment programs described in the literature are school-based guidance groups. There appear to be two major reasons for this. First, divorce-related problems are often most clearly exhibited in the child's deteriorating academic progress and classroom conduct. Kalter and Rembar (1981) found academic problems and poor school conduct to be among the most frequent symptoms in children of divorce. Loss of concentration and declining grades were observed in a majority of latency age boys and girls studied, while over half the boys exhibited disruptive classroom conduct. Second, parents are often resistant to seeking help from mental health agencies and practitioners. Although children of divorce account for a disproportionate share of mental health referrals, only a minority of children needing treatment actually receive it. Immobilized by personal and financial concerns and feelings of failure and guilt, parents generally welcome the offer of a school program to help their children cope with divorce (Cantor, 1977; Effron, 1980).

School-based counseling groups for children of divorce employ the guidance model, an interesting contrast to psychodynamic models of child group psychotherapy. Guidance groups are conducted for a limited number of sessions, each session structured to achieve a specific goal, usually the understanding of a particular guidance principle by group members (Hillman et al., 1975). Each session consists of a warm-up exercise and a main task. Homework assignments are often given at the end of sessions and reviewed at the beginning of subsequent sessions. The following guidance plan is adapted from several programs (Wilkinson and Bleck, 1977; B. Green, 1978; Guerney and Jordan, 1979; Effron, 1980).

Session One

Goal: Getting acquainted.

Warm-up: Each child is given an index card to write his or her favorite activity, TV show, food, and color. Children are then paired off to use the cards to interview each other and then to introduce each other to the group. Members are asked to repeat as many of each others' names as they can remember.

Main Task: Develop group goals and rules, including taking turns and maintaining confidentiality.

Homework: Each child is given a copy of *The Boys and Girls Book About Divorce* (Gardner, 1970) to read.

Session Two

Goal: Helping children become comfortable talking to one another.

Warm up: Leader and children each draw an animal that is like them in some way. They then share the pictures and the reason why they selected that particular animal.

Main Task: Children are asked who they most identify with in Gardner's book.

Homework: Finish reading Gardner's book.

Session Three

Goal: Identifying feelings about divorce.

Warm up: Viewing the filmstrip *Understanding Change in the Family: Not Together Anymore* (Guidance Associates, 1973), which presents the various feelings children experience during divorce.

Main Task: Discuss each slide, especially the feeling-behavior-consequence sequence ("How did you feel? What did you do? What happened to you as a result?"). Later on, solutions to the problems depicted on the slides may be discussed using brainstorming and role playing.

Homework: Talk with at least one person each day about how you feel.

Session Four

Goal: Talking about divorce.

Warm up: Playing *The Acting, Feeling, Choosing Game* (Keat, 1978), which presents cards asking questions related to divorce and other issues.

Main Task: Discuss the feeling-behavior-consequence sequence elicited by the game.

Homework: Each child is given three blank cards to make additions to the game.

Session Five

Goal: Solving problems related to divorce.

Warm up: Play the additions to *The Acting, Feeling, Choosing Game* made by the children.

Main Task: Discuss, brainstorm and role play alternate solutions to problems elicited by the cards.

Homework: Talk about the divorce experience with a friend.

Session Six

Goal: Solving problems related to divorce.

Warm up: Each child lists and then ranks problems related to divorce. The group then selects the two or three most important problems.

Main Task: Brainstorm and role play solutions to the problems.

Homework: Talk about the divorce with at least one family member.

Session Seven

Goal: Developing positive feelings.

Warm up: Draw a self-portrait and a family portrait.

Main Task: List positive self-statements on self-portraits, with the group adding to the list. Then list positive statements on family portraits, discussing what it is like to be a part of that family.

Homework: Say something complimentary to another person each day.

Session Eight

Goal: Sharing what has been learned in the group.

Warm up: Leader begins by giving positive feedback to each member.

Main Task: Each member is asked to relate things he or she has learned in the group. A round robin discussion, having each member respond to sentence stems ("Divorce makes life different by . . .") may be used.

Other warm-up films recommended in the literature include *Hurt, Anger and Sharing* (Selverstone, 1975), *Me and Dad's New Wife* (Wilson, 1977), and *Breakup* (National Instructional Television Center, 1973; for bibliography of films, see Bradshaw, 1977). A variety of useful guidance games have been reported: "Photos and Feelings," in which children discuss family photos they bring to the group; "Pie-of-Life," in which they depict daily routines on a pie graph and discuss how they would change these; "Time-Line," in which they portray important life events; "Grab Bag of Feelings," in which they draw a feeling and pantomime it; and "Secrets," in which they anonymously write down secrets for the leader to discuss (B. Green, 1978; Guerney and Jordan, 1979; Effron, 1980). Drawings have been used to help children portray their fantasies about pleasant and unpleasant times with their families, the reasons their parents divorced, and what they think is going to happen in their families (Wilkinson and Bleck, 1977; B. Green, 1978). Story writing about child-suggested topics, such as visiting a parent for the first time in a year, has been used to help children cope with difficult situations (Effron, 1980; Sonnenshein-Schneider and Baird, 1980). Obviously, these activities can be used to help children with problems other than divorce.

Groups using the guidance model are based on Piagetian ideas of cognitive and emotional development (Sonnenshein-Schneider and Baird, 1980). According to Piaget's theory, latency age children are in the concrete operations stage of cognitive development. They require specific stimuli in order to understand general principles. Structured activities are used in guidance groups to direct and promote learning of general principles. The discussion and role playing which follow warm-up exercises are seen as the key therapeutic elements, as they actively involve the children's experiences, ideas, and feelings. During discussion and role playing, children often exhibit age-appropriate egocentrism in which they identify with a common theme but cannot directly empathize with another child's experience. They typically listen to each other with impatience, waiting to outdo the other with their own "war stories."

Through sharing of stories of traumatic events, children obtain developmentally important peer validation of their affective and cognitive reactions. The anxiety related to these events is diffused through telling them to children who have gone through similar experiences and through hearing their matter-of-fact "oh yeah" responses, responses suggesting that traumas can be survived and overcome. Peer modeling may follow and is an important therapeutic element. Through discussing problem events, the children learn successful methods for dealing with their problems.

The anecdotally reported results of guidance groups for children of divorce suggest that these groups help diffuse feelings of anxiety, guilt, and shame. The group experience also provides peer support and problem solving skills which help children cope with the divorce process. An unexpected benefit has been the eliciting of active parental involvement. The establishment of children's groups has often resulted in the establishment of parents' groups regarding divorce and in parents' following through with referrals for family counseling. As in other types of child counseling groups, success appears to be highly dependent upon parental attitudes toward the group program (Cantor, 1977; Effron, 1980).

GROUP TREATMENT OF ABUSED CHILDREN

Over the past two decades, the problem of child abuse has elicited increased public awareness and concern. Considerable effort has been devoted to identifying abused children and placing them under the protective supervision of child welfare agencies. Placement of children in foster care or institutions has been a common solution to the problem. Unfortunately, this often results in even greater maladjustment (Nagi, 1977).

Attempts to treat abused children have been limited. In a review of federally funded demonstration projects of child abuse services, Cohn (1979) found that very few children received therapeutic attention. Parents were typically the focus of interventions, due to the widespread belief that helping the parent refrain from abuse helps the family and thus the child.

However, several studies have found abused children to exhibit a number of significant developmental and behavioral problems (Elmer and Gregg, 1967; Martin, 1976; A. Green, 1978b; Cohn. 1979). A Green (1978a) described abused children as having "an overall impairment of ego functioning associated with intellectual and cognitive deficits, acute traumatic reactions, pathological object relations, impaired impulse control, poor self-concept, masochistic and self-destructive behavior, impaired object constancy, and severe academic and behavioral difficulties in the school setting" (p. 357). Cohn (1979) found abused children to have poor social skills with adults and peers. A majority demonstrated poor attention span, low frustration tolerance, and inability to give or receive affection. Over 40 percent exhibited aggression, apathy, and problems with attachment and detachment. Significant intellectual deficits were found, especially in language development. As A. Green (1978b) noted, these children express themselves motorically rather than verbally.

Based upon their findings, Green and Cohn strongly advocate direct therapeutic intervention with children along with parent and family treatment. Their evaluations of individual psychotherapy programs for abused children suggest that a majority of these children are amenable to therapeutic intervention. A thorough review of the literature yields reports of successful group treatment programs for abused preschool children (Roberts, Beswick, Leverton, and Lynch, 1977) and adolescents (Blick and Porter, 1982), for foster children (Ludlow and Epstein, 1972) and for abusive parents (Bellucci, 1972; Justice and Justice, 1975; Roberts et al., 1977; Sgroi and Dana, 1982), but not a single report of group counseling for abused latency age children. Zuelzer (1983) notes a paucity of group treatment programs for abused children generally.

A strong need exists for establishing such groups. Abused children exhibit symptoms and characteristics similar to other children referred for group psychotherapy. Cohn (1979) found poor peer relations to be the most common difficulty among abused children, with 70 percent of the cases exhibiting this problem. Kempe (1976) recommended group therapy as the treatment of choice for abused latency age children.

In establishing group therapy for abused children, one should be aware of the severe psychopathology present in many of these children. Group structure and treatment goals should be formulated accordingly. A. Green (1978a) recommended the following treatment goals: alleviating acute traumatic reactions, strengthening ego functioning, improving object relations, strengthening impulse control, improving self-esteem, strengthening the capacity to tolerate separation, and improving school performance and behavior. Obviously these goals require a process of long-term bonding between therapist and child to correct the effects of the defective parent-child relationship. Therapist-child bonding is often needed before peer attachments can be developed.

In addition to long-term psychodynamic group treatment, it would appear that abused children could benefit from the more structured behavior modification and guidance group models described elsewhere in this chapter. Depending on the characteristics of the setting, they could be placed in a heterogeneous group with non-abused children, or in a homogeneous group. Ludlow and Epstein (1972) described a group for children in foster care, many of whom had been abused. These children shared a common anxiety caused by the absence of natural parents, lack of control over their life situations, and uncertainty about the future. They focused their discussion on reasons for placement in foster care, visitation with natural families, and legal issues. As a result of sharing experiences and information, their feelings of trauma and isolation were reduced and they obtained a better understanding concerning their natural families, their foster parents, and what to expect in the future.

In establishing therapy groups for abused children, clinicians should be sensitive to parental resistance. As A. Green (1978a) points out, abusive parents are especially resistant to treatment for their children. They tend to deny emotional disturbance in family members and scapegoat the abused child as being willfully "bad." They are threatened by any change in their special relationship with the child, upon whom they are dependent for need gratification. As a result, they fear the child's developing an attachment to the therapist and the child's improving to the point of refusing to participate in role reversal and scapegoating. To insure that the child's treatment is not undermined by parental resistance, it is important to involve abusive parents actively in the treatment program. Strong consideration should be given to establishing parallel group therapy for abusive parents to reduce their isolation, improve their self-esteem, and increase their capacity for securing dependency gratification from more appropriate sources.

REFERENCES

Allen, R. P., Safer, D. J., Heaton, R., Ward, A., & Barrell, M. (1975), Behavior therapy for socially ineffective children. *Amer. Acad. Child Psychiat.*, 14:500–509.

Bardill, D. R. (1972), Behavior contracting and group therapy with preadolescent males in a residential treatment setting. *Internat. J. Group Psychother.*, 22:333–342.

Bellucci, M. T. (1972), Group treatment of mothers in child protection cases. *Child Welfare*, 51:100–116.

Blick, L. C., & Porter, F. S. (1982), Group therapy with female adolescent incest victims. In: *Handbook of Clinical Intervention in Child Sexual Abuse*, ed. S.M. Sgroi. Lexington, MA: Lexington.

Bornstein, M. R., Bellack, A. S., & Hersen, M. (1977), Social skills training for unassertive children: A multiple baseline analysis. *J. Appl. Beh. Anal.*, 10:183–195.

Bradshaw, E., Ed. (1977), *16mm Films for Family Life Education, Development and Enrichment Programs*. New York: Family Service Association of America.

Broekhoff, J. (1977), A search for relationships: Sociological and social-psychological considerations. *The Academy Papers*, 11:45–55.

Cantor, D. W. (1977), School-based groups for children of divorce. *J. Divorce*, 1:183–187.

Clement, P.W. (1973), Children as behavior therapists. In: *Therapeutic Techniques; Working Models for the Helping Professional*, ed. A. M. Mitchell & C. D. Johnson. Fullerton, CA: Personnel and Guidance Association.

——— Milne, D.C. (1967), Group play therapy and tangible reinforcers used to modify the behavior of 8-year-old boys. *Beh. Res. & Ther.*, 5:301–312.

Clifford, M., & Cross, T. (1980), Group therapy for seriously disturbed boys in residential treatment. *Child Welfare*, 59:560–565.

Cohn, A. H. (1979), An evaluation of three demonstration child abuse and neglect treatment programs. *J. Amer. Acad. Child Psychiat.*, 18:283–291.

Coolidge, J. C., & Grunebaum, M. G. (1964), Individual and group therapy of a latency age child. *Internat. J. Group Psychother.*, 14:84–96.

Cowen, E. L., Pederson, A., Babigian, H., Izzo, L. D., & Trost, M. A. (1973), Long-term follow-up of early detected vulnerable children. *J. Consult. & Clin. Psychol.*, 41:438–446.

Cunningham, J. M., & Matthews, K. L. (1982), Impact of multiple-family therapy approach on a parallel latency-age/parent group. *Internat. J. Group Psychother.*, 32:91–102.

Durlak, J. A. (1977), Description and evaluation of a behaviorally-oriented school-based preventive mental health program. *J. Consult. & Clin. Psychol.*, 45:27–33.

Effron, A. K. (1980), Children and divorce: Help from an elementary school. *Social Casework*, 10:305–312.

Elmer, E., & Gregg, G. S. (1967), Developmental aspects of abused children. *Pediatrics*, 40:596–602.

Frey, L. A., & Kolodny, R. L. (1966), Group treatment for the alienated child in the school. *Internat. J. Group Psychother.*, 16:321–327.

Gardner, R. A. (1970), *The Boys and Girls Book About Divorce.* New York: Bantam.

Ginott, H. (1961), *Group Psychotherapy with Children.* New York: McGraw-Hill.

Gottman, J. M., Gonso, J., & Rasmussen, B. (1975), Social interaction, social competence, and friendship in children. *Child Devel.*, 46:709–718.

Green, A. H. (1978a), Psychiatric treatment of abused children. *J. Amer. Acad. Child Psychiat.*, 17:356–371.

——— (1978b), Psychopathology of abused children. *J. Amer. Acad. Child Psychiat.*, 17:92–103.

Green, B. J. (1978), Helping children of divorce: A multimodel approach. *Elem. School Guid. & Counsel.*, 12:31–45.

Green, R., & Fuller, M. (1973), Group therapy with feminine boys and their parents. *Internat. J. Group Psychother.*, 23:54–68.

Guerney, L., & Jordan, L. (1979), Children of divorce: a community support group. *J. Divorce*, 2:283–294.

Guidance Associates (1973), *Understanding Change in the Family: Not Together Anymore* (Filmstrip). Pleasantville, N.Y.: Guidance Associates.

Hillman, B. W., Penczar, J. T., & Barr, R. (1975), Activity group guidance: A developmental approach. *Personnel & Guid. J.*, 53:761–767.

Hock, R. A. (1977), A model for conjoint group therapy for asthmatic children and their parents. *Group Psychother., Psychodrama & Sociometry*, 30:107–113.

Hoffman, T. E., Byrne, K. M., Belnap, K. L., & Steward, M. S. (1981), Simultaneous semipermeable groups for mothers and their early latency-aged boys. *Internat. J. Group Psychother.*, 31:83–98.

Hops, H. (1982), Social skills training for socially withdrawn/isolated children. In: *Enhancing Children's Competencies*, ed. P. Karoly & J. Steffen. Lexington, MA: Lexington.

——— (1983), Children's social competence and skill: Current research practices and future directions. *Behav. Ther.*, 14:3–18.

Johnson, W. G. (1975), Group therapy: A behavioral perspective. *Behav. Ther.*, 6:30–38.

Justice, R., & Justice, B. (1975), TA work with child abuse. *Transact. Anal. J.*, 5:38–41.

Kalter, N., & Rembar, J. (1981), The significance of a child's age at the time of parental divorce. *Amer. J. Orthopsychiat.*, 51:85–100.
Keat, D. B. (1978), *The Acting, Feeling, Choosing Game: A Multimodal Game for Children*. Harrisburg, PA: Professional Associates.
Kelly, E. W., & Matthews, D. B. (1971), Group counselling with discipline-problem children at the elementary school level. *School Counselor*, 18:273–278.
Kempe, R. S. (1976), Play therapy, issues and commentary. *National Child Protection Newsletter*, 4:3–4.
Kern, R. M., & Hankins, G. (1977), Adlerian group counselling with contracted homework. *Elem. School Guid. & Counsel.*, 2:284–290.
Ladd, G. W. (1981), Social skills and peer acceptance: Effects of a social learning method for training social skills. *Child Devel.*, 52:171–178.
Leone, S. D., & Gumaer, J. (1979), Group assertiveness training of shy children. *School Counselor*, 27:134–141.
Lovasdal, S. (1976), A multiple therapy approach in work with children. *Internat. J. Group Psychother.*, 26:475–486.
Ludlow, B. B., & Epstein, N. (1972), Groups for foster children. *Social Work*, 17:96–99.
Martin, H. P., Ed. (1976), *The Abused Child*. Cambridge, MA: Ballinger.
McFall, R. M. (1982), A review and reformulation of the concept of social skills. *Behavioral Assmt.*, 4:1–33.
Nagi, S. (1977), *Child Maltreatment in the United States: A Challenge to Social Institutions*. New York: Columbia University Press.
National Instructional Television Center (1973), *Breakup*. Bloomington, IN: National Instructional Television Center.
Pasnau, R. O., Meyer, M., Davis, L. J., Lloyd, R., & Kline, G. (1976), Coordinated group psychotherapy of children and parents. *Internat. J. Group Psychother.*, 26:89–103.
Patterson, G. R. (1974), Interventions for boys with conduct problems: Multiple settings, treatment and criteria. *J. Consult. & Clin. Psychol.*, 41:471–481.
Pevsner, R. (1982), Group parent training versus individual family therapy: An outcome study. *J. Behav. Ther. & Experimental Psychiat.*, 13:119–122.
Putallaz, M., & Gottman, J. M. (1981), Social skills and group acceptance. In: *The Development of Children's Friendships*, ed. S. R. Asher & J. M. Gottman. New York: Cambridge University Press.
Roberts, J., Beswick, K., Leverton, B., & Lynch, K. A. (1977), Prevention of child abuse: Group therapy for mothers and children. *The Practitioner*, 219:111–115.
Roff, M., Sells, S. B., & Golden, M. M. (1972), *Social Adjustment and Personality Development in Children*. Minneapolis: University of Minnesota Press.
Rose, S. D. (1973), *Treating Children in Groups*. San Francisco: Jossey-Bass.
Schiffer, M. (1977), Activity-interview group psychotherapy: Theory, principles and practice. *Internat. J. Group Psychother.*, 27:377–388.
Selverstone, R. (1975), *Hurt, Anger and Sharing* (Film). Westport, CT: Educational Films.
Sgroi, S. M., & Dana, N. T. (1982), Individual and group treatment of mothers of incest victims. In: *Handbook of Clinical Intervention in Child Sexual Abuse*, ed. S. M. Sgroi. Lexington, MA: Lexington.
Slavson, S. R. (1956), *The Fields of Group Psychotherapy*. New York: International Universities Press.
Sonnenshein-Schneider, M., & Baird, K. L. (1980), Group counselling chil-

dren of divorce in the elementary schools: Understanding process and technique. *Personnel & Guid. J.*, 59:88–91.
Soo, E. S. (1974), The impact of activity group therapy upon a highly constricted child. *Internat. J. Group Psychother.*, 24:207–216.
—— (1979), Premature terminations in activity group psychotherapy. *Internat. J. Group Psychother.*, 29:116–118.
Speers, R. W., & Lansing, C. (1964), Group psychotherapy with preschool psychotic children and collateral group therapy of their parents. *Amer. J. Orthopsychiat.*, 34:659–666.
Stedman, J. M., Peterson, T. L., & Cardarelle, J. (1971), Application of a token system in a pre-adolescent boys' group. *J. Behav. Ther.& Experimental Psychiat.*, 2:23–29.
Wallerstein, J. S. (1983), Children of divorce: The psychological tasks of the child. *Amer. J. Orthopsychiat.*, 53:230–243.
—— Kelly, J. (1980), *Surviving the Breakup: How Children and Parents Cope with Divorce*. New York: Basic Books.
Weisselberger, D. (1977), Developmental phases in activity-interview group psychotherapy with children. *Groups*, 8:20–26.
Westman, J. C., Kansky, E. W., Erikson, M. E., Arthur, B., & Vroom, A. L. (1963), Parallel group psychotherapy with the parents of emotionally disturbed children. *Internat. J. Group Psychother.*, 13:52–60.
Wilkinson, G. S., & Bleck, R. T. (1977), Children's divorce groups. *Elem. School Guid. & Counsel.*, 11: 205–213.
Wilson, D. (1977), *Me and Dad's New Wife* (Film). New York: Time-Life Films.
Zuelzer, M. (1983), Personal communication.

Chapter 7
A Two-Stage Model for Group Therapy with Impulse-Ridden Latency Age Children

JUDY CRAWFORD-BROBYN, C.C.W.
ANDREA WHITE, M.S.W.

The significance of peer groups in the life of the latency age child is well documented (Bornstein, 1951; Erikson, 1959, 1963). Scheidlinger (1966) not only stressed Bornstein's two major divisions of latency but also interrelated theories of libidinal, social, and ego development to underscore the significance of peer relations for the latency child. Frank and Zilbach (1968) discussed the latency child's strong thrusts for mastery, strivings for independence, and need to gauge the success of his developing skills. They point out that "still-needed support and sense of belonging are now obtained from the peer group rather than the family" (p. 447). Thus, theory tells us of the importance of two major areas: achievement (skill performance) and peer relations. Our experience supports the theory in that the majority of latency children referred to our outpatient clinic present with poor school performance, poor peer skills, or both.

The development of peer skills takes on additional importance in the light of research which links social skill deficits with more severe psychopathology (Zigler and Phillips, 1961). The need to help children acquire social skills is further supported by investigations showing that peer skills deficits can be related to a wide variety of presenting problems (Gambrill, 1977). It is therefore essential that latency children learn the basics of peer relations. Fortunately, they much prefer to be in a group and tend naturally to attempt to band together. As a result, they respond readily to group experiences, and a number of different group approaches have been developed.

S. R. Slavson (1943), the father of group therapy for children, developed activity group therapy, which led to a much greater understanding of how children function in groups and of the child's ability to use this approach. However, we are faced now with large numbers of children so deficient in ego equipment that they are unable to use this approach in its pure form. In addition, Slavson's approach is considered today to be something of a "luxury" (Frank, 1976), as it demands that children be in treatment for up to three years, that there be a large pool of referrals so that a well-balanced group can be selected, and that staff be extensively trained. Due to the "luxury" of this method, and to the high proportion of children referred who cannot use this approach, a number of clinicians have attempted variations and alternative approaches.

Schamess (1976) reviewed a number of these new approaches and classified them as applying to four patient categories: preoedipal, atypical, impulse-ridden, and neurotic children. He stressed the importance of matching children with the appropriate model. The model we have developed fits into Schamess's category of impulse-ridden children, who engage in antisocial behavior. In conception and practice our model owes much to the work of Ganter, Yeakel, and Polansky (1967), in that we too were very concerned with increasing each child's capacity for self-observation and impulse control. However, our model goes beyond that of Ganter et al. in that we expect greater group interaction.

THE CHILDREN

This model was developed in response to an increase in impulse-ridden, antisocial boys being referred for treatment, frequently with the request that they be placed in a residential setting, at a time when our center was increasingly moving away from residential care. It was felt that these boys would be better served by keeping them in their own homes and communities and offering them outpatient therapy.

These boys were described typically as having poor impulse control, and as being destructive, aggressive, and overactive. Histories revealed multiproblem families who had generally been involved with social agencies for extended periods of time. All the boys were in special classes for behavior problems, learning difficulties, or both. Presenting problems included lying, stealing, fighting, and fire setting. The boys were between eight and nine years of age.

When seen, the boys were demanding, impulsive, aggressive, and extremely needy. All presented with low self-esteem and did not trust adults. They were also very anxious and tended to be preoccupied with primitive fears, especially of injury or punishment. Most had been physically abused in the past.

They were ego-impaired, with very poor verbal skills, and tended to use behavior as their major means of communication. Poor language skills left them unable to express nuances of feeling, and they were often found to have experienced life itself in similarly coarse and undifferentiated ways.

Their occasionally extreme aggression was seen both as a means of relating and as a way of coping with a sense of vulnerability and pseudoautonomy.

THE MODEL

Clearly a model was needed that would provide opportunities for growth and for the development of basic peer skills. It was obvious to us that these boys were lacking in even the most basic social skills. Certainly group therapy was the treatment of choice, but how to establish a group in which they would not simply attack each other and wear out the therapists was the problem. One issue was how to provide a group which would be safe for both boys and therapists. With these boys there was a real danger that they might get out of control, resulting in a runaway boy or a runaway group. A second issue was their impoverished level of peer skills, which left them unable to cope with the interactional demands of a group.

Given the characteristics of our target population, it was felt that an approach was needed that would combine a knowledge of the developmental stage of latency with some of the emerging theories and practice from social learning theory. In particular, it was necessary to incorporate more recent information available about social skills acquisition, especially as related to the specific behavioral components of peer skills and the hierarchy of peer and play skills (Jackson, Jackson, and Monroe, 1983). In addition, a model was required that would help these boys acquire skills within the context of a therapy group.

Since it was clear that all these children could not be put together to start with, a model was developed using dyads (groups of two children) gradually put together to form a larger group. It was only later that we discovered Fuller's work (1977a, 1977b) using the dyad as a treatment modality in itself. Fuller used dyads as minigroups for children who had been recommended for group therapy when it was unavailable.

Each boy was matched with a similar boy. Each of two group therapists started dyads whose goals were to acquire basic peer skills, to get to know each other, and to develop some trust in one of the therapists. Once the boys had acquired some very basic skills, these dyads were merged to form a group led by the same two group therapists. The group was similar in structure and goals to the dyads. It was felt that the boys needed to have the same therapists for dyad and group in order to ensure a continuing sense of safety, security, and support. The group was composed of five boys (one boy who was seen in dyad moved before the group was started).

The group was then used both to review and to build on skills learned in the dyad, as well as to introduce gradually the expectation that group members would interact more and more with one another. Over the life of the group (nine months), the members were expected gradually to take more responsibility for each other and for group planning.

In the next two sections we will discuss the two stages of this model dyad and group.

Dyad

Before placing children in dyad it was essential to assess family history and family dynamics. It is difficult to understand a child's behavior in group without first understanding how his family operates and his place in the family. In addition we obtained information about the child's school behavior, not only in terms of level of ability and learning style but also in terms of their roles within the classroom. Finally, each child was seen individually to assess informally his abilities, interests, intelligence, level of verbal skill, usual coping styles, physical traits, and characteristic roles (follower, leader, scapegoat, clown, distractor, etc.). Despite similar levels of functioning, the boys had differences in their coping styles, so that it was possible to get a range of styles that might later be useful in obtaining a balanced group composition.

For dyad we paired boys with similar characteristics and styles. This was done deliberately in order to increase their attractiveness to each other, to enable them to relate more quickly, and to decrease their ambivalence about being in dyad. This was done also in hope that the boys would be able to move more quickly past the initial uncertainty and into the stage of acquiring new skills.

The stages of group and dyad development were conceptualized according to the framework developed by Garland, Jones, and Kolodny (1973). They described groups as having five stages: preaffiliation; power and control, intimacy, differentiation, and separation. All the boys in dyad passed easily through the initial stage and into the second. Their speedy transition into the power and control stage was likely facilitated by their deliberate assignment to partners they viewed as similar to themselves. We learn by seeing ourselves in others.

In addition, the dyad was deliberately structured so that the boys started with activities in which they had already expressed interest. It was planned that the dyad would be fun and would be perceived as enjoyable and attractive.

Initially the expectations placed on each child in dyad were very minimal: that they stay in the room with one other boy and one therapist without leaving or engaging in physical battles. The boys were not expected to tolerate much (if any) interactive play in the early stages. Accordingly, materials for each activity were plentiful, so that there was no expectation that the boys share materials or otherwise interact. Parallel play was rewarded. Gradually, as each boy became more comfortable with the therapist and his one peer, the supply of materials was slightly limited, so that some minimal sharing was expected. At the same time, the activities were gradually shifted from parallel play activities to activities requiring brief interactive play. Throughout it was essential to set attainable expectations, then increase them slightly and hold them steady (or decrease them slightly) before increasing them again.

Throughout this period the therapists continued to assess the boys, not only to better understand their functioning levels and what behaviors could reasonably be expected on an ongoing basis, but also to learn about their special skills and abilities. In addition, strategies were tested for their later usefulness in group. For example, boys were assessed in terms of their ability to be distracted, their ability to use confrontation, and their ability to use alternative suggestions when these were offered.

The dyad was structured so that particular social skills (sharing, taking turns, taking part, etc.) were clearly defined, explicitly modeled, and then worked on. Rewards, both social and concrete, were earned by the dyad for producing these targeted skills. In both dyad and group, rewards were contingent on group behavior and jointly earned. Such treats as model airplanes or special foods were earned when the dyad or group members together accumulated a requisite number of stars.

The overall structure of the dyad was made intentionally similar to that of the group: both had clearly defined behavioral goals, both included an activity that was appealing to the members, both ended with a snack and discussion, and both stressed jointly earned rewards. Food was given at the end of every session, a token of the therapist's acceptance of the boys regardless of any turmoil that might have occurred. This was seen as nurturing and not as an earned reward, and helped bring about a warm closure.

Throughout the time the dyad was meeting, reference was frequently made to the fact that other boys were also meeting in dyads and that the dyads would be getting together to form a group. Before beginning dyad, each boy was screened by both group therapists. The boys were frequently reminded of this "other" therapist, whom they had met earlier and who would eventually be included in their group.

We were surprised to discover that after the first few group sessions the dyad partners did not generally pair. Explanations for this phenomenon include (1) in dyad boys tended to relate more to the therapist, who was perceived as being safer, than to their peer; (2) boys attended dyad for a relatively brief period (six to eight weeks on average, thirteen being the longest); (3) dyads did not generally develop much past the power and control stage of development; and (4) these boys had such impoverished social skills that they were unable to make or keep friends.

Group

The group met after school once a week for an hour from fall to late spring, a total of 28 sessions. The preaffiliation stage passed quickly and without major difficulties, probably because each child already knew one of the therapists and one other boy. Interestingly, there was less testing of limits then initially expected; although these boys did test, they responded well to clearly set limits. In addition, the therapists knew from the dyad experience the best way to intervene with each boy and the signs that indicated whether he would be able to handle a particular issue on his own or would need prompt "hurdle help" (Redl and Winemen, 1952). The therapists also knew what expectations were reasonable for each boy.

Although the group appeared very unstructured, there was a great deal of hidden structure. The group room was divided into three distinct areas. One contained mats and a punching bag, a second was set up with craft materials, and a third held a table and chairs where the boys ate snacks and had their end-of-group discussions. The boys could also use this area for crafts or board games. In addition, there was a small open space that could be used for games.

The group had temporal structure as well as physical: 45 minutes could be used by the boys to move from mats to crafts to games as they wished. The last 10 to 15 minutes of group was for snack, discussion, awarding of stars (see below), and planning. This routine was consistent throughout the life of the group.

Further structure was provided by clear limits and rules. The rules were few: come regularly, no hitting unless both boys are on the mat, and no destroying of each other's property. These rules were strictly enforced. A group member who broke one was promptly removed from the room by one of the therapists, who would go out with him to discuss how he could get ready to reenter the group. This time-out was rarely used and was always brief. Time-out was seen not as punishment but as a boy's needing individual attention.

Therapists carefully planned crafts and games for the boys. A craft was available should they wish to try it, but it was not an expectation that they try or persist with a particular craft. They could use the materials in different ways or choose to do something completely different. Generally these children had little or no idea of things they would like to do, as their environments were impoverished and provided little stimulation. Introducing new activities and games thus served to broaden their repertoire of pastimes.

The programs were carefully planned so that the level of skill and interaction required was appropriate and so that group members could experience successes. Early programs were very simple, requiring little or no group interaction. Gradually they were made more complex and demanded more interaction.

It was essential that programs be tried out in advance so that the therapists would be familiar with them, ensuring that all the necessary materials were available and that the craft was not too difficult. An extra craft or game was always available as backup. Gradually the therapists placed more and more responsibility on the boys for planning group programs.

Cotherapy

To conduct this type of group it was essential to have two therapists. The group was tiring on a variety of levels. On a practical level, it was necessary to have a cotherapist so that one therapist was available to deal with any child who required time-out. Boys may also need individual attention as they struggle with group-related problems or may arrive with individual concerns. It is important to offer them individual assistance as they face difficult situations, so that they are not forced to act out in order to command attention. Only with two therapists is it possible to free one person to assist individuals while the other continues with the group.

Groups of this kind are exhausting, not only in terms of the sheer amount of energy needed to work in the group but also in terms of the number of transference issues that must be dealt with. In therapy groups with latency children the therapist is often the most threatened person in the room. Because latency age children do not usually give feedback regarding the usefulness of the group experience, it is easy to become emotionally drained. It is therefore of immense value to have a partner to remind one of gains made, especially after a trying session.

It is accepted that in order to do group therapy with children a wide range of knowledge is needed. It was therefore useful to have therapists with different training and backgrounds: a child care worker and a social worker. Between us there was a real respect for each other's skills and abilities. Considering ourselves partners, we worked out a mutually rewarding cotherapy relationship. This was crucial since we were dealing with children who are exceptionally skilled in divide-and-conquer tactics.

There is some question as to whether it is possible to have two female therapists with an all-boys group. Our experience supports the work of MacLennan and Rosen (1963), who found that a female therapist can work satisfactorily with most of the problems dealt with in activity group therapy. Certainly with boys of this age a therapist of either sex can work effectively. However, with older boys (eleven or twelve) facing a crisis in their masculine identity, a male therapist would be desirable.

Group Contingencies

The awarding of stars as secondary reinforcers deserves a separate section. A way of keeping both the individual and the group in mind all the time and not simply a behavior modification technique, stars were used to help these children develop the capacity for self-observation. These boys had little or no ability to observe or track their own behavior. They were frequently surprised when their behavior was pointed out to them and were generally unable to recognize their own behavioral patterns. They saw themselves as passive victims of fate rather than as responsible for their own actions.

A chart was drawn up with two basic behaviors related to peer skills already worked on in dyad. Additional targeted behaviors were added as the group progressed. At snack time each boy was asked if he should get a star for these targeted behaviors. To earn a star all the child had to do was to say that he had earned it and to give one example from group of his having performed the targeted behavior. The important goal here was to get each child to develop an observing ego so that he could learn not only to observe but to track his behavior, recognize specific pieces of it, report on his own activity, and take responsibility for it. For the latency child, the capacity for self-observation is roughly equivalent to insight.

Stars were a motivator both for negativistic children and for the group as a whole; the total number of stars earned by the group led to group rewards. No individual rewards, other than social ones, were ever given. Boys soon realized that it was advantageous to help each other so that the group rewards they had chosen (such as model cars for everyone) could be gained sooner. The boys helped each other not only at the end of group (by remembering each others' positive behaviors) but also during group—for example, by asking others to share materials with them so that they both could earn stars.

Talking about their successes and counting stars at the end of group also ensured that each session ended on a positive note for each boy. Achievements were described in terms of behavior rather than introspection and interpretation, as these are not readily understood or achieved by the latency child. Indeed, any form of insight is actively avoided by children in this age group.

In addition, the stars were an essential part of the developing group process; in the early stages it was only in talking about stars that the group members interacted at all. Later the boys took real pride in their ability to earn stars, and this led to an increase in self-esteem.

One concern was that the behaviors learned in group would not transfer to situations outside the group; gradually we began asking the boys to recall occasions on which they had used their newly acquired skills in other contexts. At first they had difficulty answering, but gradually they came to know they would be asked this and came prepared. Conversations with teachers after the group ended indicated a definite transfer of the gains made in group to other situations.

Clearly the stars not only rewarded the boys for acquiring specific peer skills but also helped them develop a capacity for self-observation; both of these are essential for growth.

Fighting

Fighting was certainly the single most important issue, both for the boys and for the therapists. It was expected that the boys could greatly curb their fighting in the dyad, where there was less stress and fewer expectations. The therapist was a stronger force and lent them her superego. However, it was assumed that the boys would not be able to keep from fighting in the group. There more peers were available, stress was increased, and contagion was a strong factor. A safe way to fight was therefore organized, though fighting was not expected to be a behavior that members could control—at least not in the early stages. Therefore, aggression was allowed within safe limits. Any boy could stop the fighting if it overwhelmed him, simply by stepping off the mats. They soon felt safe to express anger, knowing that the therapists were there to provide safety and control. They also realized that nobody would be allowed to lose control to such an extent that he would frighten himself or the group.

A lot of aggressive fighting was allowed and the therapists did not interfere as long as the boys were on the mats. The boys soon learned how to use these limits to provide safety for themselves. However, every group therapist must make a decision about the amount of aggression that will be tolerated. To decide this issue therapists must consider the child factors, therapist factors (the degree to which the therapist is comfortable with fighting and is confident that the group members will not hurt each other), and each person's idea of curative factors. This group was composed of aggressive, impulsive boys whose major difficulties lay in fighting. We knew the boys well and knew that they would respond to firm limits if these were few, not too demanding, but absolute. It was essential for therapeutic gain that the boys deal directly with their fighting and its results. To avoid this aggression was to have a pleasant but nontherapeutic group. In the early stages the boys used the mats and punching bag extensively for much of the group time. In fact, they demolished a punching bag. Gradually, over many sessions, the use of the mats diminished markedly, finally reaching a point where they were used only occasionally, by an individual boy who was angry about some personal issue. At times boys would come in and head for the mats, stating that they needed some "angry time" first and would then move on to something else. In the last stages of the group the mats came to be used as a place to play cards.

The issue of touch requires special mention. These were all impulse-ridden boys and it was felt that the less they were touched the better. For these boys there was a real danger that touch would be seen as sexual stimulation or as an attack, especially as many of these boys had been abused in the past. In addition, their sense of their own boundaries was so primitive that touching them led to a feeling of loss of boundaries and panic. It was a sign of major progress when these boys would allow us to touch them. By the end of group, however, they were actually beginning to appreciate that touch could mean comfort and reassurance.

RESULTS

Before the boys entered the group, information about areas of difficulty and strength was obtained from teachers and parents. Reports were requested from them again at the end of group. While a standardized questionnaire was not used, the feedback from parents and teachers alike was positive. It seems that the gains observed in group did in fact transfer to behavior outside the group. Teachers were able to give clear examples of areas of improvement. One teacher, for example, reported that one boy had grown and developed into a real person and not just a bundle of aggression. Parents reported that their sons finally made friends outside the group for the first time.

All the boys in group were also seen with their families. We have experimented with involving some children in group only, but now only children whose families are also in treatment are accepted. When the family is also in treatment it is possible to maximize the learning that occurs in group. Newly acquired skills can not only be expected at home, but can also be monitored by the family therapist.

SUMMARY

A model of group therapy for impulse-ridden latency age children was described using a gradual progression from dyad to group, both structured in similar ways. The model relies on social learning theory as it relates to social skills acquisition. The group is aimed at helping children acquire baseline peer skills in a supportive and structured therapeutic environment. It is not intended that the group be seen as doing the whole job of treatment. Indeed, only children whose families are also prepared to work with us are accepted. Children are also encouraged to graduate from this group into more usual, community-based groups (such as Cub Scouts) to further reinforce and develop their peer skills.

This method has been developed to its present state over the space of several years and several different groups. Many things have been learned over time, including the importance of having therapists in partnership, the crucial need for careful planning before each group, and the need to review each group session afterward. It was important to pay careful attention to issues of transference and countertransference and to identify these early in order to maintain a therapeutic perspective throughout. Routine and predictability were essential, as any sudden unplanned change was seen by these boys as a threat and could lead to disruptiveness.

A number of areas need further work if the effectiveness of the group is to be improved and the model investigated more scientifically. First, a hierarchy of social skills must be constructed so that therapists can be more precise as to which skills are basic and the most desirable order in which to add them. Second, the problem of working with children whose social skills are very uneven (often they seem to lack some of the more basic skills but to have elements of some higher-order one) must be addressed. Finally, there is a need to develop a research component so that the types of gains made may be defined more clearly and measured more precisely. To this end the current group is being filmed. In addition, it is necessary to use a questionnaire that can be given to parents and teachers before and after the group experience.

To date the only way of judging the progress made by group members is through the subjective impressions of people involved with the boys outside the group and the comments of the boys themselves at the end of the group experience. Asked about the group and what they had learned, the boys said: "I learned to share and not get mad," "I learned to speak up and not get pushed around," "I learned to make friends," and "I learned to have fun."

REFERENCES

Bornstein, B. (1951), On latency. In: *The Psychoanalytic Study of the Child*, 6: 279–285. New York: International Universities Press.
Erikson, E. H. (1959), Identity and the Life Cycle. *Psychological Issues*, Monograph 1. New York: International Universities Press.
——— (1963), *Childhood and Society*. 2nd ed. New York: Norton.
Frank, M. G. (1976), Modifications of activity group therapy: Responses to ego-impoverished children. *Clin. Soc. Work J.*, 4: 102–109.
——— & Zilbach, J. (1968), Current trends in group therapy with children. *Internat. J. Group Psychother.*, 18: 447–460.
Fuller, J.S. (1977a), Duo therapy: A potential treatment of choice for latency children. *J. Amer. Acad. Child Psychiat.*, 16:469–477.
——— (1977b), Duo therapy case studies: Process and techniques. *Social Casework*, 58:84–91.
Gambrill, E. D. (1977), *Behavior Modification: Handbook of Assessment, Intervention, and Evaluation*. San Francisco: Jossey-Bass.
Ganter, G., Yeakel, M., & Polansky, N. (1967), *Retrieval from Limbo*. New York: Child Welfare League of America.
Garland, J. A., Jones, H. E., & Kolodny, R. L. (1973), A model for the stages of development in social work groups. In: *Explorations in Group Work*, ed. S. Bernstein. Boston: Milford House, pp. 17–71.
Jackson, N., Jackson, D., & Monroe, C. (1983), *Getting Along with Others*. Champaign: Research Press.
MacLennan, B. W., & Rosen, B. (1963), Female group therapists in activity group therapy with boys in latency. *Internat. J. Group Psychother.*, 13:34–42.
Redl, R., & Winemen, D. (1952), *Controls from Within: Techniques for the Treatment of the Aggressive Child*. New York: Free Press.
Schamess, G. (1976), Group Treatment Modalities for Latency-Aged Children. *Internat. J. Group Psychother.*, 26:455–473.
Scheidlinger, S. (1966), The concept of latency: Implications for group treatment. *Social Casework*, 47:363–367.
Slavson, S. R. (1943), *An Introduction to Group Therapy*. New York: International Universities Press.
Zigler, E., & Phillips, L. (1961), Social competence and outcome in psychiatric disorder. *J. Abnorm. & Soc. Psychol.*, 63:264–271.

Part V
The Therapist

Chapter 8
Countertransference: In and Beyond Child Group Psychotherapy

FERN J. CRAMER AZIMA, Ph.D.

The *raison d'être* for the development of group psychotherapy for children was the desire to provide an intensive experience in peer socialization, which favors specific therapeutic observations and interactions not possible in a dyadic setting. Theory and technique—play therapy, activity group therapy, and subsequent integrations with a variety of discussion, behavioral, and interpretive techniques—were borrowed or modified from individual, adult, and child psychoanalysis. Common to all these approaches, regardless of their idiosyncratic philosophies, is the need for the therapist to understand, empathize with, and modify aberrant child behavior. There is probably no other therapeutic situation except that with the psychotic that produces such chaotic responses in the therapist and so threatens confusion, regression, and loss of control—what is loosely termed countertransference.

Present-day group theory and technique for children have changed in most instances from a child guidance model to a multidisciplinary approach. The impact of family and behavioral therapies and, equally, systems theory has resulted in the psychotherapist's having to relate and function with cotherapists, a treatment team, parents, and community. As the title of this chapter suggests, countertransference is now "beyond" the children's group per se, and radiates out to and rebounds from network groups.

This chapter will focus on clarification and modification of the concept and process of countertransference for the group therapist working with emotionally disturbed children. Clinical material will be provided to illustrate the complexity and range of countertransference in an intensive psychotherapeutic/psychoeducational center, and to demonstrate the author's theoretical and therapeutic approach with this age group.

COUNTERTRANSFERENCE

In 1910 Freud reported that he had become aware of the countertransference in himself which had occurred as a result of the patient's influence on his unconscious feelings. He further stated that it was necessary to recognize this countertransference and to overcome it, in order not to block or damage the treatment.

In subsequent papers Freud further insisted that the analyst remain opaque like a mirror, showing nothing more than is shown to him. This cautionary attitude continued until 1947, when Winnicott spoke out boldly about "hate in the countertransference" as related to psychotic patients. Winnicott was among the first to divide countertransference reactions into "objective," those stemming from conscious sources, and "subjective," those stemming from unconscious psychopathology in the analyst. In 1950 Paula Heimann recognized the great importance of countertransference as a potent tool for the treatment.

Racker (1968), in his search for the reason for the dormancy of the concept, suggested that it was related to the analyst's omnipotent wishes to remain a perfect adult and to have total control over his infantile needs. Further, the fear was obvious that the doctor would be discredited if he were found to possess any psychological disturbance, especially if he were to be sexually attracted to patients, or to become angry or act out with them.

A variety of scientific changes were simultaneously taking place that set the stage for an imperfect world. In physics the Newtonian mechanical model was replaced by models of relativity, interaction, and field theory. Similar concepts were borrowed by psychological theorists in describing the reciprocal, mutually influencing effects of the individual in his subjective and social worlds.

Kurt Lewin's group and field theory, the introduction of interpersonal theory by Harry Stack Sullivan, the impact of object relations theory, and new research in child development led the way to a study of reciprocal interaction of therapist and patient. It is not surprising that it was Anna Freud's work with children (1965) that led to a further consideration that not all the ego's operations were defensive, that the "real" person of the therapist played a decidedly important therapeutic role. Anna Freud also cautioned that not all of the unconscious irrational feelings of the therapist could be completely mastered.

The nondefensive "conflict-free," "real," or "authentic" self of the therapist and the effects of the analyst's personality on treatment are well reviewed by Ticho (1975). It is more than likely that the growth of group therapy and group dynamic theory provided a marked impetus for the humanization of the therapist, increased self-disclosure, and a reconsideration of conscious "here-and-now" reactions.

DEFINITION OF COUNTERTRANSFERENCE FOR INDIVIDUAL AND CHILD GROUP THERAPISTS

There appear to be three types of definition operative in the analytic literature: (1) The narrow or "traditional" approach defines countertransference as the unconscious reaction of the psychotherapist to the patient's transference. (2) The broad or "inclusive" approach defines it as all thoughts, feelings, and reactions of the analyst with regard to the patient in the treatment situation. This approach encourages the active use of countertransference for the understanding of the patient (Winnicott, 1947; Fromm-Reichmann, 1950; Heimann, 1950; and Green, 1975). (3) An intermediate position is expressed by Greenson (1978) and others, who include not all of the therapist's responses to a patient but only those evoked by the patient transference. Greenson defines countertransference as "all the analyst's transference reactions toward his patient" (p. 506)—distorted, inappropriate responses activated by unconscious conflicts of the analyst's past.

Among child and adolescent group therapists, Slavson (1950), Rosenthal (1953), Schamess (1976), and Soo (1980) are adherents of the traditional narrow application of countertransference, while Azima (1973) Rachman (1972), and Sugar (1979) utilize a broader framework including conscious reactions to parents, peers, and other figures in the psychological network. In 1972 I defined countertransference as:

> The therapist's subjective, emotional and conflictual response to an individual patient or to the pressures of the group as a whole . . . which stretches horizontally in the present and verti-

cally in time and integrates both intrapsychic and interpersonal phenomena. It is a myth to consider that any therapist can escape manifestations of countertransference reactions. If, however, the leader's irrational responses become overabundant, his therapeutic function fails; this failure often leads to the destruction of the group. The issue for the therapist is how to diminish his distorted behavior, and at the same time profit from the awareness of transference communications. [Azima, 1972, p. 52]

By contrast to the countertransference in individual therapy, in group therapy the therapist is enmeshed in a multiperson system demanding more alertness, self-disclosure, and confrontation. In children's groups the pressures on the therapist are more direct by virtue of the children's activity and impulsivity, their actual physical invasion of the therapist, and the preverbal communications, which further foster regression and acting out. The therapist's position of importance as compared to adult groups is greatly diminished. Therapists are less able to understand the inarticulate or averbal child, and in a parallel way their own "words" are much less meaningful than in adult therapy. It is only through continued exposure in an ongoing group situation that the child's behavior and fantasies are observed in reference to other children, adults in the group, toys, food, etc. When the actual behavior is kicking another child, spitting in the therapist's face, or dismembering a doll, the impact on the therapist is very intense and triggers immediately both counterresponses and possible countertransferences. In these circumstances, it is virtually impossible to separate the conscious spontaneous feelings of anger, fear, disgust, etc. from unconscious countertransferences that have surfaced. For this reason the broader, more inclusive conception of countertransference appears to be more useful for the child group therapist. Further, the increasing regard for both the real person of the therapist and the interactional reciprocal relationship to the patient and group are necessary considerations for the definition of the complexity of transference-countertransference. It is clear that children, especially active boys, who make up about 90 percent of all treatment groups, relate differently to male and female therapists, especially in the early stages of treatment. The children are quick to express their feelings about the therapist's sex, age, physical strength, dexterity, attractiveness, warmth, protectiveness, authority, etc. Should the therapist become pregnant, sick, moody, even change hair styles, these changes will trigger reciprocal counterreactions in the other children, the cotherapist, and other team members.

The crux of the definition of countertransference would appear to be the degree to which the therapist's behavior, verbal and nonverbal, impedes and obstructs the treatment, and prevents the formation and growth of a true psychotherapy group. Transitory feelings of anger, loss of control, jealousy, etc. occur more swiftly for the group therapist who is buffeted by children, parents, and staff members within, or liaisoned to, the treatment team. It is not "humanly" possible to remain "neutral," and in many circumstances such neutrality is in fact read as cold and rejecting. It is fair to say that when such therapist behavior becomes repetitive, and is reflective of a projection of inner unsolved personal problems, that the term countertransference is applicable. The goal is the early recognition and reduction of inappropriate countertransference behavior. Insight into one's own unresolved infantile conflicts provides an empathic reverberation with the child's suffering and strengthens the therapeutic alliance. I am in agreement with Tower (1956) that countertransference is not only potentially useful but even desirable and necessary. The acceptance or rejection of the various definitions of the concept would appear to depend on the theoretical bias of the therapist and the nature of the setting and the latitude of permissiveness, limit-setting and interpretation.

As a supervisory concept the distinction between normal counterreactions and distorted countertransference is valuable and is similar to Winnicott's clarification of objective and subjective countertransference (1947).

SOURCES AND PROCESS OF COUNTERTRANSFERENCE

The focus of this discussion will be on those features within the psychotherapist and the psychotherapy process which reactivate countertransference in the interactional process with the children, the psychotherapy group, treatment team, parents, and important others in the surrounding community network.

The Psychotherapist

It is beyond debate that every therapist, no matter how well trained, has some remnants of infantile conflicts which become activated at critical points of the therapy, especially with children who are more primitive and direct in their expression. The decision itself to become a psychotherapist is based on conscious as well as unconscious determinants. The desire to understand and help others may in part be a sublimation of narcissistic dependency and omnipotence. Money-Kyrle (1956) aptly stated that the analyst's motive is a blend of scientific curiosity and parental and reparative drives. (Further, good therapists are "born" optimists who believe that things can always improve.) Yet another dimension of the therapist's countertransference may spring from present problems in the therapist's life which render him vulnerable.

We may speculate that the therapist's choice of working with children has something to do with his own relationship to his parents, siblings, and friends and with his unwillingness to completely surrender his own childhood. The elements of spontaneity, playfulness, and nonverbal empathy are indeed the stock and trade of child therapists. It is not unfair to say that our psychotherapy work with children gives us a second chance to recapture and undo our own propensities for regression, defiance, acting out, rivalry, narcissistic devaluation, and helplessness. The dictum "in helping others we help ourselves" applies as well to the therapist.

It seems unwise to generalize about the constellation of personality factors that determine why one clinician chooses dyadic therapy, and others family and group therapies. Group therapists enjoy emotional and cognitive stimulation, self-disclosure, and sharing the roles of leadership. Perhaps group therapists enjoy the challenge of overcoming their own stranger anxiety.

The Psychotherapy Process

Basic to the psychotherapy process is the need to understand and modify an individual's inner turmoil and defective relationships with others. To accomplish this the therapist must make a therapeutic alliance with the patient to allow him access to his inner thoughts and feelings. (A task doubly difficult with children.) The therapist moves cautiously from empathic intuition guided by diagnosis to a split or double identification. The first is with the patient himself, the second with the recipient object—the therapist's own response makes him cognizant of the way "others" would respond to this patient's behavior. Racker (1968) used the term "concordant identification" with the patient and "complementary identification" as meaning the response of the object to the patient.

Schematically the process may be conceived of as involving the following phases: (1) the therapist becomes the object of the child's transferred conflicts; (2) the therapist introjects those transferences;

(3) he gradually forms a double identification, one with the child and a second with the object recipient; (4) after a sufficient period of sampling and "digestion" the therapist projects back to the child an adequate empathic response and/or interpretation. Over time the therapist imparts to the child object constancy, trust, and reliability—empathic stages anterior to conceptualization.

At any point in this process distorted countertransferences can occur. (1) At the point of introjection a therapist may be reluctant to accept the child's emotionally laden behavior, sensing that he has similar problems in himself. The therapist may tune out, evade, or deny the material. Otto Kernberg (1965) gives the example of the therapist who remains defensively distant with the narcissistic patient who ignores him as a true other person. Here the therapist's defensive distance and withdrawal can be seen as a mirror of the patient's reflection. This mimicking of the patient is often noted in supervision and can if analyzed lead to the unraveling of the therapist's countertransference. (2) The therapist introjects the patient's conflicts but cannot tolerate his level of discomfort and so immediately reacts before having really formed a deep emotional understanding. The therapist cannot "stay with the material" because of the reactivation of primitive feelings such as rage, jealousy, shame, etc. The child usually reacts to the therapist's inappropriate attitude by further negative behavior. The analysis of such countertransference difficulties often reveals early problems related to listening and hearing unpleasant quarrels of the parents, or angry rejections and scoldings he received as a child. A child in the group may also demonstrate this vividly to the therapist by blocking his ears or saying "I don't want to hear you." (3) The therapist becomes so enmeshed in his overidentification with the child that he loses his objectivity and self-control and behaves like a symbiotic twin acting out, regressing, withdrawing, or becoming enraged or depressed. These countertransferences are so drastic that immediate action is usually taken to reduce them. However, overprotectiveness, overcloseness, undue touching and holding the child, etc. are often libidinal countertransferences not easily recognizable. (4) The therapist is unable to express his feelings or thoughts for fear he may be incorrect or what he has to say is not "good enough." The countertransference is expressed in prolonged obsessive silence with inability to "produce" or make a decision. This type of countertransference is often disguised by an intense, perfectionistic, overpatient attitude. In the early stages of therapy, in fact, this attitude may even be desirous. The problem is one where the therapist's fear of failure and independence are so great that he becomes hesitant and helpless. It is other team members who begin to object to this overpermissive, silent, postponing attitude, which forces them to make major decisions and interpretations because the therapist is always "hedging his bets." The therapist himself will often admit to his slow and boring attitude, but is not conscious of the degree of anger and alienation it produces in others. (5) The therapist has not really understood the patient and his projections are of his own transferential conflicts. A six-year-old boy in an activity group told the therapist in a tone of exasperation: "I don't want to play with you—you just want to play your own game." This countertransference if repetitive reveals a basic lack of bonding and a significant relationship deficit. In fact, one could say that the therapist has chosen a children's group in order to learn how to play.

One can conclude that the psychotherapy process itself engenders countertransference reactions. At any point along the trajectory of empathy, introjection, identification, and projection, the therapist's conflictual memories may become intertwined with those of the patient. However, it is important to recognize that there are many instances in which the psychotherapist's anxiety responses are realistic and objective. One cannot simply assume that the therapist's reactions are countertransference, in the sense that they stem from reactivation of unsolved personal trauma. An example of realistically based anxiety is the situation where there is virtually no interaction between therapist and child because the latter has not yet reached the maturational level of either identification or object relations. Instead the child remains in a pre-object stage of fusion with the mother.

COUNTERTRANSFERENCE IN CHILD GROUP THERAPY AND THE TREATMENT NETWORK

Unlike the situation in adult dyadic therapy, the child group therapist is interacting within a matrix of the children and the co-therapist, and this group is itself embedded in an outer network system. Both therapists and children are simultaneously involved in reciprocal relationships to treatment team members, parents, surrogate parents, community social workers, police, judges, etc. Multiple apperceptions, both conscious and unconscious, impinge on the group therapist, and the result is a multiplicity of rival identifications, for and against the child. The present-day child clinician must combine advances in both the intrapsychic and the interpersonal fields. There is on the one hand the continued search to understand the earliest bonding of mother and child, and on the other the multiple therapeutic inputs from the total treatment-parent-community team (Azima, 1985).

Depending on level of pathology, level of cognitive and language development, and strength of socialization skills, the psychotherapeutic and group processes may be considerably delayed. No true therapeutic alliance may be possible for a considerable length of time. In addition, very little group bonding or cohesion is seen in the early stages. Many children remain isolates, while others may relate in pairs. Only older children, those with stronger egos, may form a type of clique, with a dominant leader.

The group therapist working with children is placed in an actual and symbolic parental role, which revives directly his own childhood craving, fears, rivalry, rage, etc. As noted elsewhere (Azima, 1977), the younger the age group the more the psychological and physical boundaries of the therapist are invaded, and the more apt he is to lose control, identify with the child, regress, and act out. Identification with the parent occurs when the emotional crescendo of the group mounts and the children's demands for immediate gratification overwhelm the therapist, and he must resort to authoritarian active control, restraint, and lecturing.

Therapists differ in their vulnerability to the children's expressions of rage, rivalry, greed, physical attack, scapegoating, verbal tirades, silence, helplessness, clinging, weakness, bizarre associations and fantasies, etc. As to the possibility of countertransference to the group as a whole, this may occur if the membership is too homogeneous, dependent, demanding, or rejecting. A therapist often recognizes which group troubles him excessively. An apt analogy is possibly the mother who is unable to satisfy her "family." She does not single out one child but complains that the entire family's demands are excessive.

The concept of the "mother group" (Schindler, 1966; Scheidlinger, 1974) may be applicable to groups in which the children have sufficiently advanced intrapersonal object relations. The notion of the group as a "transitional object" (Winnicott, 1971; Kosseff, 1975; Levin, 1982), is an important one for children who show severe developmental arrests—narcissistic, borderline, and autistic disorders. This type of child remains fused to the mother, not recognizing her as a separate person, but taking her unreflectingly as part of himself. His rage, therefore, is basically that he cannot satisfy himself, and he has no idea that anyone else can. Similarly, there is no consideration of, or identification with, the therapist. This lack of regard and communication creates in the therapist reactions of helplessness and incomprehension. He feels like an object with no personal identity. His feelings and reactions are based on reality and cannot be termed countertransference. Groups for such children may serve to stimulate transitional object development and object constancy. The gradual growth of empathy in the therapist and the experience of gratifying communication between other children and the therapist set examples of the psychological "holding" the child can receive from others.

EXAMPLES OF COUNTERTRANSFERENCE

Traditional child guidance centers have given way to multimodal treatment systems in both inpatient and clinic settings. The following examples are gleaned from an intensive psychotherapeutic/psychoeducational day hospital setting. Children five to twelve years old, predominately boys, are referred for acting out, school-related problems, and personality, neurotic, and borderline disorders. The children are seen in the school setting in individual, family, and various group therapies. A combined activity/interpretive approach is integrated with the total treatment team (Epstein & Altman, 1972; Dannefer, Brown, and Epstein, 1975; Lockwood, 1981). Permissiveness is combined with limit-setting and interpretation. Parents are a mandatory part of the program and are seen in groups alone with their child.

Intellectualization

This defensive maneuver is frequently seen in the bright scientific therapist who dwells on understanding but lacks the empathic warmth to deal with children. Dependent upon their highly organized cognitive systems, they become lost without the music of words and are overwhelmed by "childish" behavior. The young therapist complains that the latency child is playing, not taking the therapy "seriously," that he is mocked and scorned. In the playroom he may be either too explanative or too silent. At times he cannot cope with his own impulsive cravings to smear and ventilate his rage; at other times he is blind to nonverbal communication. The therapist's anxiety may express itself in a number of ways. He may prepare a variety of tasks to occupy the children, write extensively, or relentlessly research his "interesting" case. A young child in the center once screamed at a therapist, "You make me tired—words, words, words. I can't listen so much." Another retorted, "They are my secrets. I know what you are after—you are not so clever."

Boredom

The therapist shows little interest or curiosity. He complains that he is bored by the children's repetitive nonverbal behavior. Sarnoff (1976) has called this reaction "lulling." The therapist is, as it were, rocked or cradled into the sleep he craved as an infant. Doodling, preoccupation with one's fantasies, drowsiness, fatigue, and yawning are often in evidence. When deciphered, the therapist's yawning, his "closed" eyes and ears, may reveal themselves as techniques to ward off and evade his own mounting anger against the children, who are not gratifying or feeding him. As this process continues, the children often resort to irritable nagging in order to regain the therapist's interest.

Smothering

Overattentiveness and overcloseness to the child is aroused in the therapist who wishes to make up for the child's deprivation and lack of mothering. Some children immediately respond in an overdependent manner, while others cannot tolerate the closeness. Again, as therapy continues the children begin to test the limits and see how far they can push the therapist before he voices his frustration and anger. Frequently the therapist is manipulated as a peer. More and more is demanded by the children; on one occasion, a therapist had to resort to bringing candies to the session—oral bribes with which to restore his status. It may be noted that libidinal gratifications, touching and physical closeness with the child, are often disguised as maternal or paternal behavior.

Overidentification with the Child

This transference is seen in a variety of forms and is related to smothering. The therapist becomes a playmate and indulges in activities that often were forbidden by his own parents. It is an opportunity for superego lacunae to be exposed. The therapist may sit on the floor and dress in a childish manner. Often his vocabulary becomes regressive. His wish is to provide the child and himself primary pregenital pleasures, and to rebel against stringent parental demands. Frequently parents and other team members complain of the therapist's overpermissiveness, noting that they are left with the discipline problem. Sometimes quiet, conservative therapists are involved in such overidentification, but this is not always readily apparent. The following is a case in point. Two analytically oriented therapists started a group in a home for delinquent boys. Both were quiet, neutral, attentive, and showed little emotional response to the boys' anger. At one point the leaders happened to observe that "some of the rules and regulations here are difficult." In the third session the boys destroyed the entire group room. In supervision it became clear that the therapists had given the message that they were on the boys' side and against the "establishment." Since they set no rules and gave no emotional response themselves, they gave tacit assent for the boys to escalate their anger and to viciously act out their own desires to get rid of the bad place. There is no such thing as completely neutral behavior. Every therapist communicates, even by his "hmms," his shrugs, his body language, his eyes, whether he agrees or disagrees, and if he wishes the conversation to continue.

Sexual Countertransference

Sexual countertransference may underlie some of the therapist's difficulties and is disguised by coldness or vagueness, or openly evidenced by overconcern. The therapist must be secure enough in his own sexual role not to become overly provocative or seductive, or, at the other extreme, a "cold fish." Spontaneity and a good sense of humor are important parts of the therapist's emotional repertoire with children.

Overidentification with the Parent

With the naughty or acting-out child, the therapist becomes critical, irritable, and censuring, and at times acts out impulsively. It is difficult for most therapists to express anger, and frequently reaction formation disguises it. Usually there is a period of "laying down the law," but when rules are broken (at times by the therapist himself), the therapist will glare angrily and end the session ahead of time with a convenient excuse. We have frequently seen that when a session ends on this note, the therapist is often late for the next one, or forgets it, develops a headache, or has some other excuse. Stealing and cheating is thus encouraged in the patient, that he may regain what has been stolen from him. None of this is consciously noted by the therapist, who, when confronted with his behavior, must deal with his own guilt and shame. With very aggressive, acting-out children, the therapist is hard put to observe and interpret what occurs while limits are being set.

Omnipotence

Omnipotent therapists encourage dependency and prevent autonomous growth. The therapist who needs to be too brilliant and too powerful prevents the patient from seeking solutions for himself, and quite frequently causes withholding—"Since you know everything even before I say it, why bother?" The therapist is afraid to look weak and vulnerable, and is unable to admit that he can make mistakes. His perfectionism blocks competition, as the children soon sense that if they argue or disagree the therapist's narcissism will be wounded. At the same time the omnipotent overambitious therapist insists on the "best group," the fastest cures, and cannot easily tolerate failure.

It is important to note that the children in the early stages of treatment may push for an omnipotent, all-saving therapist. Therapists who cannot admit their limitations will maintain dependent, helpless patients. The transferential dream of regaining the perfect parent or savior must be exposed. Omnipotent therapists may vary from being exhibitionistic and overly assertive to being overly silent, distant, and mysterious, maintaining the image of the silent sage, the only one in the group possessed of the capacity for understanding.

Fear of Self-disclosure

In the last decade group therapists have in general become more active in group interaction. The dilemma is clearly that the more active the therapist becomes the more he reveals of himself and the more vulnerable he becomes. The professional, distant calm of the overneutral therapist is a way of keeping aggressive and libidinal drives in check. The therapist who must overprotect his public image is usually rigid and fearful, and elicits the child's anger.

A defense overused by therapists in the past is to answer a question with a question, especially if it encroaches on his privacy. The calm and flexible therapist answers many questions about himself but draws a line at the point at which he wants no further encroachment.

Somatizations and Blind Spots

The therapist becomes alerted to his own anxiety or depression by such symptoms as headaches, flushing, nausea, cramps, urinary frequency, etc. Yawning and falling asleep may at times be due to fatigue, but most often are related to flight from anger and attack. Therapists become aware of their blind spots by being observed from behind a one-way screen, or in group supervision in which peers identify behavior not otherwise noted. A supervisor who listens only to retrospective reports or audiotapes is often quite surprised when he watches his supervisee on video or conducting an actual session. Paulina Kernberg (1978) confirms that work with latency age groups is a valuable adjunct to the training of child psychiatrists; it offers, we believe, a very important opportunity to deal with countertransference issues.

TECHNIQUES FOR REDUCING COUNTERTRANSFERENCE IN THE GROUP AND PROGRAM SETTING

A few strategies have been helpful in reducing recognized countertransference difficulties.

1. *A third therapist* has been added to certain groups in which the children are overactive, impulsive, or regressive, thereby diminishing such therapist countertransference manifestations as overcontrol, acting out, and rivalry. The third therapist sits beside an empty chair and is designated as a special person for the disruptive child. At times it is enough simply to invite the child to take the special seat and have a quiet talk. At other times he must be taken from the room and told that he can return when he feels he is under control. To be in the peer group is seen as a privilege. The time-out is seen not as a punishment but as a way for the child to gain control and self-reflection. After the session, this therapist can relate what was going on in the provoked child. This technique relieves the cotherapists and also diminishes their rivalry over who will be the more persuasive or authoritarian. Theoretically, the third member is conceived as an *auxiliary ego* who helps the child gain control and self-reflection.

2. The inclusion of *male cotherapists* and staff members in groups for older boys realistically diminishes the countertransference difficulties of female therapists, especially at the beginning of treatment.

3. A *one-way screen room* allows team members to observe intake and some ongoing groups. At times a senior supervisor is asked to

observe a group with whom the therapists are experiencing special difficulties.

4. Active use is made of *TV playback* with the children, the therapists, and at times the parents. Clarification of what really happened is of great help in dealing with the complicated set of transference-countertransference interactions. The TV is used judiciously with parents to help them understand how the children and the therapists interact and how the latter intervene. TV is, of course, used also for supervision.

5. *Sequential planning* is done for many children who are initially poor group candidates. Depending on the specific relationship, deficit, the child is seen individually, with one other child, in small groups engaged in nonstressful activities, etc. In essence, the psychotherapeutic intervention must be congruent with developmental level, the presence or absence of language, and specific conflicts. These guided interventions may be regarded as transitional steps in the separation process.

6. *Parent forum and group therapy* are helpful in diminishing countertransference to children and staff. Involving the parents in special programs with the children provides actual observations of parent-child interaction and tends to make them allies rather than antagonists.

7. *Supervision and training* for psychotherapists involves the deeper discussion of personal dynamics and countertransference. For other team members, broader issues, problems, and errors are discussed at weekly staff meetings. Weekly case conferences around each child involve only the primary therapists. When a member continues to display inappropriate countertransferential behavior which has not been assuaged by the usual supervisory method, he may be advised to enter therapy or, in particularly serious cases, asked to leave the service. A well-functioning team with open and sharing professionals creates the necessary therapeutic milieu for the children. Intrateam rivalries and quarrels sabotage treatment and usually re-create scenarios similar to those that brought the children into therapy in the first place.

CONCLUDING REMARKS

Countertransference for the group therapist may be defined as the therapist's subjective, emotional, and conflictual responses reactivated in the interaction with an individual patient or the group as a whole, and extends horizontally in the present and vertically in time. It includes both intrapsychic and interpersonal phenomena. It is recognized that even the very well trained therapist retains residues of unresolved infantile conflicts that become particularly operative in the often chaotic children's group. Further, the very nature of the psychotherapy process engenders countertransference.

It is important to recognize that not all a therapist's reactions are subjective countertransferences; they may well be objective reactions to a presently stressful interaction. Further, it seems unwarranted to use the concept of countertransference with a child who has not matured to the level of identifications and object relations. In such cases, the therapist does not exist as a real and separate person for the child. Recognition of the potent tool of countertransference as an aid in diagnosis, treatment planning, and training programs allows more open disclosures in team and supervision meetings. The concept of the "real" self of the therapist, and of the interactive nature of treatment, is of further value in counteracting the rather negative and threatening notion of countertransference that until only recently prevailed.

REFERENCES

Anthony, E. J. (1957), Group analytic psychotherapy with children and adolescents. In: *Group Psychotherapy*, eds. S.H. Foulkes & E.J. Anthony. Baltimore: Penguin.

Azima, F. J. C. (1972), Transference-countertransference issues in group psychotherapy for adolescents. *Int. J. Child Psychother.*, 4:51–70.

——— (1973), Transference-countertransference in adolescent group psychotherapy. In: *Group Therapy for the Adolescent*, ed. N. S. Brandes & M. L. Gardner. New York: Jason Aronson, pp. 101–126.

——— (1977), Group therapy for latency children. *Canadian Psychiat. Assoc. J.*, 21:210–212.

——— (1985), Outpatient therapeutic servicing of children and adolescents: review and preview. In: *Outpatient Psychiatry: Progress, Treatment, Prevention*, ed. R. E. Kogan & J. T. Salvendy. University: University of Alabama Press.

Bornstein, B. (1951), On latency. In: *The Psychoanalytic Study of the Child*, 6:279–285. New York: International Universities Press.

Dannefer, E., Brown, R., & Epstein, N. (1975), Experience in developing a combined activity and verbal group therapy program with latency age boys. *Internat. J. Group Psychother.*, 15:331–337.

Epstein, N., & Altman, S. (1972), Experiences in converting an activity group into verbal group therapy. *Internat. J. Group Psychother.*, 22:93.

Freud, A. (1965), *Normality and Pathology in Childhood: Assessments of Development*. New York: International Universities Press.

Fromm-Reichmann, F. (1950), *Principles of Intensive Psychotherapy.* Chicago: University of Chicago Press.
Green, A. (1975), The analyst, symbolization and absence in the analytic setting. *Internat. J. Psycho-Analysis,* 56:1–22.
Greenson, R. R. (1978), *Explorations in Psychoanalysis.* New York: International Universities Press.
Heimann, P. (1950), On counter-transference. *Internat. J. Psycho-Anal.,* 31:81–84.
Kernberg, O. (1965), Notes on countertransference. *J. Amer. Psychoanal. Assn.,* 13:38–50.
Kernberg, P. (1978), Use of latency-age group in the training of child psychiatrists. *Internat. J. Group Psychother.,* 28:95–108.
Klein, M. (1948), *Contributions to Psychoanalysis: 1921–1945.* London: Hogarth Press.
Kosseff, J. (1975), The leader using object-relations theory. In: *The Leader in the Group,* ed. Z. A. Liff. New York: Aronson, pp. 212–242.
Levin, S. (1982), The adolescent group as transitional object. *Internat. J. Group Psychother.,* 32:217–232.
Lockwood, J. (1981), Treatment of disturbed children in verbal and experiential group psychotherapy. *Internat. J. Group Psychother.,* 31:355–366.
Money-Kyrle, R. (1956), Normal countertransference and some of its deviations. *Internat. J. Psycho-Anal.,* 37:360–366.
Racker, H. (1968), *Transference and Countertransference.* London: Hogarth Press.
Rachman, A. (1972), Group psychotherapy in treating the adolescent identity crisis. *Internat. J. Child Psychother.,* 1:97–119.
Rosenthal, L. (1953), Countertransference in activity group therapy. *Internat. J. Group Psychother.,* 3:431–440.
Sarnoff, C. (1976), *Latency.* New York: Aronson.
Schamess, G. (1976), Group treatment modalities for latency-age children. *Internat. J. Group Psychother.,* 26:455–474.
Scheidlinger, S. (1974), On the concept of the "mother group." *Internat. J. Group Psychother.,* 24:417–428.
Schiffer, M. (1977), Activity-interview group psychotherapy: Theory, principles, and practices. *Internat. J. Group Psychother.,* 27:377–388.
Schindler, W. (1966), The role of the mother in group psychotherapy. *Internat. J. Group Psychother.,* 16:198–200.
Soo, E. S. (1980), The impact of transference and countertransference in activity group therapy. *Group,* 4:27–41.
Slavson, S. R. (1950), *Analytic Group Psychotherapy with Children, Adolescents and Adults.* New York: Columbia University Press.
——— Schiffer, M. (1975), *Group Psychotherapies for Children.* New York: International Universities Press.
Sugar, M. (1979), Integration of therapeutic modalities in the treatment of an adolescent. *Internat. J. Group Psychother.,* 29:509–522.
Ticho, E. A. (1975), The effects of the analyst's personality on psychoanalytic treatment. *Psychoanal. Form,* 4:137–151.
Tower, L. W. (1956), Countertransference. *J. Amer. Psychoanal. Assn.,* 4:224–255.
Winnicott, D. W. (1947), Hate in the countertransference. In: *Collected Papers.* New York: Basic Books, 1958.
——— (1971), *Playing and Reality.* New York: Basic Books.

Chapter 9
Training and Supervision in Child and Adolescent Group Psychotherapy

EDWARD S. SOO, M.S.

Slavson and Schiffer's format on supervision and training (1975) stresses primarily individual supervision. Weekly individual conferences review and discuss the protocols of each session with emphasis on (1) the pattern and meaning of group members' behavior as related to their problems; (2) discussion of the therapist's response to the members and the group as a whole ("but no effort must be made to identify the therapist's psychological reactions and attitudes. The supervision should be pragmatic . . . not involving the therapist's own feelings"); and (3) informal discussions with a group of therapists led by the same supervisor (pp. 267–268).

The broad spectrum of emotional disorders in children and adolescents receiving treatment in various settings requires different group therapy models and tasks to address the different treatment needs and goals (Kraft, 1980). This challenges supervisors to incorporate an understanding of advances in group treatment to develop a training method that addresses the dynamics of group formation, the emotional impact of children and adolescents (and the group as a whole) on the therapist, and his role in the management of individual and group transferences. The training process should equip a child or adolescent therapist to be a group therapist for children and adolescents according to the AGPA guidelines established for training mental health professionals.

TRAINING AND SUPERVISORY FORMAT

This chapter will discuss the role of the supervisor of a beginning group therapist. The combination of individual supervision and group training leading to group supervision is the supervisory format that will be presented. In order to expand and develop the supervisory model suggested by Slavson and Schiffer, training objectives should include the understanding of group formation and dynamics, subgroup and group resistances, the use of countertransference in the management of individual and group transference resistances, and the activity of the therapist's role based on the model for each client group. Rosenthal (1977) affirmed that the task of the group therapist is the comprehension of the developmental norms and emotionality of children, the understanding of the individual member's dynamics, the capacity to handle the group as an entity in recognizing group resistances, and self-awareness of the therapist regarding the feelings induced by the group interaction. The training process for the potential group therapist should address such issues. Experience dictates that a combination of individual supervision, training group participation, and group supervision geared specifically toward an integrated approach is required. Individual supervision addresses the supervisee's specific learning needs, knowledge of children's group psychotherapy, and the understanding of clinical material.

TRAINEE AND TRAINING GROUP

The training group allows the trainee to experience the emotional impact of group formation and dynamics, understand subgroup and group resistances, and observe the supervisor's activity in the group. The trainee participates in an arena, studying the interaction among members and the feelings induced by their participation. The regressive influences of the group process activate individual and group resistances that can be demonstrated and observed. The group as a whole becomes more meaningful for the trainee, and the process adds a dimension to individual supervision. Once the trainees are sensitized to the group training experience, the group is ready to serve as an arena for group supervision.

The supervision of group psychotherapy involves a triangular relationship of supervisor, group therapist, and client group. The symbolic role of the supervisor as an authority and parental figure must be considered in the trainee's interrelationships and the influence this role has on the learning situation. The supervisor's individualization of the trainee's learning needs and his reactions to the expression of acceptance, approval, dependency, and various other feelings of compliance by the supervisee must be considered in all three forms of supervision. The interrelationships must be taken into account in order to assess the obstacles which may be created as a result of the training process.

Training is an anxiety-producing process. As each supervisee faces individual supervision and a new group experience in the training group, he is subjected to performance anxieties. He brings into the arena a wide range of feelings, defenses, and behavioral attitudes which are reflected in a learning situation with the supervisor and the group members. He is vulnerable to exposure and threats to his self-esteem and self-image as a learner. The supervisor's recognition of the skills and attitudes each supervisee brings to the supervisory and training process, and the effects they have upon his learning, will enhance the supervisor's understanding of the individual and group resistances that will develop. The supervisor's handling of developing resistances becomes an important part of the training process. Each supervisee will be confronted with his reactions to the clinical material and the anxieties provoked by the children's interaction and behavior in his group.

COUNTERTRANSFERENCE

Rosenthal (1953) reported on countertransference issues that typically arise in activity group therapy. He noted that therapists who are initiated in children's group psychotherapy must endure the reawakening of repressed conflicts from unresolved feelings in their childhood and familial experiences. Inherent in child and adolescent group psychotherapy are varied and complex transference and countertransference reactions activated by the group members and the therapists. Although similar to adult transferences, those displayed by children and adolescents are not identical with them. An admixture of life experiences and developmental and maturational needs are revealed in the transference, as well as the reenactment of family pathologies and repressed conflicts.

If the action derived from the countertransference goes unrecognized, transferences may develop into group resistance. If this is left unattended, the group will be established on the emotional level of the supervisee's personality dynamics. The supervisor must recognize such feelings and assist the supervisee in understanding the operation of individual and multitransferences in the group.

Countertransference feelings can be used to good effect if the supervisee learns to differentiate subjective countertransference feelings from objective ones as a means of emotional communication (Soo, 1980). The identification of the objective countertransference reactions that emerge from the group members and process, plus the subjective countertransferences that are rooted in the group therapists' personality dynamics becomes a focus of study in supervision.

The analysis of the objective countertransference will provide clues and insights into the dynamics of member and group transferences. When the supervisee understands the objective countertransference reaction, he can use the induced feelings as a mode of emotional communication to develop an intervention appropriate to the context of the transference resistances. The understanding of individual and group transferences will enhance the therapists' skill in using countertransference reactions, adding a valuable dimension to their treatment repertoire. Using himself to monitor the induced emotional communication from the transference, the supervisee can be an effective instrument in the management of transference in child and adolescent group psychotherapy.

SUPERVISOR'S TASK

The supervisor must create a receptive atmosphere of trust and ensure that the supervisee's revelation of countertransference feelings be subject to analysis as a constructive means of understanding the content of transference resistances. This process lends assistance to the supervisee's control of his subjective countertransference reactions. A major task for the supervisor is to maintain the narrow line between supervision and treatment. The supervisory and training process may have therapeutic value, but the main concern is to develop the supervisee's competence as a child and adolescent group psychotherapist.

INDIVIDUAL SUPERVISION

While supervisees are participating in the training group, each may form a group and be individually supervised. The supervisee's choice of an appropriate model is based on the children's age group, which may be preschool, latency age, preadolescent, or adolescent. Each format will address itself to the needs and problems of a specific age group.

The process of forming the group will provide the supervisee an opportunity to become reacquainted with children's or adolescents' developmental levels, emotional needs, and pathology. The supervisee learns and understands each member's life history and dynamics and how these factors contribute to the transferences in the group. The suitability and appropriateness of a potential group candidate leads to the subject of selection and group balance.

SELECTION OF MEMBERS

Special attention is given to the selection of children and adolescents in order to achieve group balance (Slavson, 1955). Balance involves the placing of children with varying degrees of developmental levels and emotional needs, adaptive and defensive systems, and a spectrum of pathological issues to promote a broad continuum of interaction and behavior in the group. The interpersonal conflicts created by contrasting behavioral styles promotes therapeutic interchanges among the children. In a properly balanced group, each child's need to express affect and regressive behavior is attenuated by the established group culture. A balanced group serves as an ego boundary for the members whereby anxieties, hostile aggression, and destructive behavior can be tolerated and contained (Soo, 1974).

An unbalanced group composed of impulsive and highly aggressive members will produce a chaotic rather than therapeutic climate. Fearful children will be driven out or be overwhelmed by the aggression. On the other hand, a collection of fearful, passive, and withdrawn youngsters will create a depressed atmosphere and members will withdraw further. Contraindicated for inclusion are psychotic, brain-damaged, or retarded children with no inner resources or few controls. Psychopathic or highly narcissistic and pleasure-seeking children will exploit the other group members in the interest of self-gratification and require a special format, structure, and task dealing specifically with their developmental and emotional defects. For this the selection of a homogenous membership is indicated.

THE SCREENING INTERVIEW

After each prospective member is studied for appropriateness, the child is screened to validate the selection. The screening interview can provide the supervisee the opportunity to observe the child's presentation of his problem, his attitude toward joining the group, his expectations, and what he wants from the therapist. Through induced feelings conveyed by the child in the interview, his functioning in the group may be anticipated. Screening interviews can provide the supervisee clues as to how to relate therapeutically to each member in the group. With the knowledge of each member's emotional and developmental needs, and a dynamic understanding of the member's life history, the supervisee can anticipate the problems to be recapitulated in the transferences.

The supervisee's training in selection and screening methods provides an assessment of his learning needs, his understanding of children and adolescents as members of a group, and his role in relating to each member and to the group as a whole. His countertransference reactions in the selection is part of this training. The subjective countertransference influences the process of selection, and the supervisee's awareness of subjective countertransference minimizes the unconscious bias that contributes to premature termination in children's group psychotherapy (Soo, 1977).

CLINICAL EXAMPLE

Two eight-year-old boys were referred for activity group therapy. Each of the youngsters was from a broken family with an absence of positive male figures and had suffered from poor peer relationships.

Jay had witnessed fighting between his parents, and his alcoholic father had abused his mother physically. After the father separated from the family, the mother complained about Jay's abusive behavior toward her. She acted helpless and felt victimized by Jay. In school, the teacher complained that Jay fought and bullied other children.

Thomas was a product of an unknown father and a mother who died in childbirth. He was cared for by his maternal aunt, who had saved him from foster care. He was described as disruptive in school, unable to share with his classmates, and often scapegoated.

At first the supervisee thought that both boys were appropriate for activity group therapy. The group would provide male objects for identification, and the group interaction would resolve their peer problems. However, upon further scrutiny, the supervisee realized from their histories that if Jay and Thomas were placed in the same group they would come into conflict. Thomas would be scapegoated by Jay, thus insuring further scapegoating by the group. A member may provoke scapegoating as a role in a group, as part of a process in group formation, or as symptomatic of group resistance (Soo, 1983), but Jay was seen as a youngster who had a need to abuse and victimize. His placement in a permissive group with Thomas would reenforce his sadism.

Thomas's early trauma—his mother's death at childbirth—was being reinforced by rejection by his aunt. He carried with him a heavy burden of guilt. His attempts at expiation through being a scapegoat would be at risk in any group, but nonetheless his need to be scapegoated could best be dealt with in a group setting. For Thomas to be included, the group should have a balance that would contain his acting out and counteract his need for rejection with an accepting "family group."

THE SUPERVISEE'S REACTIONS

Upon completion of the group's composition and the necessary preparations made with the parents and their therapists for the youngsters' entry into the group, the supervisee faces the common anxiety of beginning group therapists: the initial exposure and encounter with his group. The supervisee's anxieties about his performance and acceptance by the group are alleviated through the supervisory process, but the basic reactions toward authority, toward judgment, praise, and criticism of his performance, will remain. These emotional currents are part of the supervisor-supervisee relationship and will be transferred into the training supervisory group.

The supervisee brings with him his experience as a child and adolescent individual therapist. There is a tendency for the supervisee to relate to individuals in the group rather than to the group as a whole; his observations and his relationships with members will be reported from an individual perspective. He needs help with the transition from individual therapist to group therapist without losing sight of individual needs in the group. When the group as a whole is recognized, the dynamics of group formation, the process of equalization among the members, the development of individual, subgroup, and group transference resistances, and the therapist's reactions to the emotional impact of the group can be identified, studied and discussed during supervision.

The didactic approach to supervision is essentially geared toward enhancing the cognitive and technical abilities of the supervisee, which limits the integration of his observations on group phenomena. The training group as an experiential method enhances the integration of theoretical knowledge with clinical practice. Through participation as a member of a group, the supervisee experiences the process of group formation, engages in the development of individual and group resistances, observes the role of the supervisor in handling the group, and learns to apply the didactic material. Observation of interactions in the training group will enhance his skill in handling the group process and group resistances in preparation for the transition to the supervisory group.

APPLICATION OF OBJECT RELATIONS

MacLennan (1977) and Schamess (1976) observe that the various models of children's group psychotherapy differ according to the task and focus of each model, the structure of the group, and the therapist's role and activity. Whenever children enter a group, both the group as a whole and the individual members can be seen as reflecting phases of object relations in sequential developmental lines. The inherent factors of the group process facilitate the unfolding of defects and malformations in object relations, the revelation of psychosexual arrests, and the recapitulation of family pathogenic issues.

SYMBOLIC REPRESENTATIONS

The symbolic representation of the group as an "all-good mother" (Scheidlinger, 1974) and the combination of this group and the adult-therapist viewed as a "new object" (A. Freud, 1965, p. 38) reconstitutes the symbolic family. The reconstituted family group establishes an arena in which members receive corrective emotional experiences through the process of group formation, members' interaction, and the therapist's stance toward each member and the group as a whole. The group's curative potential regarding object relationships will address itself to members' specific deficits. The therapist and the symbolic family group support the individual's and the group's need for both distance and proximity in relationships. The therapist's management of transference resistances, and the working through of psychosexual arrests and family pathologies, will result in the reconstruction of object relations in children's group psychotherapy (Soo, 1985).

GROUP FORMAT AND STRUCTURE

Preschool play groups, latency age activity groups, activity-discussion groups, and interview-discussion groups for adolescents in an interpretive group psychotherapy have different formats and structure based on age-specific developmental stages. The supervisor's knowledge must encompass the developmental continuum of preschool children, latency age children, and adolescents. The groups formed are determined by the specific developmental needs and pathological issues requiring treatment. A thorough understanding of the choices appropriate to the needs of each age group in each model is essential.

THE SUPERVISOR-LEADER'S ROLE

Depending on the supervisor's theoretical orientation, his role in the training group is defined by his activity in resolving the supervisees' and the group's resistances against the task of learning child and adolescent group therapy. To develop the training group as a viable training method, the task of the group is defined and an agreement made with the supervisees; the agreement is part of the learning process. It is explained to them that as members they will experience the feeling of being a member of a group, participate in the interaction of the group, and observe the supervisor's role in handling resistances in the group's interaction. The goals in the agreement are that each member will learn to become a better group therapist will assist the others in becoming the same, and will present his group for shared learning and supervision. The sessions of the group will start promptly and will end as scheduled.

TRAINING GROUP PROCESS AND RESISTANCES

Arriving late to sessions is a common manifestation of resistance, and the leader should explore each instance to clarify whether it is an individual or a group resistance. Typical excuses include "I was delayed because of a case conference" and "I had a session that ran over."

The significance of tardiness as symbolic of resistance in the group is important to explore. It may be a precursor of regressive influences in the group. In order to establish limits to group regression, the working out of lateness is essential.

When the training group is given a choice to decide on a topic and format, the members begin to struggle with divergent wishes to learn. The regressive pull of the group will influence some members toward dependence on the leader for direction. As a defense against regression, other members will wish to determine their method and agenda of study themselves. A power struggle then develops from attempts by both sides to impose their point of view. A struggle for position ensues which creates for the membership a state of conflict, anxiety, confusion, frustration, and anger. For many of the members the power struggle will revive previous emotional struggles in familial and peer relationships which may be projected and displaced onto the group as "splitting" into subgroups. An impasse develops over the group's inability to gain a consensus and the group falls into a state of resistance. Hostile confrontations between members, a tendency toward scapegoating, acting "silly," complaints against authority, and "being stuck" are all expressions of resistances stemming from the reaction to regressive pulls in the group process. The group's inability to resolve the impasse requires an intervention by the leader. His resolution of the impasse as a group resistance will facilitate group development.

In one instance in which a stalemate was explored by the leader, he asked if his handling had contributed to the group's immobility. This brought on a series of complaints: "This group is crazy!" "There are too many arguments." "We can't agree on anything." "It's too much like group therapy."

The leader agreed that the group seemed confused, frustrated, and "stuck," and that the training group was not meant to be a therapy group. The trainees were reminded there was no agreement to reveal one's life history, dreams, or conflicts; however, it was legitimate for the members to discuss their feelings as members in the group and to discuss the leader's role and his handling of the group.

Other complaints were made about the leader's role: "You're too laid back." "You should be more active instead of just sitting there." The leader was blamed for permitting the group to get out of hand: "You should be teaching us children's group therapy instead of fooling around."

A defender exclaimed that the experiential method should be continued and that the leader's handling of the group was a positive learning experience for him. Even after extensive discussion, the rift between the subgroups persisted; the resistance finally was dealt with by the leader's accommodating the subgroup that requested a more didactic approach.

A reading list was proposed and required readings assigned. When the assignments were to be reported on, the group's reluctance was obvious. Members protested that they were inundated with paperwork and that they found the leader's assignment unrealistic; they preferred him to lecture. Others suggested guest speakers. However, the question of honorariums was discussed and since neither the agency nor the group was willing to contribute, the group resigned itself to local talent.

The showing of Slavson's film on activity group therapy was presented, and the leader continued with lectures on various types of child and adolescent group therapy. The group became restless, and it was evident they had had their fill of didactic material. The observation was made that the group's lethargy may be due to the leader's having "overfed" the group. A member responded that he would be interested in hearing about the groups run by other members. The group agreed, but expressed reluctance in presenting their groups; each felt vulnerable in risking exposure to the group's aggression and hostility. The supervisees' hesitation was accepted as a realistic concern, and the members recognized the need for a group atmosphere of mutual trust before each could fully participate in cooperative learning.

The training group accomplished several tasks. First was the supervisees' involvement as members of a group. Their participation in the process of group formation, the development of group resistances, and exposure to an arena in regressive interaction and behavior simulated the emotional impact and atmosphere of children's groups. The process created sensitivity toward the gamut of feelings encountered and enabled the members to develop some emotional insulation against the intensity of feelings produced by children and adolescents in group therapy. A second accomplishment was the evolution of the training group into a supervisory group. The effective working out of resistance in the training group created an atmosphere of trust and cooperation which enabled the supervisees to expose their work to scrutiny and to learn to use countertransference reactions in managing group transferences. The continuing role of the supervisor-leader was to maintain this atmosphere of trust and to deal with the resistances in learning child and adolescent group psychotherapy.

GROUP SUPERVISION

The impact of children's groups upon supervisees is reflected in the supervisory group's acting-out behavior. A member asked if the group had seen *Animal House*. Some had seen it or heard about it, and the group responded immediately with laughter and hilarity. The supervisor recognized the members' overstimulated mood and a member wondered anxiously whether his activity group would develop into an "animal house" group. He presented his group's interest in water play and visualized the group room being flooded; the other members, to disguise their anxiety, made jokes about his needing scuba gear. The discussion led to concerns over messing, scapegoating, and other regressive behaviors that might surface in their groups.

SUBGROUP RESISTANCE

A subgroup in a supervisory group may be symptomatic of group resistance. Two members supported each other in encouraging a member to present her group; although she had not intended to present, she readily complied with their request. The leader commented on her cooperativeness with the subgroup, and wondered why she was helping them in their resistance. When the subgroup, who worked together as cotherapists, revealed that their adolescent group was suffering an attrition of members, the core group of three were successful in convincing them that they were not ready to receive new members constructively. New members were not welcomed and were discouraged from staying. The cotherapists had convinced themselves that the group should remain a "small family" because improvement and movement was evidenced in the treatment. They stated that the "small family" was cooperative in revealing their problems and accepting the therapists' interpretations, but could not tolerate new members. They felt that the character of the group would be altered and that their "working through" in the group would be incomplete. The cotherapists were influenced by this group "press" plus their own subjective countertransferences and decided to maintain the small group.

To encourage members to present their groups, resistances against presenting need to be resolved. The individual and group resistances manifested in the supervisory group often disguise latent resistances induced by the transferences in the members' groups, and the material presented in the supervisory group will induce reactions and behavior that will reflect and provide insights into the dynamics of these groups. Analysis of these reenactments assists the supervisee in the management of the transferences and countertransferences in his group.

Focusing on the supervisee's activity prematurely draws attention to himself and makes him more concerned with his emotionality. The supervisee becomes less available emotionally to understand the dynamics and transference resistances in his group. The supervisor's focus should be on understanding the history of the members, the dynamic interaction in the group, and the impact on the supervisee.

A sense of security is necessary if the supervisory group is to be led to a more open revelation of induced feelings. The goal of the group is to create an atmosphere in which collective concern for mutual learning is felt and in which the feelings of the group can be used for associative and affective experiences that meet each member's supervisory needs. Each of the supervisees can identify with the process and the leader in developing an awareness of, and a respect for, defenses and resistances, and skill in using countertransference reactions to read emotionally the individual and group transferences.

SUMMARY AND CONCLUSION

In summary, the combination of individual supervision and group training leading to group supervision transcends the didactic supervisory approach to training child and adolescent group psychotherapists. Not only does it encompass specific knowledge and theoretical understanding of children and adolescents, but it allows the supervisee the opportunity of developing his group, choosing an appropriate modality to address specific problems and age groups, forming the group through appropriate selection and group balance, and learning to use countertransference reactions in the management of transferences.

Training groups based on the experiential model provide supervisees experience as members of a group, an understanding of resistances arising out of group interaction, and the chance to see how the supervisor handles these resistances. As members of the training group, supervisees experience the process of group formation, as well as individual and group resistances to fulfilling the agreement. The training group provides an arena in which regressive interaction and behavior will simulate the emotional atmosphere and impact of child and adolescent groups. The process enables the supervisees to develop an emotional insulation against the onslaught of feelings and behavior produced by children and adolescents in group treatment.

The task of the supervisor in combined individual supervision and group training is to facilitate the transformation from an atmosphere of distrust and negativism to one of trust and cooperation. The supervisee must feel secure in his vulnerability and find the supervisory group supportive in the disclosure of countertransference reactions induced by his group. Then the supervisee can present the group for supervision and learn to use the induced countertransference feelings for the management of transference resistances. The training process—individual supervision, the training group, and group supervision—provides a comprehensive experience and understanding of the emotional impact felt by a child and adolescent group psychotherapist.

REFERENCES

Freud, A. (1965), *Normality and Pathology in Childhood Assessments of Development.* New York: International Universities Press.

Kraft, I. A. (1980), Group therapy with children and adolescents. In: *Treatment of Emotional Disorders in Children and Adolescents: Medical and Psychological Approaches to Treatment*, ed. R.M. Benson, B.J. Blinder, & G.F. Sholevar. New York: Spectrum, pp. 109–132.

MacLennan, B. W. (1977), Modifications of activity group therapy for children. *Internal. J. Group Psychother.*, 26:85–96.

Rosenthal, L. (1953), Countertransference in activity group therapy. *Internat. J. Group Psychother.*, 3:431–440.

——— (1977), Qualifications and tasks of the therapist in group therapy with children. *Clin. Soc. Work J.*, 5:191–199.

Schamess, G. (1976), Group treatment modalities for latency age children. *Internat. J. Group Psychother.*, 26:455–475.

Scheidlinger, S. (1974), On the concept of the "mother group." *Internat. J. Group Psychother.*, 24:417–428.

Slavson, S. R. (1955), Criteria for selection and rejection of patients for various types of group psychotherapy. *Internat. J. Group Psychother.*, 5:3–30.

——— Schiffer, M. (1975), *Group Psychotherapies for Children.* New York: International Universities Press.

Soo, E.S. (1974), The impact of activity group therapy upon a highly constricted child. *Internat. J. Group Psychother.*, 24:207–216.

——— (1977), The impact of collaborative treatment on premature termination in activity group therapy. *Group*, 1(4):222–234.

——— (1980), The impact of transference and countertransference in activity group therapy. *Group*, 4(4):27–41.

——— (1983), The management of scapegoating in children's group psychotherapy. In: *Group and Family Therapy 1983: An Overview*, ed. M. L. Aronson & L. R. Wolberg. New York: Brunner/Mazel, pp. 115–124.

——— (1985), Application of object relations in children's group psychotherapy. *Internat. J. Group Psychother.*, 35:37–47.

Chapter 10
Research on Child Group Therapy: Present Status and Future Directions

ROBERT R. DIES, Ph.D.
ALBERT E. RIESTER, Ed.D.

The purpose of this chapter is to provide a review of the recent research on the efficacy of group psychotherapy with children. The last review of this body of literature was published nearly a decade ago (Abramowitz, 1976). Although surveys of psychological interventions with children have appeared more frequently in recent years—for example, child psychotherapy (Barrett, Hampe, and Miller, 1978; Freedheim and Russ, 1983); behavior therapy (Rickard and Elkins, 1983); cognitive-behavior therapy (Hobbs, Moguin, Tyroler, and Lahey, 1980); social-cognitive problem solving treatments (Urbain and Kendall, 1980); and social skills training (Conger and Keane, 1981; Gresham and Lemanek, 1983; Ladd and Mize, 1983)—none of these reviews stress the value of group treatments. In addition, there are comprehensive critiques of research problems and issues in the field of psychological interventions and child psychopathology, but these surveys also fail to highlight group treatments (Achenbach, 1978; O'Leary and Turkewitz, 1978; Rutter, 1983).

Reviews on group psychotherapy with adults appear with increasing regularity in the literature, and cover various aspects of group process, leadership, and therapy outcome (Dies, 1979, 1985). However, in the children's group psychotherapy literature such reviews are virtually nonexistent. Before we began our systematic search of the literature to prepare this chapter our impression was that researchers had focused most of their interest on group treatments with adults, and paid only perfunctory attention to such interventions with children. After our examination of the literature was completed, there was no doubt in our minds that this was the case.

In this chapter we will review the current status of the research findings, outline several critical issues that must be addressed before significant progress can be made, and offer specific guidelines for future clinical practice and empirical investigation.

We believe that a careful evaluation of the research literature on children's groups can help clinicians and researchers improve the quality of clinical service. The stereotypic view of research as irrelevant to the group psychotherapist is simply not valid. The publication of the first volume of the American Group Psychotherapy Association's monograph series, *Advances in Group Psychotherapy: Integrating Research and Practice* (Dies and MacKenzie, 1983), is ample testimony to this fact. It has been noted that the abilities involved in understanding the empirical literature and in formulating meaningful research are not dissimilar from the operations involved in comprehending group process and planning interventions to facilitate clinical improvement (Dies, 1983a). Kiesler (1981) reports that practitioners and scientists employ identical processes: "Both start with empirical observations (systematically measured or not) from which generalities are abstracted and treatment or manipulative hypotheses are deducted, applied and subsequently validated empirically (through systematic observations or not). Both the science and practice of psychotherapy involve at their core a hypothesis-testing procedure" (pp. 213–214). The feature that traditionally distinguishes the practitioner from the researcher is that the former usually does not rely upon research instruments to document clinical practice. However, we believe that if group psychotherapists are aware of the potential value of research tools they may begin to incorporate them into their clinical work with children's groups, or at least invite their empirically minded colleagues to collaborate in this venture. Throughout this chapter we will offer recommendations for how to refine understanding of group process and therapeutic outcome by building instruments into clinical practice. We hope in this fashion to contribute toward a narrowing of the gap between research and practice.

Our literature survey includes both impressionistic and experimental reports on the efficacy of group interventions with children, ranging from preschool age through puberty (ages four to thirteen). Only reports published in English on group counseling or psychotherapy, play group therapy, and group interventions under the rubric of social skills training or cognitive-behavior therapy are included.

ANECDOTAL REPORTS

In our search of the literature we identified 18 clinical reports describing the value of various group treatments with children. A common feature among these testimonials to the efficacy of treatment is the failure to incorporate systematic assessment of therapeutic change. For the most part these authors did not employ objective measures of treament effects, nor did they compare treated and untreated groups in any quantitative fashion. Thus, conclusions are based mainly on the author's impressions regarding treatment outcome. The reports present a range of therapeutic approaches including several theme-centered groups (e.g., assertiveness training, structured self-concept counseling, groups for youngsters in transition), various action-oriented techniques (e.g., activity groups, play group therapy), a number of methods combining activity and discussion, and behavioral contracting. Nearly all of these articles discuss the author's impressions of therapeutic process and outcome based on a single treatment group. Table 1 summarizes these anecdotal reports.

The clinical settings represented in the reports include six inpatient psychiatric hospitals, six outpatient clinics, and six school-based facilities. The children range from severely disturbed psychotics to relatively normal youngsters with specific behavioral, attitudinal, or emotional difficulties.

An examination of the Author's Conclusions column of Table 1 suggests very strongly that the vast majority of the youngsters who participated in the various groups were helped considerably in overcoming the problems that led them to treatment. Statements of clear-cut clinical improvement, development of more effective coping skills, reduction in acting-out behavior, or positive changes in patterns of communication, attitudes, and general adjustment are noted in nearly every report. Although some authors temper their conclusions by citing treatment limitations, they are generally optimistic about the value of group treatments for reducing the frequency of maladaptive styles and fostering the development of prosocial behaviors.

It is no surprise that clinicians who devote significant portions of their professional time to group interventions with children should be so enthusiastic about the potential advantages of group treatments. The critical issue that must be faced, of course, is whether or not these favorable clinical reports can be buttressed by more objective and systematic evaluation of treatment outcome. Far too many critics of

TABLE 1
Anecdotal Reports (n = 18)

Source	Treatment and Setting	Group Participants	Author's Conclusions
Abramson, Hoffman, and Johns (1979)	Play group therapy in an *inpatient* setting	Early latency age, severely disturbed impulsive children	Patients showed clear-cut clinical improvement
Adams (1976)	Play group therapy in an *inpatient* setting	Children hospitalized with a life-threatening disease (very young to latency age)	Treatment facilitated the emotional adjustment of patients with serious illness
Allan and Bardsley (1983)	Group counseling in the *school*	"Transient" third-grade children, i.e., youngsters who make repeated moves to new schools	Group discussions facilitated adjustment
Bardill (1977)	Behavior-contracting groups in an *inpatient* facility	Emotionally disturbed boys ages 9–14	Patients showed reduction in acting-out behaviors and improved therapeutic responses
Barsky and Mozenter (1976)	Creative drama group in a child guidance *clinic*	Children with behavioral adjustment problems and school underachievement (8–10 years old)	Clients developed better coping skills
Bower, Amatea, and Anderson (1976)	Assertiveness training in a *school* setting	Behaviorally passive fourth-grade girls	Teachers reported that passivity decreased, and children rated themselves as more assertive

TABLE 1 (continued)

Source	Treatment and Setting	Group participants	Author's Conclusions
Cantor (1978)	Support groups in the *school* for children of divorcing parents	Third- through sixth-grade students showing recent adjustment difficulties	Teachers did not observe change, but parents reported subtle changes; children expressed positive reactions to the group experience
Clifford and Cross (1980)	Group play and verbal interaction in an *inpatient* setting	Emotionally disturbed boys diagnosed as behavior disordered or psychotic (ages 7–11)	Patients developed more effective social skills
DuPlessis and Lochner (1981)	Activity-group therapy in a special *clinic*	Learning disabled boys ages 4–12	Clients showed improvement in patterns of communication, attitudes, and general adjustment
Durbin (1982)	Structured self-concept group in the *school*	Sixth-grade girls reported to have difficulties with self-concept	Students developed more positive self-images
Hoffman, Byrne, Belnap and Steward (1981)	Simultaneous semipermeable groups in a *clinic*	Early latency age boys with adjustment reactions, and their mothers	Simultaneous groups helped children and families adjust more effectively
Lovasdal (1976)	Play and discussion group therapy in a *clinic*	Boys with aggressive behavior or social isolation (ages 9–13)	Children, parents, and teachers reported behavioral improvement
McKibbin and King (1983)	Activity group counseling in the *school*	Learning-disabled boys with behavior problems, ages 8–10	Boys were seen as more responsible, mature, and better able to relate to peers

TABLE 1 (continued)

Source	Treatment and Setting	Group Participants	Author's Conclusions
Pasnau, Meyer, Davis, Lloyd, and Kline (1976)	Coordinated group therapy (children and parents) in a *clinic*	"Psychoneurotic" boys, ages 7–9, and their parents	Clients showed improvement in behavioral adjustment, and families became more supportive
Rashbaum-Selig (1976)	Assertiveness training in a *school* setting	Fifth- and sixth-grade students chosen through self-referral, teacher referral, or counselor invitation	Students were helped to deal with a variety of problems related to lack of assertion skills
Rosenberg and Cherbuliez (1979)	Activity-discussion group therapy on an *inpatient* psychiatric unit	Severely disturbed, psychotic children, ages 8–12	It is difficult to separate group treatment effects from those attributable to the milieu, but the group seemed to serve as a corrective emotional experience
Tiktin and Cobb (1983)	Focused group therapy for children plus support groups for parents during post-divorce adjustment in a *clinic* situation	Children ages 7–12 whose parents are involved in separation or divorce	The groups have a positive impact on the children's post-divorce adjustment
Trafimow and Pattak (1981)	*Inpatient* groups with a developmental, object relations focus	Psychotic or near-psychotic children, ages 7–10	The group fostered growth by offering a number of objectal alternatives

the group psychotherapy literature have challenged the validity of impressionistic or anecdotal evidence for us to place much confidence in unsubstantiated testimony (Bednar and Kaul, 1978; Weigel and Corazzini, 1978; Kazdin, 1982). If we are to maintain a critical and unbiased perspective on the efficacy of children's group psychotherapy, we must seek corroboration in the scientific literature of clinicians' enthusiastic endorsements of the group modality.

A number of the authors of these impressionistic reports actually collected "data" on the children who participated in their groups. Thus, Bardill (1977) examined hospital records to evaluate points accumulated by boys in his behavior contracting group treatment. Bower, Amatea, and Anderson (1976) used three measures to assess pre/post changes in assertiveness: self-reports, teacher ratings, and a simulated task. DuPlessis and Lochner (1981) and Durbin (1982) used personality tests. Durbin also collected observations from therapist and teacher regarding treatment progress. Similarly, McKibbin and King (1983) and Tiktin and Cobb (1983) solicited feedback on clinical improvement from independent observers. Regrettably, none of these authors were able to report their findings on the significance of therapeutic change. In most of these projects only one group of children was evaluated. Consequently, the small sample size and lack of any comparison group prevented statistical contrasts. Yet the data collection procedures of these clinicians were similar, and in many cases superior, to those reported in the next section of this chapter, under the heading of Research Reports.

What would have been necessary to convert these anecdotal reports into meaningful clinical research? A brief excursion into the "nuts and bolts" level of research to answer this question might provide a useful framework for this chapter. Our goal is to demonstrate that the gap between the practice of group psychotherapy and its investigation is not insurmountable (Dies, 1983a).

The group psychotherapist who collects pre/post change scores on self-report tests and behavioral ratings from teachers and parents on a single group of children is not in a position to publish the results. These systematic, objective, and independent evaluations have likely enriched the clinician's understanding of the children's progress, but the limited sample and lack of any control group preclude a level of generalization that might be of value to the scientific community. As a first step, then, the clinician should replicate these data collection procedures with subsequent groups of youngsters (later we will see that the average number of groups in the published research is generally less than five).

As a second step, the clinician should go beyond the simple pre/post design and evaluate progress at regular intervals throughout treatment, and then continue for some time after the children have completed therapy. This follow-up is essential to understand the meaning of therapeutic gain. Despite replications and multiple assessments of change, however, our group psychotherapist could still not rush out to publish the results. Without a frame of reference against which to judge the significance of change, the clinician could not be certain that it is really the treatment that is producing improvement. The child's experience with repeated testing, maturational changes, modification in the family system, or a host of other factors might explain the changes on the objective measures and independent ratings.

A third step must be introduced. The presence of a no treatment control group, or a similar group of youngsters receiving a different treatment, would provide an adequate reference group. Unfortunately, many clinicians are not able to identify such control groups, so they must establish an alternative. One option is to add a process perspective to the data collection procedure. For example, it would be possible to use a sociometric technique to compare the outcomes of children who have played central roles within the group versus those who have been less popular. Other process variables might include attendance, communication patterns, relationship to the therapist, extent of parental involvement in the treatment program, and so forth. These intragroup comparisons, even in the absence of the more traditional experimental control group, might allow the clinician to evaluate differential treatment progress.

Ironically, the clinician who takes these three simple steps—replication, multiple assessment, and process evaluation—will have progressed beyond the level of sophistication of the vast majority of the published reports in the children's group psychotherapy literature.

RESEARCH REPORTS

When the clinician confronts the empirical literature on group treatments for children there is immediate "culture shock." A previous review of the research on children's groups, for example, complained that "available evidence regarding group therapy outcome with children is inconclusive, but nonetheless discouraging" (Abramowitz, 1976, p. 321). About a third of the studies yielded generally positive results, another third mixed results, and yet another null findings. Other critics share these rather pessimistic conclusions. Thus, Achenbach (1978) notes the lack of evidence for the efficacy of most mental health services for children, and Rutter (1983) observes that until very recently, "most reviews were preoccupied with the general, but basic, question of whether such therapies have any effect at all—mostly with the conclusion that they are without measurable beneficial impact" (p. 152).

The favorable impressionistic reports by group psychotherapists regarding the merits of treatment (Table 1) and the researcher's lament that child group psychotherapy has not demonstrated its effectiveness seem irreconcilable. It should be noted, however, that a parallel level of dissonance was evident in the adult group psychotherapy literature about twenty years ago. At that time reviewers could muster little evidence to support the efficacy of group treatments. Nevertheless, surveys of the outcome literature became progressively more positive. In 1962 Rickard concluded that the efficacy of group psychotherapy had been demonstrated only tenuously. Subsequent reviews by Pattison (1965) and Mann (1966) were less cautious but still tentative. By 1971 Bednar and Lawlis were quite confident: "the converging evidence is consistent with the view held by many practitioners that group therapy is a valuable tool of the helping professions" (p. 814). Seven years later a similar review prompted an equally certain generalization that "there is a large body of research that indicates that group treatments 'work' " (Bednar and Kaul, 1978, p. 792).

Quite conceivably, then, the empirical literature on group psychotherapy with children has just not grown up yet. Given the proper time and nurturing this body of literature, too, may catch up to what the practitioner already believes to be true, i.e., that group psychotherapy with children can be an extremely beneficial form of intervention. This leap of faith, however, would be inappropriate without first evaluating the nature of the research that has been conducted on children's groups. In her critique of the empirical literature, Abramowitz (1976) noted a variety of serious methodological inadequacies and basic flaws in research design. Moreover, she found that authors failed to describe their group treatments sufficiently. Documentation of therapist interventions and group process were rarely provided, and instruments used to evaluate therapeutic change were generally found wanting.

In this chapter we provide an updated review of the empirical literature on group therapy with children to determine if the conclusions drawn by Abramowitz are still warranted, and to see whether an increased "maturity" and sophistication is evident in the more recent research. In our survey we were able to identify 22 empirical investigations of children's group psychotherapy in which the authors used either a pre/post design to explore therapeutic change or at least made a reasonable effort to gather objective information in order to assess the impact of their group treatments. Table 2 summarizes the research published since Abramowitz's comprehensive review (1976).

Abramowitz identified 42 empirical studies conducted between 1950 and 1974. However, 17 of these investigations were actually unpublished reports appearing in *Dissertation Abstracts International*. Unfortunately, Abramowitz was unable to examine these latter studies in detail, but based her conclusions on the brief summaries presented in the Abstracts. We disapprove of this practice because it leaves too many questions unanswered. Our table therefore contains only published research. Our decision to be more selective, however, introduces a problem. By eliminating the dissertations from our review we are tilting the odds in favor of studies that have demonstrated the efficacy of children's group psychotherapy. Abramowitz (1976) noted, for example, that a "disproportionate number of the null verdicts" appear in the dissertation research (p. 321). Our biased perspective should not be overlooked when we come to discuss the implications of research for clinical practice.

On the basis of the publications appearing in the literature, we are able to detect only a slight increase in the number of investigations conducted on children's groups. The average is less than three published studies each year, and this gives little cause for challenging the earlier conclusion by Abramowitz that "published empirical outcome research has been especially rare" (p. 321).

Despite the relative paucity of research on children's groups, it is still possible that over the years the quality of the research has improved. A more careful analysis of the studies may furnish an answer to this question. Reading down the Treatment and Setting column of Table 2, we find that the reports are focused primarily on group treatment studies in the school. Over four-fifths of the pub-

TABLE 2
Research Reports (n = 22)[1]

Source	Treatment and Setting	Group Participants	Author's Conclusions
Amerikaner and Summerlin (1982)	Relaxation training, social skills group, and no treatment control in the *school*	Learning disabled students in the first and second grade	Treatment improves social self-concept (social skills group) and produces less acting out (relaxation training)
Bell and Ledford (1978)	Activity group, sociodrama, and no treatment control in the *school*	Students with maladaptive classroom behaviors in grades 1–3	Sociodrama has an effect on attitudes but little effect on behaviors
Berry, Turone, and Hardt (1980)	Self-concept psychotherapy group versus behavioral modification group in the *school*	Students with disruptive classroom behaviors, ages 6–9	Self-concept groups are superior to engineered classrooms. Behavioral measures reflected change but not measures of self-concept
Bierman and Furman (1984)	Individual versus group social skills training; group interaction alone, and a no treatment control in the *school*	Fifth and sixth graders low in peer acceptance and deficient in conversational skills	The interventions had strong, positive, and differential effects. Social skills training in the group was most powerful. Effects were maintained at follow-up

TABLE 2 (continued)

Source	Treatment and Setting	Group Participants	Author's Conclusions
Bleck and Bleck (1982)	Play group counseling versus a control group in the *school*	Third-grade students with disruptive classroom behaviors	Structured play had positive effects on attitudes and to a lesser extent on disruptive behavior
Clement, Roberts and Lantz (1976)	Peer therapist and mother therapist reinforcement groups versus controls in a *clinic* setting	Shy, withdrawn, and introverted youngsters, ages 6–11	Children, mothers, and teachers all report positive changes from pre- to post-therapy but not from post-therapy to follow-up. Certain behavioral changes within sessions did not generalize
Cooke and Apolloni (1976)	Behavioral group therapy in a *clinic*	Learning disabled children who failed to adapt to a regular classroom, ages 6–9	Limited and specific behavioral changes occurred but showed inconsistent generalization beyond treatment. Gains were maintained at follow-up
Downing (1977)	Group counseling versus no treatment controls in the *school*	Sixth-grade students with disruptive classroom behaviors	Treated children made greater academic achievement gains, had better school attendance records, and improved in their social behavior in the classroom

TABLE 2 (continued)

Source	Treatment and Setting	Group Participants	Author's Conclusions
Factor and Schilmoeller (1983)	Social skills training versus controls in a playroom setting in the *school*	Classes of normal preschool children	Treated children showed higher levels of sociability and less negative group behavior. There was a modest generalization effect
Franz, Berning, and Reilly (1976)	Sensory awareness groups versus controls in the *school* setting	Entire classroom of fourth graders	Treatment increased interpersonal closeness as viewed by students
Hargrave and Hargrave (1979)	Peer group socialization versus a no treatment control group in the *school*	Shy, withdrawn, and inhibited or aggressive and demanding students in grades 4–6	Group members improved significantly in task-oriented classroom behaviors but social skill improvements were less clear
Hayes, Cunningham, and Robinson (1977)	Group counseling; parent groups, and controls in the *school* setting	Students showing discipline, attendance, or academic difficulties in grades 5–6	Findings tend to support the position that counseling that is conducted indirectly through contact with parents is more effective
Kendall and Zupan (1981)	Cognitive-behavior group, individual cognitive-behavior treatment, and nonspecific group counseling in the *school*	Students with classroom behavioral problems, ages 8–11	Results indicated some improvement for all conditions yet only individual and group cognitive behavioral treatments evidenced improvements on teacher ratings of self-control at post-treatment

TABLE 2 (*continued*)

Source	Treatment and Setting	Group Participants	Author's Conclusions
Kern and Hankins (1977)	Group counseling, group counseling plus homework, and active controls in the *school*	Students in fourth- and fifth-grade classroom units showing the lowest degree of adjustment	Both treatment groups improved more than control subjects, with those in the group counseling plus homework condition showing a slight advantage
Kilmann, Henry, Scarbro, and Laughlin (1979)	Structured "affective education" versus no treatment controls in the *school*	Underachieving students with classroom behavioral problems in grades 4–6	Students in the treatment group showed significantly greater increase in reading skills and on several self-report measures
LaGreca and Santogrossi (1980)	Social skills training versus attention placebo and waiting-list controls in the *school*	Students low in peer acceptance in grades 3–5	Treated children showed greater improvements in social behavior with peers. Some generalization was evident
Leone and Gumaer (1979)	Group assertiveness training in the *school*	Nonassertive and shy children, age unspecified	Youngsters showed increased assertive behavior and improved self-esteem
Lockwood (1981)	Verbal-experiential group psychotherapy in a *clinic*	Children who ranged in psychopathology from moderate to severe, ages 9–13	Post hoc analyses showed that most of the clients improved, especially those who attended more sessions and those whose families were involved

Source	Treatment and Setting	Group Participants	Author's Conclusions
Michelson and Wood (1980)	Assertiveness training versus controls in the *school*	Entire classroom of fourth graders	Training groups showed more improvement on self-report and teacher ratings of assertiveness on post and follow-up assessments
Moracco and Kazandkian (1977)	Behavioral group counseling with or without consulting with teachers versus a behavioral group and controls in the *school*	Students with disruptive classroom behavior in grades 1–3	Behavioral group counseling produces behavior change and improved academic performance, especially when teacher consultation is included
Riester and Tanner (1980)	Group counseling, unspecified, in the *school* setting	Students who had attended group sessions two to eight years earlier for interpersonal problems and negative school attitudes	The majority of the participants reported that their group experience was beneficial for improving interpersonal skills and attitude toward school
Wodarski and Pedi (1978)	Unstructured groups, social learning (behavioral), and traditionally-structured groups in a *clinic* setting	Antisocial boys ages 8–16	Differential treatment effects were not obtained. The children showed low frequencies of antisocial behavior at the clinic, but not in other settings

[1] In addition, six other studies evaluated the effects of group treatments with children. Unfortunately, group treatments were confounded so that it was impossible to isolate the unique effects of group psychotherapy. Three of these studies evaluated "therapeutic milieus" (Abramovitch, Konstantareas, and Sloman, 1980; Ratusnik and Ratusnik, 1976; Wenar and Ruttenberg, 1976) and three examined "therapeutic comps" (Freeman, Anderson, Kairey, and Hunt, 1982; Heckel, Hursh, and Hiers, 1977; Mondell, Tyler and Freeman, 1981).

lished research has been conducted with children in their educational environment, the remaining one-fifth evaluating the effectiveness of group psychotherapy in the outpatient setting. This is in contrast to the relative balance we found for the anecdotal reports across residential, clinic, and school-based facilities (Table 1). Although many factors may account for this discrepancy, the most significant are probably the researcher's ease of entry into the educational system and the degree of experimental control feasible within that context. In addition, the school is obviously a setting in which childhood disturbances are likely to be manifest and to require immediate efforts at remediation. From this perspective it is not surprising that so many of the studies focus on children with disruptive classroom behaviors or other problems likely to produce management difficulties: learning disabilities, shyness or withdrawal, demandingness (see the Group Participants column of Table 2).

The fact that clinical agencies are underrepresented in the research introduces a bias in the generalizations that are possible regarding the efficacy of children's group psychotherapy. Studies in the outpatient or private practice setting are just not available in the recent literature. For this reason, we hope that clinicians will begin to adopt the three steps for implementing research that we suggested earlier. A few group psychotherapists utilizing comparable data collection methods with similar groups of children could pool their resources (perhaps with a researcher as consultant) to make a substantial contribution to the literature.

Achenbach (1978) notes that the setting from which children are recruited may exert significant influences on behavior: "The differential histories, motivational structures, and expectations of subjects obtained through public schools, clinics, residential institutions and courts can produce major differences in behavior despite similarities in developmental level, demographic characteristics, and diagnosis" (p. 762). Although the effects of differential recruitment strategies and the confounding influence of situational factors have been discussed in the adult group psychotherapy literature (Dies, 1978), researchers on children's groups have rarely addressed these issues. For instance, it was necessary to exclude six additional empirical investigations from the present review by virtue of our inability to isolate the unique contribution of group treatments from other aspects of the therapeutic milieu (see the footnote to Table 2). That is, the children were exposed to a number of concurrent therapeutic interventions so that the specific effects of group interaction were confounded. This same problem plagued many of the earlier research projects on group psychotherapy with institutionalized adults (Bednar and Kaul, 1978).

The group experiences listed in Table 2 are fairly diverse and generally comparable to those identified among the anecdotal reports. Theme-centered groups (self-concept, sensory awareness, assertiveness training), action-oriented techniques (play groups, activity groups), methods combining activity and discussion (sociodrama, verbal-experiential, structured groups), and behavioral groups all appear in this table as well. Overall, the group experiences featured in both the impressionistic and the empirical reports reflect fewer nonstructured groups, less emphasis on verbalization within sessions, and more activity than the groups typically described in the adult literature. These contrasts are not unexpected and are certainly consistent with developmental differences between children and adults.

The group experiences are for the most part relatively brief, the average number of sessions being approximately twelve. Moreover, the number of groups investigated is generally small (between four and five). This emphasis on short-term groups with fairly restricted sample sizes is a problem evident also in much of the adult literature (Dies, 1983b).

Most readers will immediately recognize an apparent contradiction in our presentation. Earlier we encouraged clinicians to become involved in small-scale research, but now we are faulting investigators for using limited sample sizes. How can we take both of these positions? One answer, of course, is that we believe that systematic and objective data collection can improve the quality of clinical service even when publication of results is not the goal. A second explanation is that most of the researchers who studied a small number of groups did not follow steps 2 and 3 in our set of recommendations. That is, multiple assessment with follow-up (step 2) and the integration of process measures (step 3) were not built into their research designs. Moreover, the authors of the published research often did not employ multiple perspectives on outcome (as we did in our illustration), nor did they pool resources with other clinicians and/or researchers to broaden their empirical foundation. Thus, their simple pre/post designs were inferior to the set of guidelines we listed for the practitioner building a research component into clinical practice.

It is beyond the scope of this chapter to present a detailed critique of the experimental designs used in these 22 studies, but many of the deficiencies noted by Abramowitz (1976) continue to plague much of the research. In addition to the unrepresentative and small samples, there are numerous instances of inadequate or nonexistent control groups, treatments confounded by therapeutic interventions with parents (making it difficult to determine what actually produces change in the child) or contamination due to the fact that teachers served as group counselors as well as evaluators of change (introducing an obvious bias in measures of improvement), and other fairly significant imperfections in the experimental designs. On the other hand, there are several exceptions to this rather gloomy picture. A few studies that we will highlight later in the chapter have utilized more sophisticated research designs and documented the value of group interventions (Clement, Roberts, and Lantz, 1976; LaGreca and Santogrossi, 1980; Factor and Schilmoeller, 1983; Bierman and Furman, 1984). Despite these exemplary studies, we are unable to demonstrate that the quality of research has "matured" *significantly* over the past several years. Thus, we are left with the conclusion of Barrett et al. (1978) that "child psychotherapy research is no match in quantity or quality for that with adults" (p. 412). Tramontana (1980) provided a similar generalization regarding research on psychotherapy outcome with adolescents, suggesting that the literature in this area was then at a state of development that adult outcome literature had reached more than fifteen years ago. Our analysis of subsequent research literature on group psychotherapy outcome with children and adolescents leads us to conclude that the situation has not changed to any significant degree.

We agree with Abramowitz (1976) that "research that is more sound methodologically and broader conceptually could eventuate in more effective child clinical practice. Toward this end, it is hoped that future investigators in this area will take into account . . . recent recommendations concerning the design, conduct, analysis, and reporting of psychotherapy studies" (p. 325). This was a fitting conclusion to Abramowitz's paper, but we were not content to end our chapter at this point. The slight increment in the rate of publication and the presence of several more sophisticated studies gives us some reason for greater optimism. Although the field is still in its early developmental phases, we believe that a number of important observations can be made, and that more constructive guidelines can be established regarding future directions for research and clinical practice.

As we read down the Author's Conclusions column of Table 2, it is clear that a majority of the investigators believed that their treatments were at least partially successful. Statements of increased assertiveness, improved social skills, less acting out, more positive attitudes, enhanced self-concept, and greater achievement in task-related behaviors can be found with some regularity.

The staunchest critic of this body of literature might dismiss many of these conclusions as unwarranted given the fundamental flaws in the experimental designs and the comparatively limited number of studies on which these conclusions are based (especially in light of our policy of excluding research in which null results are more prevalent, i.e., the doctoral dissertations). At this point, however, we will cling more tenaciously to our optimism that there is some substance to the claims that group psychotherapy with children can be highly beneficial.

Certainly as group psychotherapists we believe that our treatments are effective. As empirically minded clinicians, however, we demand a more convincing demonstration that our faith is not unfounded. Unfortunately, researchers have generally failed to provide the level of documentation that is essential.

In the remainder of this chapter we will turn our attention to a number of central issues that must be addressed if this body of literature is to "mature." Specifically, we will focus on (1) maintenance of treatment effects; (2) generalization of therapeutic gain; (3) isolating the unique contribution of treatment from other growth-inducing changes in the environment; (4) methods for measuring the outcome of group interactions; and, (5) defining treatment (process) more precisely. Throughout our discussion we will offer suggestions for how researchers and practitioners can introduce procedures for collecting meaningful information on the children who participate in their group treatments.

Maintenance of Treatment Effects

In his review of behavior therapy with children, Ross (1978) observed that a frequent shortcoming was the brief period over which treated children were followed to determine whether any beneficial effects were maintained. He noted that we will remain relatively naive about the effectiveness of our treatment "until objective measures are applied over three or four years" (p. 614). This position is rather extreme, but certainly highlights the importance of follow-up procedures to adequately assess the benefits of treatment. Achenbach (1978) believes that a progress check at the end of one year should become a routine part of clinical service. Rutter (1983), in his overview of treatment research with children, also argues for the necessity of evaluating the persistence of improvement. He outlined four possibilities regarding therapeutic outcome. First, psychotherapy may accelerate immediate recovery but not alter long-term outcome, so that initial effects may wash out. This might happen, for example, when members of a control group catch up due to developmental changes or to slower-acting natural interventions in the child's environment. Second, treated groups may deteriorate soon after the termination of the intervention. Thus, group psychotherapy may serve temporarily to suppress deviant behaviors which may return once the child is aware that special attention is no longer available. Third, therapeutic gain may increase over time, for instance, as overt changes have a cumulative effect due to "adaptive chain reactions" (p. 148). And finally, interventions most effective on a long-term basis may not be those with the greatest short-term effects.

Only six of the studies covered in our survey incorporate follow-up procedures, and their results were quite varied. Clement et al. (1976) investigated changes due to behavioral group methods immediately after treatment and again after six months. On self-report measures the authors discovered improvement from pre-therapy to follow-up. On measures based on rating scales completed by the children's mothers, there was improvement from pre-therapy to post-therapy, but no reliable changes occurring between post-therapy and follow-up. On the other hand, teachers' ratings showed a mixed pattern. Kendall and Zupan (1981), in their examination of individual versus group cognitive-behavioral techniques and a nonspecific group treatment, found that initial differences diminished on certain measures. Some improvement in the nonspecific group therapy condition, and reversal of gain in the cognitive-behavioral group treatment, accounted for the lack of differences across conditions two months later. Michelson and Wood (1980), studying assertiveness training, and Cooke and Apolloni (1976), using modeling and reinforcement techniques, found that initial treatment effects were still evident after four weeks. The two most recent studies to evaluate maintenance of therapeutic change focused on social skills training. Bierman and Furman (1984) found differential results during a six-week follow-up. Skill training produced strong and sustained improvements in children's conversational skills, but effects on peer acceptance, rates of peer interaction, and self-perceptions were less consistent. Treatment with individual or group coaching methods also influenced the findings. The group intervention had a more favorable effect on peer acceptance. Factor and Schilmoeller (1983) showed that social skills training with preschool children did not produce reliable results even within their one-week follow-up period. Children maintained their changes in the experimental treatment room, but did not display similar improvement in the classroom.

On the basis of these six investigations, then, it is apparent that systematic follow-up procedures are necessary to understand fully the meaning of therapeutic change. Results may vary as a function of the behaviors being assessed, who is evaluating those behaviors, the context in which they are being examined, and the age of the particular child. The collection of follow-up information should become a routine part of clinical practice. The progress of children can be assessed by telephone contacts with parents, requests that the parents and child return periodically for brief evaluation, questionnaires sent through the mail, regular examination of school records, conferences with teachers, and a variety of other procedures. It is surprising how seldom these relatively simple techniques are used to gather meaningful follow-up data on children who have participated in group treatments.

Two other studies used a post hoc follow-up procedure to evaluate therapeutic impact. Lockwood (1981) asked parents, school personnel, and group psychotherapists to rate degree of improvement among children six months after therapy had terminated. By contrast, Riester and Tanner (1980) asked the clients themselves (high school students) to reflect back on group counseling they had experienced two to eight years earlier. Although both studies indicated that treatments had produced positive results, it would be difficult to rule out the possibility that intervening events had contributed significantly to whatever changes were observed. For example, Lockwood found that parental involvement in therapy, as well as in modifying significant factors in parent-child relationships, was common among youngsters who improved. Thus, it was perhaps not the children's group psychotherapy at all that led to therapeutic gain, but change in the family system initiated by the parents. Similarly, while the high school students in the study by Riester and Tanner were able to recall many details of their group experiences, their testimonials as to therapeutic benefit may not be entirely reliable, or even related to actual changes.

Studies using a repeated measures design with appropriate control groups would inspire more confidence in the conclusions.

Achenbach (1978), from his perspective of developmental psychotherapy, makes another interesting point regarding therapeutic change. He argues that measurements repeated on the same children more than a few weeks apart are quite likely to differ as a function of development. In consequence, investigators who interpret improvement as due to their therapeutic interventions could be in error. Similarly, Rutter (1983) states that it is "necessary to measure alterations produced by therapy against the background of continuing development and behavioral change that occurs as a consequence of biological maturation and the accumulation of interacting experiences. When evaluating the long-term effects of treatment during childhood, it is essential to differentiate the benefits of treatment from the improvements that result from growing up" (p. 140).

If this field is to advance, clinicians and researchers must attend to these issues. The presence of a control group is a step in the right direction, but if we are to become more than toddlers, our efforts must be more substantial. Normative comparisons (Kendall and Zupan, 1981), careful attention to group composition to insure that children placed together are at similar developmental levels, efforts to match children in different treatment conditions, and repeated, multiperspective, and long-term assessment of changes are essential.

Generalization of Therapeutic Gains

If the behavioral changes psychotherapists observe during their group sessions are not also evident in other settings (the classroom, family interactions, peer relationships), then treatment is of very limited value. Ideally, we would hope to witness widespread behavioral effects that are apparent to observers in a range of situations. On the other hand, Ross (1978) has argued that many maladaptive child behaviors are limited to one setting; the child who is disruptive in the classroom may be quite tractable in the home. In such cases, we would hope at least for generalization from the group sessions to the school environment. Clearly, children's behavior varies tremendously with situations, and we must therefore design our group treatment studies to evaluate those settings in which generalization is most likely to occur.

Although many of the studies listed in Table 2 assess treatment effects in other settings, the investigators have rarely focused on this issue by linking the type of changes observed during treatment with those occurring in other settings, or by exploring the relationship among multiple perspectives on therapeutic change. In one of the better designed early studies, however, Clement et al. (1976) evaluated the generalization of within-therapy changes across a variety of settings. These investigators concluded that their "active treatment program made some differences in the child's behavior within the therapy sessions, but these differences did not appear to generalize to the extra-therapy measures" (p. 356).

In a specific test of the notion that group treatment provides training in a therapeutic context similar to the setting in which generalization is desired (in this instance, the classroom), Kendall and Zupan (1981) compared individual and group application of cognitive-behavioral self-control procedures. Although both treatments were effective in producing desired behavioral changes, differential treatment benefits were not detected. Consequently, the authors concluded that their group intervention did not increase the likelihood of generalization. By contrast, Bierman and Furman (1984) found that group training in school skills *was* more effective than individual methods, at least for two of their dependent measures—peer acceptance and children's self-perceptions of their social efficacy. We might expect that learning social skills in a group treatment setting would generalize more readily than learning social skills within the one-to-one treatment modality. The research on curative factors in the adult group psychotherapy literature clearly documents the importance of the unique advantages of the group in terms of interpersonal learning (Yalom, 1975). Bierman and Furman (1984) suggest that groups may be especially important for children. They note that "peer interactions play significant and unique roles in facilitating the development of appropriate assertiveness, altruistic behavior, moral reasoning, and other social competencies" (p. 151). Similarly, Gresham and Lemanek (1983) stress that social competence is an important developmental achievement. Socially unskilled children tend to have poor relationships with peers, evidence a high incidence of school maladjustment (e.g., inferior academic performance, increased drop-out rates, delinquency), and as adults often display mental health difficulties. Thus, peer group interaction may be particularly critical during earlier stages of development. This observation may in fact provide an excellent rationale for the value of group treatments with childhood disorders.

Cooke and Apolloni (1976) examined generalization from group treatment of simple social-emotional behaviors (e.g., smiling, sharing, positive physical contacting, and verbal complimenting) with children in a small experimental classroom. The investigators discovered that generalization for most of these behaviors was present, and that the "positive chain reactions" mentioned earlier (Rutter, 1983) seemed to occur. That is, given that these children were in the same classroom, the increased rates of social-emotional behavior served to facilitate each child's maintenance of such behavior. Even untrained children in the same classroom were influenced by social reciprocity or vicarious learning. The situational specificity of such generalization is apparent.

Wodarski and Pedi (1978) observed very low frequencies of antisocial behavior among children defined as antisocial on diagnostic measures used by referring agencies. The authors suggested that these aggressive children did not evince their antisocial behaviors in treatment because they did not wish to give up the opportunity of coming to the community center. These findings once again highlight the importance of situational factors in determining the generalization of behaviors. We noted earlier, too, that investigators have rarely systematically explored the relationship among multiple perspectives on therapeutic gain. With Wodarski and Pedi's children, referral sources were shown antisocial behaviors while the researchers were not. We will address this issue more fully in a later section, but we want to emphasize at this point that when researchers examine generalization it is possible that different observers may perceive different treatment results. Bierman and Furman (1984), for example, found that two measures, both focused on children's rates of peer interaction in naturalistic settings (trained observers' evaluation of lunchtime interaction rates and teacher ratings of classroom interactions), yielded differential results. Only the observers' ratings were significant at post-test and follow-up. These investigators also demonstrated that self-report and peer-sociometric evaluations produced varying results. LaGreca and Santogrossi (1980) studied the effects of social skills training in different contexts and with different raters. Children were observed during a variety of situations conducive to peer interactions, e.g., recess, gym period, and club meetings. Differences were obtained for ratings of "initiating social interactions," but not on measures of "positive social behavior." Finally, we noted earlier that Factor and Schilmoeller (1983) discovered that generalization was apparent in peer group interactions within the treatment room a week after the group intervention was terminated, but not in the classroom setting. Thus, generalization was selective. Altogether, then, these investigations indicate that the extent of generalization depends on the setting in which the effects are evaluated, who makes the observations, which measures are used to record the ratings, and what behaviors are actually scored.

Achenbach (1978) has concluded that the type of observers and their relationship to the child will invariably influence the behavior reported. In general, the greater the disparity between the situation in which observers view the children and the more the observers vary in their relationships to the youngsters, the lower the agreement among them. A few studies covered in our review have used multiple observers—self-report, teachers, independent raters, parents, therapists, and/or peers (see Table 3)—and found widely divergent results. The consistencies may not reflect unreliability in the rating process, but may rather highlight the lack of generalization of many behavioral changes. Thus, in order to comprehend the nature of therapeutic change more fully, we must incorporate a range of perspectives on treatment outcome (MacKenzie and Dies, 1982).

According to Ladd and Mize (1983), "skill generalization can be seen as a process in which the learner progresses from performing new skills in a relatively controlled, risk-free context, to one in which he or she is expected to use the skills in the course of normal social interaction in real-life situations" (p. 135). Only a few of the studies we identified in the literature evaluate this translation from therapy to outside social interactions very effectively. More work is clearly needed, especially in view of the increasing emphasis within the literature urging professionals to recognize that generalization of treatment gains should be programmed or planned and not left to chance (Barton and Bevirt, 1981).

Isolating the Unique Contribution of Group Treatment

Rutter (1983) recommends that any appraisal of the value of psychological therapies for children must take into account the extent to which the family has been involved. The vast majority of the studies covered in our review have neglected this important consideration. Earlier, however, we mentioned the post hoc follow-up investigation by Lockwood (1981), who discovered that parental interest and involvement in therapy, and in modification of critical factors in parent-child relationships, served to facilitate therapeutic progress. This finding certainly makes sense, but it also poses a dilemma, because it is unclear what factors account for clinical improvement. Was it the group psychotherapy for the children, change in family structure, or some combination of these ingredients? The research design does not permit the isolation of factors contributing to positive outcome. These same criticisms can be leveled against several of the anecdotal reports summarized in Table 1. Barsky and Mozenter (1976), for example, conducted family therapy sessions as well as creative drama in a children's group, but never mentioned the possibility that the family therapy may have contributed to the children's improved coping skills. Pasnau, Meyer, Davis, Lloyd, and Kline (1976), Hoffman, Byrne, Belnap, and Steward (1981), and Tiktin and Cobb (1983) described rather innovative techniques for involving parents in their child's treatment, but they, too, failed to address adequately the unique contribution of the children's group psychotherapy to clinical improvement. It is unknown how many of the research projects outlined in Table 2 are confounded by parental involvement, as most investigators do not provide information allowing us to make this determination.

A few of the research reports have attempted to tease out the distinct contribution of parent participation and child group psychotherapy. Clement et al. (1976) compared three types of group: Peer Therapist Groups, Mother Therapist Groups, and Contrast Mother Groups. In the first type children took turns being therapists in their own group while receiving prompting and social reinforcement from the investigators through a "bug-in-the-ear" device. A similar format was followed in the groups led by mothers. Children in the Contrast Mothers Group did not receive treatment, but their mothers attended weekly training sessions. The researchers demonstrated that both children and parents could be trained to implement behaviorally oriented group therapy with some degree of success. Although their findings were mixed, Clements and his colleagues were able to demonstrate that even children who did not participate in treatment showed some therapeutic gain, often at levels not significantly different from those manifested in actively treated youngsters.

Hayes, Cunningham, and Robinson (1977) compared direct and indirect group psychotherapy (child only versus parent only) and found tentative support for the position that counseling conducted indirectly through contact with parents may be more effective than direct group counseling with the children. Moracco and Kazandkian (1977) explored the role of another significant adult, namely the child's teacher, in the treatment process. They compared four treatments: behavioral group counseling plus consultation with teachers about the application of behavioral techniques in the classroom; consultation with teachers only; behavioral group counseling only; and a placebo control group. The results indicated that group counseling plus consultation was superior to the other three treatments, whereas the placebo group was significantly less effective than the other two methods. Thus, involvement of the teacher in the treatment process led to increased benefits for the children whether or not the students were directly involved in group counseling.

Overall, these results indicate that investigators must make a concerted effort to isolate the distinct contribution of the child's participation in a group from the role played by various types of involvement of significant adults in the child's treatment. Otherwise, claims cannot be made about the unique therapeutic potential of group treatments for children. Our inability of disentangle the benefits of group interaction from other components of the treatment environment led us earlier to reject those research projects conducted within therapeutic milieus and camps (see the footnote to Table 2).

Our conclusions do *not* suggest that parents, teachers, or other significant figures should be excluded from the child's treatment. On the contrary, most experts in this field argue that this involvement is absolutely essential (Freedheim and Russ, 1983; Rutter, 1983). The main implication for the researcher and the clinician, however, is that procedures must be developed for identifying the relative contribution of parents, teachers, or family support over and above the child's participation in group psychotherapy. It may be possible, for example, to observe variations in the extent or nature of the adult involvement and then to explore differential treatment effects.

Methods for Assessing Outcome

A wide assortment of instruments and rating procedures have been used to evaluate therapeutic change. These include self-report measures, ratings furnished by teachers, trained observers, parents, therapists, and peers, records (attendance and grades), and within-therapy ratings provided by independent observers and the group psychotherapists. Table 3 gives an overview of the 22 empirical studies outlined earlier and the types of measures administered in these investigations. The table does not list specific instruments but presents a classification of outcomes based on two ingredients: (1) the percentage of measures used by the investigator that reflect statistically reliable changes and (2) a judgment about the adequacy of those measures. The classification scheme is explained in the footnote to Table 3. We can read down the columns to identify how often particular types of measures were used, and across the columns to determine the range of measures included in each study.

The most popular research strategy was to use self-report measures of therapeutic outcome (14 of 22 students). Children were requested to complete a wide range of tests assessing their self-concept, level of anxiety, antisocial tendencies, generalized personality traits, adjustment, specific attitudes, and similar attributes. We found little standardization across measures as investigators used 22 different tests, and only two of these were replicated (a self-esteem inventory and a test of personality traits). As we read down the Self-Report column in the table it appears as though the measures have been moderately successful in demonstrating treatment effects (see the definitions of terms in the footnote to Table 3). At least from the vantage point of the children, then, group psychotherapy has been experienced as a beneficial intervention, particularly in terms of helping them to feel better about themselves and less anxious. Ladd and Mize (1983), based on their extensive review of the social skills training literature, conclude that studies with children indicate that feelings of self-efficacy (positive self-esteem) are "antithetical to anxiety, and may mediate children's persistence at performing interpersonal skills in situations where obstacles or low success rates are encountered" (p. 136). Moreover, they suggest that deflated or decreasing self-confidence is frequently accompanied by improved interpersonal performance, negatively charged emotional reactions, and lessened motivation. The finding that group treatments result in fairly consistent increases in feelings of self-efficacy is quite important.

The second most common approach to outcome assessment is to use ratings provided by teachers in the classroom setting (13 to 22 studies). As over 80 percent of the studies are conducted in the school system, this finding is hardly surprising. Again, a lack of uniformity is apparent across the studies, as 13 researchers used an equal number of measures to evaluate change. Two scales were used more than once (both of these were problem-behavior checklists), but the behavioral rating procedures used in other studies overlap quite substantially.

TABLE 3
Measures to Assess Outcome[1]

Source	Self		Observations (Extratherapy)					Observations (Intratherapy)		Records
	Report	Achievement	Teacher	Observer	Parents	Therapist	Peers	Observers	Therapists	
Amerikaner and Summerlin (1982)	Very Weak	—	Moderate	—	—	—	—	—	—	—
Bell and Ledford (1978)	Limited	—	Limited	None	—	—	Limited	—	—	—
Berry et al. (1980)	None	—	—	Moderate	—	—	—	—	—	—
Bierman and Furman (1984)	Moderate	—	None	Strong	—	—	Moderate	—	—	—
Bleck and Bleck (1982)	Moderate	—	Very Weak	—	—	—	—	—	—	—
Clement et al. (1976)	Moderate	—	Moderate	—	Moderate	—	—	Moderate	—	—
Cooke and Apolloni (1976)	—	—	—	Limited	—	—	—	Limited	—	—
Downing (1977)	—	Limited	Limited	—	—	—	—	—	—	Limited

TABLE 3 (continued)

Source	Self		Observations (Extratherapy)					Observations (Intratherapy)		Records
	Report	Achievement	Teacher	Observer	Parents	Therapist	Peers	Observers	Therapists	
Factor and Schilmoeller (1983)	—	—	—	—	—	—	—	—	—	—
Franz et al. (1976)	—	—	—	Moderate	—	—	—	—	—	—
Hargrave and Hargrave (1979)	—	—	Limited	—	—	—	Limited	—	—	—
Hayes et al. (1977)	Moderate	—	—	—	—	—	—	—	—	None
Kendall and Zupan (1981)	None	None	Limited	—	—	Limited	—	—	Very Weak	—
Kern and Hankins (1977)	Limited	—	Moderate	—	—	—	—	—	—	—
Kilmann et al. (1979)	Limited	Limited	—	—	—	—	—	—	—	—
LaGreca and Santogrossi (1980)	—	Strong	—	Moderate	—	—	None	—	—	—

TABLE 3 (*continued*)

Source	Self		Observations (Extratherapy)					Observations (Intratherapy)		Records
	Report	Achievement	Teacher	Observer	Parents	Therapist	Peers	Observers	Therapists	
Leone and Gumaer (1979)	Moderate	—	Moderate	—	—	—	None	—	—	—
Lockwood (1981)	—	—	Limited	—	Limited	Limited	—	—	—	—
Michelson and Wood (1980)	Moderate	—	Moderate	—	—	—	—	—	—	—
Moracco and Kazandkian (1977)	—	—	Limited	—	—	—	—	—	—	—
Riester and Tanner (1980)	Limited	—	—	—	—	—	—	—	—	—
Wodarski and Pedi (1978)	None	—	—	—	—	None	—	None	Very Weak	—

TABLE 3 (continued)

¹The judgment of outcome as "none," "very weak," "limited," "moderate," and "strong" was based on a classification scheme using two criteria: (1) percent of measures used which reflect therapeutic improvement; and (2) the adequacy of the measures employed.

Therapeutic Change	X	Adequacy of Measure	
1 None (0–10%)		A (self) Single, nonstandardized	or A (other) Author-devised, no reliability
2 Weak (10–35%)		B (self) Single, standardized	or B (other) Adequate but biased
3 Moderate (35–65%)		C (self) Two independent	or C (other) Standardized, no reliability check
4 Strong (65% +)		D (self) Several Standardized	or D (other) Standardized, reliability check

Classification of Outcome (percent X adequacy)
None   = 1A 1B 1C 1D
Very Weak = 2A 2B
Limited   = 2C 2D 3A 3B 4A 4B
Moderate = 3C 3D 4C
Strong   = 4D

Therefore, the lack of homogeneity across measures is less troubling than might be thought. A glance down the Teacher column of Table 3 suggests that group psychotherapy has been moderately productive in fostering behavioral change within the classroom setting.

The other perspectives on therapeutic gain have been largely underutilized. Independent observers have been used in six different studies with moderate success. These raters have been able to detect therapeutic change, sometimes when improvement was not seen by the teachers in the classroom context. Peers have been asked to rate their classmates in five studies, but evidence for the positive influence of treatment is quite meager from this perspective. The use of achievement scores (4), therapists (3), parents (2), and records (2) are too infrequent and inconsistent to allow for meaningful conclusions.

Our glance down the columns of Table 3, then, can inspire only cautious optimism as to the value of group treatments for children. Although subjective measures (self-report) and behavioral reports by teachers, and to a lesser extent independent observers, have been able to confirm a moderate degree of therapeutic improvement, several factors weaken confidence in our conclusions. The lack of uniformity of measures across studies, the limited use of certain perspectives (e.g., parents), and the sparse results with peer ratings all detract from our assurance that research has documented the effectiveness of group psychotherapy for children.

Our initial optimism is jeopardized even more when we read across the columns of Table 3 and discover that so many of the conclusions are based on narrow conceptualizations of therapeutic change and limited corroboration across data sources. Seven studies use only one data source and another six employ only two perspectives. One glimmer of hope that we can extract from Table 3, however, is that several of the more rigorously designed studies were able to demonstrate the value of group interventions with children (Clement et al., 1976; LaGreca and Santogrossi, 1980; Factor and Schilmoeller, 1983; Bierman and Furman, 1984). Each of these studies used carefully selected control groups and independent raters to assess change, examined generalization of treatment effects, and in most cases measured change during a follow-up period. It should be noted, however, that these investigations all represent a cognitive-behavioral approach to group intervention. Well-designed experimental studies to evaluate more traditional group treatments with children have not been conducted since Abramowitz's review of the literature (1976). Again, we underscore the need for clinicians to subject their treatments to empirical evaluation.

LaGreca (1983) has provided some general guidelines for evaluating the outcome of psychotherapy with children. One of the most important requirements is that the assessment process involve several persons in the child's environment, including the child. Typically, children are not self-referred for treatment, so the referral may bear little relationship to the child's feelings of discomfort. Therefore, input both from the child and from significant others is critical in obtaining an accurate impression of the problem. Then, too, a child's behavior is often situation-specific so that multiple perspectives across observational settings are required to gain a more comprehensive understanding of the child's behavioral patterns. Finally, LaGreca notes that it is "important to assess how the adults in the child's life behave toward the child and the child's problem" (p. 110).

Despite the importance of these issues, O'Leary and Turkewitz (1978) have indicated that one of the most serious deficiencies in child treatment research is the lack of multiple outcome criteria. This view is shared by Achenbach (1978), who argues that "because there is typically no single criterion situation against which to validate observations, it is important to obtain multiple measures from observers who differ in their relationships with the subjects" (p. 764). Achenbach believes that parents are usually effective informants regarding behavior because their perceptions will determine what will be done with their children. He has found that parents' reports of behavior problems are much more complete than those of teachers and observers in the school or home. Nonetheless, he concedes that the weight given to reports from other perspectives—teachers, clinicians, peers, self-reports—should depend on the extent to which they relate to the variables of interest.

Freedheim and Russ (1983) discuss the value of Strupp and Hadley's tripartite model for understanding therapeutic gain (1977). This model stresses the importance of using three viewpoints in assessment: society, the individual, and the mental health professional. "The vantage point of society would be reflected in measures of adaptive behavior. For the child, that would include measures of school achievement, behavioral adjustment, peer relations, coping strategies, etc. The point of view of the individual would be reflected in the child's sense of well-being. The vantage point of the mental health profession would be reflected in measures of cognitive and personality structure" (p. 988). The critical issue is that outcomes should demonstrate "social validity" (Gresham and Lemanek, 1983), i.e., not only represent statistical significance but also display socially important outcomes. Walker and Roberts (1983) provide an excellent compendium for the assessment of children. Their chapters on diagnostic evaluation cover interviewing and behavioral observations, intellectual and educational testing, neuropsychological assessment, and objective and projective tests.

Barrett et al. (1978), reviewing the research on psychotherapy with children, argue that instruments capable of use by several informants (e.g., client, therapist, independent observers) are needed. Although such measures may be difficult to devise, initial steps can be implemented by having different observers judge the same behavioral domain, e.g., disruptive behaviors in the classroom as seen by child, peers, teacher, and observers (a reliability check across perspectives); disruptive behaviors across many situations by the same observers (a check on generalization); or even disruptive behavior as seen by child, teacher, and parents in diverse situations.

If this field is to "mature" and to demonstrate a more sophisticated understanding of treatment effects, investigators must begin to heed the recommendations offered by critics of the literature. If it is acknowledged that the research is indeed in a "rudimentary stage, it should be clear that development of standardized procedures for assessing pathologies and competencies and for measuring change in them should command a high priority" (Achenbach, 1978, p. 773). Researchers must show a greater understanding of the problems inherent in various assessment strategies (O'Leary and Turkewitz, 1978) and begin to incorporate measures with demonstrated success. Achenbach and Edelbrock (1978), for example, indicate that there are now instruments for which a considerable body of data exist on substantial samples. These include measures of both broad-based syndromes and more differentiated symptomatology, measures that can be used by multiple observers. The integration of individualized outcome criteria (MacKenzie and Dies, 1982) and nonreactive measures of gain (Patterson and Sechrest, 1983) are also necessary. The need for researchers and clinicians to collaborate in the selection of measures is important (Dies, 1983a), and will be addressed in the conclusions to this chapter.

Defining Treatment (Process) More Precisely

The paucity of outcome research on children's groups is overshadowed by the even greater dearth of studies on group process.

This stands in contrast to the large body of literature on process in adult therapy groups as summarized in numerous reviews: cohesion, feedback, and self-disclosure (Bednar and Kaul, 1978); curative factors (Bloch, Crouch, and Reibstein, 1981; Butler and Fuhriman, 1983); group composition (Melnick and Woods, 1976); patient perceptions of the therapeutic relationship (Gurman and Gustafson, 1976); leadership variables (Dies, 1977, 1983b), and others. Surveys of process research on children's groups are rare and only a smattering of information is available from individual studies.

Many critics of the research literature on group psychotherapy with children note that a principal shortcoming is the failure to specify treatment beyond global or categorical descriptions of the interventions (Hobbs et al., 1980). O'Leary and Turkewitz (1978) encourage authors to provide a detailed definition of their treatments to enhance the possibility of replication of the research and to facilitate an understanding of the interventions. Moreover, these authors argue that when researchers make comparisons between different group therapies they should provide reliable and objective information to document the actual procedural differences that distinguish the treatments. Of the 22 studies we cover in our review only three conduct a "therapy manipulation check" and note that the therapists were indeed offering the treatment conditions as described (Kern and Hankins, 1977; LaGreca and Santogrossi, 1980; Kendall and Zupan, 1981). A number of other investigators furnish an outline of the structure for each session, but their descriptions are rather sparse.

Five of the research projects referenced in Table 2 incorporate measures of events occurring within the sessions. Cooke and Apolloni (1976) trained observers to record four simple social-emotional behaviors (smiling, sharing, positive physical contacting, and verbal complimenting) within a group of handicapped youngsters. Similarly, Wodarski and Pedi (1978) trained independent observers to register instances of prosocial, nonsocial, and antisocial behaviors exhibited by children during their treatment sessions. As noted earlier, Cooke and Apolloni were able to demonstrate the generalization of therapeutic changes to extratherapy settings. By contrast, Wodarski and Pedi, because of the low frequency of nonsocial and antisocial behaviors within their treatment sessions, were unable even to test their hypothesis. Clement et al. (1976) used a time-sampling procedure to score each child on eight behavioral dimensions including, for example, statements to other children, questions, symbolic and verbal aggression, solitary play, and proximity. Similarly, Factor and Schilmoeller (1983) used seven behavioral categories in their study of preschool children in their social skills training play group: unoccupied, onlooker, solitary, parallel, group positive, group negative, and child-directed. Finally, Kendall and Zupan (1981) instructed their therapists to complete an evaluation form at the end of each session to record such behaviors as time spent with each child, the child's ability to follow instructions, number of tasks completed, and closeness of the therapist-child relationship. In the latter three studies the investigators were able to demonstrate a few connections between group process variables and treatment outcome, but the findings were relatively modest.

As many critics have noted, the question of whether group psychotherapy "works" is anachronistic and not very likely to inspire sophisticated research on group treatments. Advancement in the field will follow only from a more precise articulation of the treatment conditions that contribute to varying therapeutic outcomes with different children (Barrett et al., 1978). Efforts to delineate the linkage between specific group process variables and particular therapeutic gains are at best rudimentary in the children's group therapy literature. Kendall and Zupan (1981) noted tentative associations between children's perceptions of the therapist-child relationship, but did not report their findings. Similarly, Wodarski and Pedi (1978) collected information on various dimensions of therapist behavior, but they, too, because of limited statistical significance, did not report their results. Ladd and Mize (1983) suggest that interventions with children depend on the quality of the relationship established between the child and the leader. The authors note that this conclusion has not been adequately tested in the child social skills training literature, but argue that evidence is available in related fields: nurturance and warmth are regarded as important in the parent-child relationship; adult warmth plays a significant role in the socialization of children's self-esteem; children are more likely to imitate prosocial behaviors demonstrated by warm as opposed to aloof adult models; and teacher characteristics such as warmth, enthusiasm, and directiveness affect attitudes toward learning and the actual learning process. Regrettably, investigators have not adequately addressed this issue in group psychotherapy with children. However, there is ample evidence in the adult group treatment literature to confirm the importance of the therapist-client relationship (Dies, 1983b).

Other researchers have developed methods for tabulating group process variables but have not explored the relationship of these measures to therapeutic gain. Howe and Silvern (1981) describe the preliminary development of a Play Therapy Observational Instrument that reliably combines 13 behaviors to form three subscales (emotional discomfort, use of fantasy play as a coping method, and the quality of the child's relationship with the therapist). Heckel, Hursh, and Hiers (1977) examined patterns of group development on a number of critical dimensions including initiating activity, seeking information, group-building roles, giving opinions, and therapist-directed responses. Further research on these instruments has not been published.

Riester and Tanner (1980) attempted to evaluate the relation between therapeutic outcome and group process by interviewing junior and senior high school students about group counseling they had experienced as students in elementary school. The authors found that the "curative factors" cited most frequently by the students were interpersonal learning, group cohesiveness, and catharsis (Yalom, 1975). Furthermore, Riester and Tanner found that each problem area elicited different opinions concerning how the group was helpful. For example, the goal of improving grades was related more to the guidance factor whereas the goal of improving the students' relationships with parents was linked more to identification, interpersonal learning, and insight. Regrettably, the post hoc nature of this study and the subjective quality of the findings make it difficult to place much confidence in the results. Nevertheless, their conclusions and the few other findings we examined suggest that efforts to explore the process-outcome connection are essential in fully comprehending the nature of group psychotherapy with children. Certainly these efforts have begun to yield a rich body of information in the adult group therapy literature (Bednar and Kaul, 1978; Dies, 1983b).

Rutter (1983) states that there are strong reasons to believe that specific therapeutic mechanisms producing differential treatment effects will be identified. Although the findings are not compelling, several of the studies covered in our review support this position. Amerikaner and Summerlin (1982) found that their two treatments were most influential in the areas they were designed to affect. Their social skills group influenced social self-concept scores, while their relaxation group had a greater impact on the children's ability to control undesirable acting-out behaviors. Downing (1977) demonstrated that contracting with children in the group setting for individualized goals was effective at bringing about specific desired changes, especially since the treatment sessions were tailored to focus on the goals the children had formulated in collaboration with the therapist. Similarly, Kern and Hankins (1977) demonstrated that Adlerian group counseling, combined with the use of homework in the form of behavioral contracts, was more effective than group counseling alone. Presumably the contracts, because of their specificity and continuity of structure across sessions, were a source of clarification of the principles presented during the sessions.

LaGreca and Santogrossi (1980) compared social skills groups, attention-placebo groups, and waiting-list controls. The treatment group was consistently superior on measures of outcome and generalization. However, the lack of differences between the attention-placebo and the waiting-list controls prompted the authors to conclude that "efforts to increase merely a child's social contacts, without additionally providing the child with instruction on appropriate social behaviors to employ with peers, are not likely to have any impact on the child's peer interactions" (p. 225). That is, the structure introduced during treatment produced changes that were not effected through peer group interaction alone. The findings of Bierman and Furman (1984) support this conclusion. These authors compared four treatment conditions: individual social skills coaching; group experience; group experience with coaching; and no treatment. Their interventions produced strong, positive, and differential effects on the social competencies of the children. Skill training (both individual and group coaching) promoted increases in conversational skills and rates of peer interaction. Peer involvement (both group conditions versus individual and no treatment conditions) was more likely to effect classroom sociometric status and feelings of social efficacy. Yet the group experience coupled with social skills training had an added advantage. Only the children in this combined condition shared general and sustained improvements in peer acceptance as well as social skills and peer interaction rates. Once again the increased structure facilitated changes that were not influenced by peer group involvement alone. Although both of these studies demonstrated the value of social skills training, particularly in a group context, the authors could not pinpoint the precise components of treatment that stimulated the positive behavioral changes: instructions, behavioral rehearsal, prompting, modeling, or performance feedback.

Ladd and Mize (1983) argue that "one of the most pressing needs is for the assessment of the function and efficacy of component manipulations and their relative contributions to skill learning and behavior change" (p. 151). They also note that there is little precedent for using process measures in social skills research and that therefore very few instruments have been developed for this purpose. Similarly, Conger and Keane (1981) concluded from their review of social skills interventions with children that although treatments have demonstrated some effectiveness, they have failed to reveal the exact nature of the relationships among process variables and their role in producing specific changes. The social skills training literature is far more extensive and sophisticated than the group psychotherapy for children literature. Obviously, the deficiencies noted in that body of research are even more apparent in the empirical work on more traditional forms of children's group psychotherapy. Clearly, more attention must be directed toward the delineation of critical group parameters that foster therapeutic growth.

In selecting process measures, both clinician and investigator have a number of issues to consider. One is the relevance of behavioral versus phenomenological (self-report) assessment. In the adult group psychotherapy literature the predominant emphasis has been on the client's perspective on group process. A variety of measures on group process have been used to evaluate perceptions of leadership (Dies, 1983b), curative factors (Butler and Fuhriman, 1983) group climate (MacKenzie, 1983), and many other variables. In the child literature, the few efforts to assess group process have relied mainly upon observations of the child's behavior within the group sessions. Our review has provided examples of these rating systems. The child's more limited conceptual abilities may favor the use of behavioral recording, but self-report methods should not be overlooked. The child's perceptions of the therapist-child relationship, attitude about treatment, and expectations regarding therapeutic progress may be crucial.

A second consideration relates to the use of process measures to explore differential treatment outcomes. This was step 3 in our recommendations for converting impressionistic studies into publishable results. Even with a relatively small number of groups it is possible to identify certain children whose experience of psychotherapy is different along important dimensions from that of other children in the group. This could be in terms of the child's own sense of the difference (e.g., compatibility with peers) or independent evaluations of that child's status (e.g., sociometric ratings by peers, activity level as tabulated by an observer). For example, with five treatment groups the two highest and lowest ranking children from each group could be compared on outcome: thus the ten youngsters who receive the most verbal praise from peers might be expected to show more treatment progress than the ten who receive comparatively little peer reinforcement. Although large-scale treatment studies might offer greater scientific respectability, carefully conducted small-scale projects of this nature, which link process variables to therapeutic outcome, can contribute substantially to our understanding of group treatments.

A final issue is the difference between intra- and extratherapy process measures. Researchers in the adult group psychotherapy literature have long been chastised for their failure to evaluate the impact of current nontreatment variables on therapeutic outcome (Dies, 1979). Client change is generally attributed to events within treatment, whereas changes in the person's life circumstances (e.g., moving to a new job, receiving a promotion) may in fact produce the therapeutic gain. An awareness of such extratherapy events is probably even more critical for an understanding of behavioral change in children, who presumably are more dependent on significant others and the situations around them. Fortunately, researchers in the area of children's psychotherapy are in a much better position than their adult-oriented colleagues to gather information about the circumstances affecting a child's behavior. Teachers and parents are usually willing and able to furnish considerable information about the child's experiences throughout the day. Regrettably, researchers have scarcely tapped these rich sources of information.

CONCLUSIONS

Throughout this review we have struggled to maintain our optimism regarding the efficacy of group psychotherapy with children. Yet we have found that the research evidence to support the value of group treatment is limited. The few positive indices of therapeutic effects, whether self-reported or perceived by teachers or observers, are derived from a small number of groups and research projects often characterized by methodological inadequacies. We have shown that maintenance and generalization of treatment effects have barely been tested, that researchers have only begun to identify specific mechanisms of change (process) and have often failed to isolate the unique contribution of group treatment to the child's progress, and that conceptualizations of outcome are frequently narrow and insufficiently standardized.

On the other hand, there is another perspective we might take on this entire body of literature, one that would place the rather sparse results in a completely different light. This novel perspective requires one more brief inspection of the research summarized in Table 2. We will ask three questions: (1) Who are the therapists? (2) What are the treatments? (3) Who are the clients?

Who are the therapists? In many studies we simply do not know the answer to this question because the investigators have provided no description of the therapists' credentials, their levels of experience with children's group psychotherapy, or their actual interventions within the treatment context. However, investigators have demonstrated the value of group therapy using "therapists" as diverse as children six to ten years old, mothers, teachers, relatively untrained undergraduates, graduate students, master's level professionals with three to four years experience, and even a set of audiotapes. If these novice "therapists" can effect significant therapeutic progress, it is certainly conceivable that well-trained and highly experienced clinicians might do even better. This assumption does not appear to require any significant leap of faith.

What are the treatments? We noted earlier that a partial answer is that the treatments are *very* brief. Yet we are able to identify in the research projects numerous illustrations of significant therapeutic changes reported by the children and, even more important, recognized by their teachers and independent observers. Thus, reduced acting out, improved achievement scores, increased assertiveness, and other behavioral changes are found in treatments of 5, 6, 7½, and 10 hours' duration. Similarly, significant self-esteem changes were reported by children in several groups lasting only 6 or 7 hours. If these abbreviated group experiences can produce treatment effects of this magnitude, it is well within the realm of possibility that somewhat longer (but not necessarily long-term) treatments may generate even more significant results. This assumption, too, does not require much faith. In fact, two of the research projects in our survey offer some initial evidence that more extended treatments may be more effective (Michelson and Wood, 1980; Lockwood, 1981). The group therapies reported in the literature, besides being very brief, are often generic educational interventions (e.g., sensory awareness, affective education, and relaxation training with tapes) and not remedial treatments with clinical populations. This leads to our third question.

Who are the clients? The vast majority of the group members are not clients in the "real" sense (i.e., children referred for therapy), but rather youngsters recruited to participate in the research to satisfy the experimental requirements of the investigator. Thus, the researcher typically sought the children, and it was not the children, their families, or even their teachers who sought treatment for the child.

The fact that the researchers were able to document significant improvements in self-esteem and meaningful behavioral changes with inexperienced "therapists" conducting nonclinical "treatments" with "clients" who were not seeking "therapy" is quite astonishing. If our confidence was at all in doubt, we should at this point feel rejuvenated and experience a renewed optimism regarding the potential growth in this field as investigators gain in research sophistication and begin to address some of the basic issues we have outlined throughout this chapter.

Achenbach (1978) has stated that in the face of the insubstantial evidence for the efficacy of psychotherapy with children, mental health professionals must assume greater initiative in determining how children with mental disorders and behavioral problems can be helped. He cites the widening gulf between the two "cultures" of researchers and practitioners as a major factor for the developmental arrest in this field. He urges that researchers "gear their work as closely as possible to the needs of practitioners and . . . provide practitioners with usable results in a constructive fashion. It is only through implementation in practice that researchers can obtain feedback on the effectiveness of their efforts" (p. 775). Future attempts to evaluate the efficacy of group treatments must be guided more by clinical realities than by research expediency. The active collaboration of researchers and practitioners is absolutely essential. Many of the guidelines for this working alliance have already been established (Dies and MacKenzie, 1983; Barlow, Hayes, and Nelson, 1984), and it is time for clinicians and researchers in this field to begin their joint venture in earnest. We cannot afford to wait fifteen or twenty years for the field of children's group psychotherapy research to arrive at the state of the adult group therapy literature today.

To accomplish the goal of bridging the gap between experimentation and practice, researchers must spend more of their time observing and interacting with clinicians, who in turn must be prepared to invite their empirically minded colleagues to participate in evaluating their treatment interventions (Dies, 1983a). Clinical agencies must provide experienced group psychotherapists and relevant clinical populations, and allow the researchers to work with them to integrate into their treatments appropriate measures for evaluating critical dimensions of change (process) and clinically meaningful indices of therapeutic outcomes.

The luxury of our childhood, with all its naive conceptualizations, underdeveloped methodologies, nascent efforts to study inexperienced therapists conducting inadequately defined treatments with poorly selected clients, and primitive measures to assess outcome, should be behind us. It is time to grow up.

REFERENCES

Abramovitch, R., Konstantareas, M., & Sloman, L. (1980), An observational assessment of change in two groups of behaviourally disturbed boys. *J. Child Psychol. & Psychiat.*, 21:133–141.

Abramowitz, C. V. (1976), The effectiveness of group psychotherapy with children. *Arch. Gen. Psychiat.*, 33:320–326.

Abramson, R. M., Hoffman, L., & Johns, C. A. (1979), Play group psychotherapy for early latency-age children on an inpatient psychiatric unit. *Internat. J. Group Psychother.*, 29:383–392.

Achenbach, T. M. (1978), Psychopathology of childhood: Research problems and issues. *J. Consult. & Clin. Psychol.*, 46:759–776.

——— Edelbrock, C. S. (1978), The classification of child psychopathology: A review and analysis of empirical efforts. *Psychol. Bull.*, 85:1275–1301.

Adams, M. A. (1976), A hospital play program: Helping children with serious illness. *Amer. J. Orthopsychiat.*, 46:416–424.

Allan, J., & Bardsley, P. (1983), Transient children in the elementary school: A group counseling approach. *Elem. School Guid. & Counsel.*, 17:162–169.

Amerikaner, M., & Summerlin, M. L. (1982), Group counseling with learning disabled children: Effects of social skills and relaxation training on self-concept and classroom behavior. *J. Learn. Disabil.*, 15:340–343.

Bardill, D. R. (1977), A behavior-contracting program of group treatment for early adolescents in a residential treatment setting. *Internat. J. Group Psychother.*, 27:389–400.

Barlow, D. H., Hayes, S. C., & Nelson, R. O. (1984), *The Scientist Practitioner.* New York: Pergamon Press.

Barrett, C. L., Hampe, I. E., & Miller, L. C. (1978), Research on child psychotherapy. In: *Handbook of Psychotherapy and Behavior Change: An Empirical Analysis*, ed. S. L. Garfield & A. E. Bergin. New York: Wiley, pp. 411–435.

Barsky, M., & Mozenter, G. (1976), The use of creative drama in a children's group. *Internat. J. Group Psychother.*, 26:105–114.

Barton, E. J., & Bevirt, J. (1981), Generalization of sharing across groups: Assessment of group composition with preschool children. *Behav. Modif.*, 5:503–522.
Bednar, R. L., & Lawlis, G. F. (1971), Empirical research in group psychotherapy. In: *Handbook of Psychotherapy and Behavior Change*, ed. A. E. Bergin & S. L. Garfield. New York: Wiley, pp. 812–838.
——— Kaul, T. J. (1978), Experiential group research: Current perspectives. In: *Handbook of Psychotherapy and Behavior Change: An Empirical Analysis*, ed. S. L. Garfield & A. E. Bergin. New York: Wiley, pp. 769–815.
Bell, S., & Ledford, T. (1978), The effects of sociodrama on the behaviors and attitudes of elementary school boys. *Group Psychother. Psychodrama & Sociometry*, 31:117–135.
Berry, K. K., Turone, R. J., & Hardt, P. (1980), Comparison of group therapy and behavioral modification with children. *Psychol. Reports*, 46:975–978.
Bierman, K. L., & Furman, W. (1984), The effects of social skills training and peer involvement on the social adjustment of preadolescents. *Child Devel.*, 55:151–162.
Bleck, R. T., & Bleck, B. L. (1982), The disruptive child's play group. *Elem. School Guid. & Counsel.*, 17:137–141.
Bloch, S., Crouch, E., & Reibstein, J. (1981), Therapeutic factors in group psychotherapy. *Arch. Gen. Psychiat.*, 38:519–526.
Bower, S., Amatea, E., & Anderson, R. (1976), Assertiveness training with children. *Elem. School Guid. & Counsel.*, 10:236–245.
Butler, T., & Fuhriman, A. (1983), Curative factors in group therapy: A review of recent literature. *Small Group Behav.*, 14:131–142.
Cantor, D. W. (1978), School-based groups for children of divorce. *J. Divorce*, 1:183–187.
Clement, P. W., Roberts, P. V., & Lantz, C. E. (1976), Mothers and peers as child behavior therapists. *Internat. J. Group Psychother.*, 26:335–359.
Clifford, M., & Cross, T. (1980), Group therapy for seriously disturbed boys in residential treatment. *Child Welfare*, 59:560–565.
Conger, J. C., & Keane, S. P. (1981), Social skills intervention in the treatment of isolated and withdrawn children. *Psychol. Bull.*, 90:478–495.
Cooke, T. P., & Apolloni, T. (1976), Developing positive social-emotional behaviors: A study of training and generalization effects. *J. Appl. Behav. Anal.*, 9:65–78.
Dies, R. R. (1977), Group therapist transparency: A critique of theory and research. *Internat. J. Group Psychother.*, 27:177–200.
——— (1978), The human factor in group psychotherapy research. In: *Group Therapy 1978: An Overview*, ed. L. R. Wolberg, M. L. Aronson, & A. R. Wolberg. New York: Stratton Intercontinental Medical, pp. 91–104.
——— (1979), Group psychotherapy: Reflections on three decades of research. *J. Appl. Behav. Science*, 15:361–373.
——— (1983a), Bridging the gap between research and practice in group psychotherapy. In: *Advances in Group Psychotherapy: Integrating Research and Practice*, ed. R. R. Dies & K. R. MacKenzie. New York: International Universities Press, pp. 1–26.
——— (1983b), Clinical implications of research on leadership in short-term group psychotherapy. In: *Advances in Group Psychotherapy: Integrating Research and Practice*, ed. R. R. Dies & K. R. MacKenzie. New York: International Universities Press, pp. 27–78.
——— (1985), Research foundations for the future of group work. *J. Spec. Group Work*, 10:68–73.

———— MacKenzie, K. R., Eds. (1983), *Advances in Group Psychotherapy: Integrating Research and Practice.* New York: International Universities Press.

Downing, C. J. (1977), Teaching children behavior change techniques. *Elem. School Guid. & Counsel.*, 11:277–283.

DuPlessis, J. M., & Lochner, L. M. (1981), The effects of group psychotherapy on the adjustment of four 12-year-old boys with learning and behavior problems. *J. Learn. Disabil.*, 14:209–212.

Durbin, D. M. (1982), Multimodal group sessions to enhance self-concept. *Elem. School Guid. & Counsel.*, 16:288–295.

Factor, D. C., & Schilmoeller, G. L. (1983), Social skill training of preschool children. *Child Study J.*, 13:41–55.

Franz, W. K., Berning, L. W., & Reilly, E. M. (1976), The effect of sensory awareness training on interpersonal social distance in fourth graders. *Psychol. Schools*, 13:58–63.

Freedheim, D. K., & Russ, S. R. (1983), Psychotherapy with children. In: *Handbook of Clinical Child Psychology*, ed. C. E. Walker & M. C. Roberts. New York: Wiley, pp. 978–994.

Freeman, R. W., Anderson, C., Kairey, I., & Hunt, P. F. (1982), Evaluation of camp Tortuga, a two week children's therapeutic day camp via goal attainment scaling and locus of control. *Children Youth Serv. Rev.*, 4:375–388.

Gresham, F. M., & Lemanek, K. L. (1983), Social skills: A review of cognitive-behavioral training procedures with children. *J. Appl. Devel. Psychol.*, 4:239–261.

Gurman, A. S., & Gustafson, J. P. (1976), Patient's perceptions of the therapeutic relationship and group therapy outcome. *Amer. J. Psychiat.*, 133:1290–1294.

Hargrave, G. E., & Hargrave, M. C. (1979), A peer group socialization program in the school: An outcome investigation. *Psychol. Schools*, 16:546–550.

Hayes, E. J., Cunningham, G. K., & Robinson, J. B. (1977), Counseling focus: Are parents necessary? *Elem. School Guid. & Counsel.*, 12:8–14.

Heckel, R. V., Hursh, L., & Hiers, J. M. (1977), Analysis of process data from token groups in a summer camp. *J. Clin. Psychol.*, 33:241–244.

Hobbs, S. A., Moguin, L. E., Tyroler, M., & Lahey, B. B. (1980), Cognitive behavior therapy with children: Has clinical utility been demonstrated? *Psychol. Bull.*, 87:147–165.

Hoffman, T. E., Byrne, K. M., Belnap, K. L., & Steward, M. S. (1981), Simultaneous semipermeable groups for mothers and their early latency-age boys. *Internat. J. Group Psychother.*, 31:83–98.

Howe, P. A., & Silvern, L. E. (1981), Behavioral observation of children during play therapy: Preliminary development of a research instrument. *J. Pers. Assmt.*, 45:168–182.

Kazdin, A. E. (1982), *Single-Case Research Designs: Methods for Clinical and Applied Settings.* New York: Oxford University Press.

Kendall, P. C., & Zupan, B. A. (1981), Individual versus group application of cognitive-behavioral self-control procedures with children. *Behav. Ther.*, 12:344–359.

Kern, R. M., & Hankins, G. (1977), Adlerian group counseling with contracted homework. *Elem. School Guid. & Counsel.*, 11:284–290.

Kiesler, D. J. (1981), Empirical clinical psychology: Myth or reality? *J. Consult. & Clin. Psychol.*, 49:212–215.

Kilmann, P. R., Henry, S. E., Scarbro, H., & Laughlin, J. E. (1979), The

impact of affective education on elementary school under-achievers. *Psychol. Schools*, 16:217–223.
Ladd, G. W., & Mize, J. (1983), A cognitive-social learning model of social-skill training. *Psychol. Bull.*, 90:127–157.
LaGreca, A. M. (1983), Interviewing and behavioral observations. In: *Handbook of Clinical Child Psychology*, ed. C. E. Walker & M. C. Roberts. New York: Wiley, pp. 109–131.
——— Santogrossi, D. A. (1980), Social skills training with elementary school students: A behavioral group approach. *J. Consult. & Clin. Psychol.*, 48:220–227.
Leone, S. D., & Gumaer, J. (1979), Group assertiveness training of shy children. *School Counsel.*, 27:134–141.
Lockwood, J. L. (1981), Treatment of disturbed children in verbal and experiential group psychotherapy. *Internat. J. Group Psychother.*, 31:355–366.
Lovasdal, S. (1976), A multiple therapy approach in work with children. *Internat. J. Group Psychother.*, 26:475–486.
MacKenzie, K. R. (1983), The clinical application of a group climate measure. In: *Advances in Group Psychotherapy: Integrating Research and Practice*, ed. R. R. Dies & K. R. MacKenzie. New York: International Universities Press, pp. 159–170.
——— Dies, R. R. (1982), *CORE Battery*. New York: American Group Psychotherapy Association.
Mann, J. (1966), Evaluation of group psychotherapy: A review in evidence. In: *The International Handbook of Group Psychotherapy*, ed. J. L. Moreno. New York: Philosophical Library, pp. 129–148.
McKibbin, E., & King, J. (1983), Activity group counseling for learning-disabled children with behavior problems. *Amer. J. Occup. Ther.*, 37:617–623.
Melnick, J., & Woods, M. (1976), Analysis of group composition research and theory for psychotherapeutic and growth-oriented groups. *J. Appl. Behav. Science*, 12:493–512.
Michelson, L., & Wood, R. (1980), A group assertive training program for elementary school children. *Child Behav. Ther.*, 2:1–9.
Mondell, S., Tyler, F. B., & Freeman, R. W. (1981), Evaluating a psychotherapeutic day camp with psychosocial competence and goal attainment measures. *J. Clin. Psychol.*, 10:180–184.
Moracco, J., & Kazandkian, A. (1977), Effectiveness of behavior counseling and consulting with non-Western elementary school children. *Elem. School Guid. & Counsel.*, 11:244–251.
O'Leary, K. D., & Turkewitz, H. (1978), Methodological errors in marital and child treatment research. *J. Consult. & Clin. Psychol.*, 46:747–758.
Pasnau, R. O., Meyer, M., Davis, L. J., Lloyd, R., & Kline, G. (1976), Coordinated group psychotherapy of children and parents. *Internat. J. Group Psychother.*, 26:89–103.
Patterson, D. R., & Sechrest, L. (1983), Nonreactive measures in psychotherapy outcome research. *Clin. Psychol. Rev.*, 3:391–416.
Pattison, E. M. (1965), Evaluation studies of group psychotherapy. *Internat. J. Group Psychother.*, 15:382–397.
Rashbaum-Selig, M. (1976), Assertive training for young people. *School Counsel.*, 24:115–122.
Ratusnik, C. M., & Ratusnik, D. L. (1976), A therapeutic milieu for establishing and expanding communicative behaviors in psychotic children. *J. Speech & Hearing Disorders*, 41:70–92.

Rickard, H. C. (1962), Selected group psychotherapy evaluation studies. *J. Gen. Psychol.*, 67:35–50.
——— Elkins, P. D. (1983), Behavior therapy with children. In: *Handbook of Clinical Child Psychology*, ed. C. E. Walker & M. C. Roberts. New York: Wiley, pp. 958–977.
Riester, A. E., & Tanner, D. L. (1980), Group counseling: Follow-up viewpoints. *Elem. School Guid. & Counsel.*, 14:222–230.
Rosenberg, J., & Cherbuliez, T. (1979), Inpatient group therapy for older children and preadolescents. *Internat. J. Group Psychother.*, 29:393–405.
Ross, A. O. (1978), Behavior therapy with children. In: *Handbook of Psychotherapy and Behavior Change: An Empirical Analysis*, ed. S. L. Garfield & A. E. Bergin. New York: Wiley, pp. 591–620.
Rutter, M. (1983), Psychological therapies: Issues and prospects. In: *Childhood Psychopathology and Development*, ed. S. B. Guze, F. J. Earls, & J. E. Barrett. New York: Raven Press, pp. 139–164.
Strupp, H. H., & Hadley, S. W. (1977), A tripartite model of mental health and therapy outcomes. *Amer. Psychol.*, 32:187–196.
Tiktin, E. A., & Cobb, C. (1983), Treating post-divorce adjustment in latency age children: A focused group paradigm. *Soc. Work Groups*, 6:53–66.
Trafimow, E., & Pattak, S. I. (1981), Group psychotherapy and objectal development in children. *Internat. J. Group Psychother.*, 31:193–204.
Tramontana, M. G. (1980), Critical review of research on psychotherapy outcome with adolescents: 1967–1977. *Psychol. Bull.*, 88:429–450.
Urbain, E. S., & Kendall, P. C. (1980), Review of social-cognitive problem-solving interventions with children. *Psychol. Bull.*, 88:109–143.
Walker, C. E., & Roberts, M. C., Eds. (1983), *Handbook of Clinical Child Psychology*. New York: Wiley.
Weigel, R. G., & Corazzini, J. G. (1978), Small group research: Suggestions for solving methodological and design problems. *Small Group Behav.*, 9:193–220.
Wenar, C., & Ruttenberg, B. A. (1976), The use of BRIAC for evaluating therapeutic effectiveness. *J. Autism & Childhood Schizophr.*, 6:175–191.
Wodarski, J. S., & Pedi, S. J. (1978), The empirical evaluation of the effects of different group treatment strategies against a controlled treatment strategy on behavior exhibited by antisocial children, behaviors of the therapist, and two self-rating scales that measure antisocial behavior. *J. Clin. Psychol.*, 34:471–481.
Yalom, I. D. (1975), *The Theory and Practice Of Group Psychotherapy*. New York: Basic Books.

Part VI
Looking Forward on the Foundation of the Past

Chapter 11
Activity Group Therapy Revisited

MORTIMER SCHIFFER, M.S.

The first planful use of a small group design in psychological treatment, activity group therapy (AGT), was made by S. R. Slavson in the early 1930s with a carefully selected patient population of latency age children. This represented a second major revolution in therapy, the first being individual treatment.

There were earlier attempts with groups of adult patients, notably the work of T. Burrow, J. Moreno, J. Pratt, P. Schilder. L. Wender, and others. These experimental groups were large, and they lacked discrimination with respect to the selection of patients. Some of the initial psychological concepts and treatments, formulated and implemented in empirical fashion, became incorporated in present practices. Notable was Schilder's application of Freudian psychoanalytic principles with groups, a brilliant exploration of dynamic group psychotherapy, much of it still relevant. Despite some theoretical differences between various "schools," group psychotherapy has formulated a formidable body of knowledge of the dynamics of behavior in groups.

It is of more than passing interest that group therapy of children and adolescents has languished in comparison to that of adults. The clinical merit of using a group modality in treating children is not a consideration with respect to this unfortunate situation. Moreover, the lag in its growth becomes even more anomalous when viewed against the fact that the group modality has proven its value incontrovertibly in correcting a wide range of children's emotional problems.

The need for peer group experiences is critical in children's development, especially during latency. Interpersonal interactions in children's groups—both normal and therapy groups—are psychologically complementary. An important consequence of this is that children demonstrate much less resistance to the implementation of group therapy than they do to individual treatment.

In light of this, how are we to account for the relatively limited use of children's groups?

There are few facilities specifically oriented to training in children's group therapy, and only a small number of senior, experienced therapists capable of serving as teachers and supervisors.

Furthermore, despite the limited use of children's groups, there have also been a number of significant departures from standard group methods, a circumstance which seems to imply that already validated methods are inadequate, if not altogether inappropriate. While there may be a present need for some modifications of group treatment with special child-patient populations, questions must be raised as to the validity of some purportedly "new" methods.

Perhaps of greater importance, there are misconceptions of fundamental psychological principles underlying child group therapy which, when applied in actual practice, produce deleterious results. This is particularly so with respect to AGT, a method that is extraordinarily efficacious for a wide range of emotional problems of latency age children.

This chapter is addressed to these and other subjects concerning children's group therapy, particularly AGT, which lay the foundation for child group treatment and the later development of analytic groups.

Over a number of years, reports have been presented at annual meetings of the American Group Psychotherapy Association, as well as in its international journal and other professional publications, concerning modifications in standard AGT. Slavson had stated early that AGT would be vitiated as a clinical instrument if significant departures were made from its standard techniques with the kinds of problems for which AGT is specifically indicated. He believed that of all forms of child psychotherapy—both individual and group—AGT tolerates least any alterations in its well-defined methodology if it is to remain effective, a view shared by the writer. This conviction does not imply that AGT is the sole group method, or that other procedures are invalid. Slavson himself devised additional group treatments for children.

Reports on adaptations of AGT reveal the following alterations of basic methodology: (1) an active, participatory role on the part of the therapist in contrast to his characteristic neutral, nonintrusive role in purely activity therapy; (2) a less permissive group climate and the use of direct interventions by the therapist, again in marked contradistinction to the extraordinary freedom allowed children in the standard format; (3) verbal interpretations of children's behavior by the therapist, intended to point up to them the motivations, meanings, and consequences of their actions and to suggest alternative ways of behaving; and (4) still other interventions to limit children's acting out. These, and additional techniques which may be appropriate in other methods of child group therapy, are entirely eschewed in standard AGT.

It is undeniable that pure AGT is counterindicated, or of limited value, for some problems of latency age children, a fact established decades ago (Rosenthal and Nagelberg, 1956). Slavson and others, including this writer, recognized the need for other methods for some children, particularly those with neurotic problems and severe ego impairment (Hallowitz, 1956; Scheidlinger, 1965; Slavson and Schiffer, 1975). Several were devised, including activity-interview group psychotherapy for older latency age children and play group therapy for young ones, both methods utilizing activity and analytic procedures. They successfully met the needs of a large child-patient population, used either as exclusive treatment or in conjunction with, in preparation for, or following a course of individual treatment.

What present circumstances necessitate modifications in these proven methodologies of child group therapy, AGT in particular? Is it true, as some aver, that standard AGT does not provide for a "new breed" of child patient? Finally, is it conceivable that departures from standard methodology may be a result of insufficient training and inexperience, compounded by minimal or no supervision from senior group therapists? These and other practical questions demand our attention if the practice of child group therapy is to proceed along reasonably objective lines.

There are realistic circumstances which lend credibility to one adaptation of activity therapy. Accommodations have to be made for a growing population of ego-impaired children with impulse-ridden behavior. Their behavior is often antisocial, asocial, and sometimes chaotic, and the standard methods of individual and group treatment are ineffective, if not aggravating, to already mordant problems. One adaptation of AGT will be described later in this chapter.

During the past two decades dramatic alterations have taken place in family life and in social phenomena because of an astonishing increase in separations and divorces, out-of-wedlock children, and single-parent families, as well as the changing role of women and other cultural and philosophical issues affecting social mores. These changes have produced palpable effects on individuals and families. Values and behavior have become "liberalized"; social, ethical, and religious concepts and practices have been challenged and modified; and what may be termed a "social superego" has become modified and weakened as a monitoring influence on group behavior. Such social changes are further intensified by pervasive national and international stresses—the threat of nuclear destruction, cold war, economic crisis. All this has affected families and individuals by exacerbating existing emotional problems and creating entirely new ones. Children and adolescents in this environment have been subject to unusual stress.

Practices of psychotherapy have also been altered by these broad social changes. A pressure for psychological relief from a patient population increased both, in number and in the complexity of its problems, is discernible in the large number of character disorders and borderline personalities in adults, and impulse disorders in children and adolescents. It is understandable that therapists would look for new treatments to service such a burgeoning patient population.

However, in the rush to meet the exigencies of what is tantamount to an emergency situation, the danger arises of hurried experimentation with techniques lacking any substantive relations to fundamental human psychology. No method of treatment has merit unless it relates causally to the etiology of emotional disorders and is in compliance with an individual's needs and capacity for change. Unfortunately, some innovative techniques become extrapolated into "methods" too easily, or what may represent a valid technique in a specific situation becomes elevated to a paradigm of psychotherapy.[1]

Group therapists have not been without fault in abetting less than worthy innovative procedures. Authors have been permitted, if not encouraged, to rush into print on the basis of a single experience with

---

[1] Somewhat revealing of this in the practice of psychotherapy are the following: *The Psychotherapy Handbook* by R. Herink; also, a statement by a writer who reported that there are more than 300 different *group* procedures used to alleviate human distress. It is inconceivable that the human race requires more than 500 different methods of psychological correction to restore its emotional equilibrium.

one treatment group, with perhaps five or six children. Good case history studies are valuable and they deserve a forum in conferences and journals. It is another matter, however, when a report on the basis of a limited experience, often one not repeated by the author or duplicated by another therapist, is presented as a "new" method. Just as the desperate hope that laetrile would be a universal cure for cancer proved futile, in like measure it is improbable that a "psychological laetrile" will be discovered to remedy emotional problems.

It is not my intention to discourage critical examination of AGT, or to deny a forum for new ideas. Rather, my purpose here is to examine a professional dilemma concerning modifications of AGT, to ascertain the present reality, and to evaluate methodologies.

The psychology underlying AGT will be described in detail to point out the specificity of this treatment for problems affecting a large number of troubled latency age children. Against this background some modifications of standard practice will be examined.

Much of the present practice of AGT is based on misconceptions as to how children assimilate normal developmental experiences with significant libidinal objects and how emotionally troubled children in activity groups react in psychologically homologous transference relationships with a therapist. For the sake of clarity, it is necessary to understand AGT in context with our knowledge of children's early growth and development. Several premises will be examined: (1) the validity of AGT for specified problems; (2) its ability to influence and modify personality and character structure; (3) whether it is true that modifications in its standard procedures are really necessary; and (4) whether AGT is, as some therapists would seem to imply, an archaic treatment incapable of meeting present needs.

Some fail to comprehend how, in the absence of analytical investigation, group treatment can influence personality and character structure. This was the reaction in 1934, when AGT was first introduced at the Madelaine Borg Child Guidance Institute of the Jewish Board of Guardians. It is interesting that clinical resistance to the employment of group treatment was expressed in the very agency which gave birth to it, which was later recognized as a major training center for various forms of group psychotherapy with patients of all ages. Under the guidance of its creative director, John Slawson, the agency was a prestigious, psychoanalytically oriented center engaged in treating children and families. In keeping with its clinical orientation, all patients were seen individually. The introduction of a group modality was looked upon askance by the staff, and there was notable opposition to its employment, to the extent that few referrals of children to group therapy were forthcoming. Only when the efficiency of AGT was demonstrated did staff opposition decrease.

It is not difficult to understand why in the early years experienced analytically-trained therapists could not accept a treatment in which verbal communication played little or no part. Such a radical departure from classical interpretive therapy had literally a shock effect. Similar resistance to AGT persists today with an appreciable number of therapists. This resistance still prevents some therapists of a Freudian orientation from using groups with children. This is anomalous inasmuch as many therapists using group methods today were trained in Freudian psychoanalytic psychology.

CAN THERAPY BE EFFECTIVE IN THE ABSENCE OF ANALYTIC METHODOLOGY?

Psychological treatment, especially with adolescent and adult patients, requires that they become aware of the nature of their emotional problems, including conscious and unconscious elements. They must be helped to reflect upon and verbalize their feelings in order to comprehend the relatedness between etiology, the precipitation of problems, and their resolution. In the usual processes of psychotherapy therapists utilize questions, explanations, and interpretations to deal with resistances and other elements of patients' habituated, dystonic emotionality. This clinical "mental set," if a reductionist frame of reference may be permitted for the moment, determines in large measure a therapist's conceptions about what constitutes psychotherapy, and it influences his techniques. Given such a traditional orientation, it is understandable why some persons question (and challenge) a purely activity group treatment with child patients, a method which abjures questioning and interpretation. If there is no insight, they ask, how does a child derive awareness and understanding of emotional problems? Indeed, can a child's psychic nature—and consequently his behavior—be influenced appreciably without involving him cognitively in the therapy?

In this chapter I have to demonstrate that AGT provides opportunities for meaningful interpersonal interactions between members of a group, including the therapist, and that without recourse to analytic procedures these experiences are assimilable psychologically and capable of modifying the psyche—with, I must emphasize, those emotional problems for which AGT is the treatment of choice.[2] AGT is intended for use with children of latency age to prepuberty as an exclusive treatment for primary behavior (conduct) disorders (Van Ophuijsen, 1961) and some character disorders, particularly problems in sexual identity; immature but not overly infantile children, as well as nonschizophrenics who withdraw from social contact with peers, may also benefit from exclusive treatment with AGT (Slavson and Schiffer, 1975).[3]

Neurotic children whose conflicts are accompanied by extraordinary feelings of guilt, anxiety, and marked ambivalence may find only palliative relief in AGT. They require combined treatment, activity and analytic, e.g., activity-interview group psychotherapy and play group therapy or, perhaps, individual play therapy. In some instances, AGT is used as a "tapering-off" treatment following individual therapy or to prepare resistive children for individual therapy.

AGT provides selected children with a long-term opportunity (minimally two years) to express normal and conflicted feelings in a treatment climate characterized by extraordinary freedom. It offers opportunities to engage in crafts, games, and other activities with materials of intrinsic interest for this age group. A permissive therapist accepts the children as they are, including their acting-out behavior which, in other places and with other adults, would ordinarily be responded to with criticism, restraints, and punishments.

While not interfering in the children's activities, the therapist is always accessible to them when they need him. The therapeutic effects flow from significant interactions involving the children with one another and with the therapist. In time, the group, as a social gestalt, acquires corrective potency as a behavior modifier and helps to reeducate its members. The net effect of AGT is to alter maladaptive behavior and the child's personality and character. The therapist's nonintrusive role can be sustained by virtue of a careful selection of

---

[2] Two reports are included in a book by the writer that effectively adapt some aspects of noninterpretive activity therapy to a special patient population. In my estimation this represents the only substantiated use of modified AGT reported to date. (See Schiffer, 1984.)

[3] Therapists thoroughly trained in children's group therapy, who act as instructors, supervisors, and consultants, may find some of this information redundant. Nevertheless, it merits repetition. On the basis of my experience as a trainer and supervisor over an extended period of time, I conclude that a significant proportion of those who work with children's groups lack a fundamental understanding of the psychology governing children's behavior in groups.

clients for whom AGT is specifically indicated and maintenance of a psychologically balanced group (aggressive and passive children, leaders and followers, etc.). This group becomes capable of tempering its own intermember conflicts, sparing the therapist unnecessary interventions.

THE NATURE OF CHILDREN'S EXPERIENCE

Since AGT has been described as an "experiential" treatment, it would be helpful to describe how experiences are internalized and integrated, and how they affect ego function, personality, and character. The corrective effects of exceptional experiences in AGT will become more comprehensible in the light of what occurs in normal development.

Experience consists of two components: an event and the individual's reactions to it. With respect to children, one element bears unusual weight: events which children find intrinsically interesting (and these are legion) tend to engage them in *action* responses, more so than is the case with older persons.

All young children possess insatiable curiosity. They are sensitive and responsive to external stimuli, especially as these relate to relationships within the family, their developmental needs, the nature of psychic and emotional constitution, and their interests and preoccupations. Thus, infants and young children are hypersensitive to a host of impinging stimuli: sounds, sights, smells, touches, inanimate objects, people, personal interactions, animals, etc. Children have yet to learn about physical, biological, human phenomena which older persons have already experienced and have become less sensitive to through habituation.

Children possess an innate epistemophilic drive, a need to know. This impels them toward active, physical engagements and mental activity while they acquire their first knowledge of animate and inanimate objects and happenings within their immediate purview. Innate curiosity persistently mobilizes them toward physical, participatory involvements unless extraordinary external circumstances frustrate and otherwise inhibit this healthy, natural tendency to explore. Such hindrances, stemming initially from unknowing parents and later from many educators, can, if sufficiently immobilizing, effectively stifle children's normal predisposition toward active exploration of the world.

Maturing young children are narcissistic and self-centered. Despite their growing social parameters, significant libidinal objects and events affect them centripetally; the child feels himself the focus of experiential absorption. This narcissistic centrality is normal in all young children. It is responsible for their heightened perceptivity of persons and events—those which gratify needs and wishes, and others which frustrate them, either of which may tend, over time, to harm growth and emotional development.

New experiences become internalized and incorporated with prior learnings, and gratifying ones produce feelings of well-being and potency. Mastery of situations and exploratory success foster a sense of self, identity, and ego strength. Thus, through a multiplicity of experiences a child touches the world, learns about it, tries to accommodate it to his drives and wishes, and becomes psychologically molded by it. He must discover the reality of frustration and learn that he cannot bend all persons and circumstances to his will. Despite maturing ego capacities and a puerile sense of omnipotence, he learns that he is incapable of eliminating or even influencing all situations which are stressful.

This innate, burgeoning curiosity of children to learn the nature of reality and their desire to "manage" it has been described by many observers. Freud (1931) compared this quality in young children with the capacities of adults: "Think of the depressing contrast between the radiant intelligence of a healthy child and the feeble intellectual process of the average adult. . . . A child tries to *do* itself what has just been done to it" (p. 225, italics mine). In another paper he equated a child's play with the products of creative writers, "in that he creates a world of his own or rather rearranges the things of his world in a way which pleases . . ." (Freud, 1908, p. 143).

Piaget's prodigious investigations revealed infants' and young children's avid interest in external events. Their remarkable qualities of solipsism and syncretism enable them to formulate idiosyncratic "answers" for observed phenomena whose complexity exceeds their abilities to comprehend them fully. He also noted their biological need to engage actively in the quest for affirmations and new discoveries.

René Spitz (1965) made similar observations, alleging that an infant is constrained to learn more in his first year than in all the rest of his life. In still another study (Spitz, 1945) he revealed the terrible consequences to physical and emotional development when infants and young children are subjected to extremes of sensory deprivation and denied opportunities for motor activity and manipulative engagements. Those who were massively frustrated in these respects suffered from physical and emotional marasmus, some to the point of death.

These eminent researchers revealed the true nature of children's compelling drives to comprehend events in the world surrounding them; to become physically manipulative in drawing sensations and discovery to their persons; to acquire adaptative responses to external objects and situations; and, in summary, to be actively involved as much as possible in learning experiences. Thus, participatory activity is a necessary component of biological growth, ego development, and personality and character formation. Few events impinge upon infants and children without mobilizing them to participate in some fashion and degree, unless special circumstances bar this process.

It is this global conceptualization of the nature and scope of young children's mental and physical activities—the manner in which they explore and experience events, people, and novel circumstances—which bears critically on the practice of AGT. The integral importance of normal children's activity in acquiring coping behavior illuminates how a noninterpretive activity therapy can modify personal attributes and deviant behavior.

AGT has been described as "experiential" therapy because of the absence of interpretations. However, the term is used also to refer to some adult group methods in which verbal communication is a sine qua non. In both instances it is a loose employment of the word, because *all* human behavior is experiential, whether it be active or passive, verbal or nonverbal. What was probably intended in describing some methods of group treatment as "experiential" is that patients will become aware of how their feelings and behavior affect others and how they are influenced in turn.

With respect to children, some therapists construe "experiential" as denoting purely motoric behavior, the active involvement of children in individual play or with one another. Within the limited context of such a definition, a group might be considered dysfunctional if it is relatively quiet. A more accurate assessment of an activity group's viability requires a broader conceptualization of the nature and meanings of children's varied activities. Much more than motor activity must be subsumed under children's activity, especially in therapy, whether individual or group.

WORDS AND DEEDS: THEIR RELATIVE EFFECTS ON CHILDREN

In AGT a therapist's influence on a child's emotional problems stems from the therapist's role as an "ideal parent," a role in which verbal communication of any kind is kept to a minimum and is secondary in influence to helpful ministrations by the therapist at psychologically propitious moments. Characteristically, his verbalizations deal mostly with practical circumstances related to the children's work and play and the maintenance of the meeting room, with only rare references to a child's, or the group's, behavior. The evolving positive transference of children to the therapist stems mainly from their perception of him as a consistently helping, understanding, *doing* person.

As young children acquire language capability and begin to comprehend and use it, even minimally, single words and phrases become symbolic supplements of feelings, intentions, and actions (secondary process). At certain developmental stages (the anal-aggressive period, for instance), words become significant "instruments" of ego function, particularly as they express the infant's sense of power and control for the first time. Also, words become expressions of negativistic feelings which earlier were demonstrated mainly in nonverbal ways (Spitz, 1957). Children also become increasingly sensitive to language as it is used by others, particularly their parents. They begin to learn that language, which was functionally meaningful and effective as *they* learned to use it, also generates confusion when parents misuse it in communicating "mixed" messages. Further, parental discipline is usually accompanied by verbal and nonverbal "messages" of disapproval, anger, and threat. Thus, both the deeds and the words of mistreatment can be sorely experienced by a child.

When emotionally debilitating environmental conditions affect early and later development, much of the parents' language is negatively cathected for the child. Perforce, he must learn to defend himself against harmful actions and the accompanying verbalizations, having been betrayed by both.[4] Typically, children often demonstrate negativism against parents with a seeming "deafness." Thus, the common parental refrain: "What I say goes in one ear and out the other!"

---

[4] Of interest is the childish refrain, "Sticks and stones can break my bones, but names can never hurt me!" (a denial?). This is truly an apt jingle about the harmfulness of both words and deeds as experienced by children.

When brought for therapy, emotionally troubled children are little impressed by a therapist's spoken intention to "help" them with "problems." Children are not inclined to aggrandize such words and intentions, however honestly presented, especially when they come from a complete stranger. Parenthetically, it is unwise for therapists to tell child patients that they want to "help." Children seek understanding. The child feels that his parents need more help than he does.

Adult language begins to exert penetrating influence in psychotherapy when a therapist becomes cathected as a significant libidinal object in the positive transference.[5] Initially, children automatically associate the therapist with the adult world, and his words are therefore suspect. Children require time to confirm the uniqueness of a "new" kind of adult, one who will remain accepting, supportive, and understanding regardless of the children's behavior. Thus, in AGT it is the therapist's total demeanor, *particularly his behavior and his not taking retaliatory action when children act out*, which is impressive. It establishes the positive transference, which then reinvests language with psychologically corrective potency.[6]

RESTITUTIVE EXPERIENCE

Harmful effects of maldevelopment in latency age children can be tempered and reversed and more healthy qualities instilled in them, given a corrective experience psychologically homologous to that of a benevolent, health-sponsoring "family." Under suitable therapeutic influences, noxious experience which has adversely affected development becomes reversible. A group must meet certain requirements if it is to provide this restitutive experience, to allow and encourage children's active participation in a special "life" environment with a therapist (symbolic parent) and group members (symbolic siblings).

---

[5] Melanie Klein (1932) wrote how a child becomes a "willing guide to the mind," as soon as a therapist helps him become aware, for the first time, of the relationship between a current anxiety or fear and the repressed experience that was responsible for generating his distress. Following such an initial insight, which is an entirely novel experience, not only does the child begin to formulate the needed transference, but the therapist's language registers more significantly.

[6] The late Haim Ginott told me of an incident which, more than anything in my entire career, bespoke the nature of troubled young children and their needs. Immediately following a helpful, encouraging comment from him to a girl of about four, a member of a play therapy group, she took his face in both hands—he was bent over close to where she played—and said, glowingly, "You *unnerstan'* me."

In large measure AGT is restitutive therapy: the love, security, and protection which were denied children or inappropriately provided them in their families during critical developmental periods of early life in AGT become available to them in massive, symbolic forms. Activity groups, as ideal "families," provide the psychological equivalent of developmental nurturance.

INTERNALIZATION OF CORRECTIVE EXPERIENCE

Young children are still psychologically prone to internalize "good" and "bad" experiences. *A child tends to become what he does*: he is a psychological amalgam of innumerable experiences involving himself and significant libidinal objects. Fortunately, by virtue of his developing, as yet uncrystallized emotional state, the young child remains psychically resilient, capable of being changed, given the influence of proper therapy over sufficient time. Young children in latency are still capable of assimilating experiences which can alter personality and character for the better.

Experiences in AGT acquire increasing therapeutic potency as they bear upon both circumstances of early development responsible for creating unusual pain, anger, fear, guilt, and anxiety, and ongoing experiences within families that reinforce such debilitating emotions. Because the etiology of children's difficulties relates mainly to parents and siblings, it is in the context of homologous, symbolic relationships in a therapy group that health-producing change becomes feasible. Children who were forced to "learn," consciously and unconsciously, to accommodate to stress-producing circumstances, in AGT become resensitized to the influence of persons and events that in their cumulative effects are psychologically corrective. Thus, the penetrating influence of AGT.

In brief, what children actively experience in the fundamentally positive transference with the therapist, and through interactions with sibling substitutes, becomes a mutational corrective force. This differs from the psychological treatment of adolescents and adults, both of whom can be *helped* through psychotherapy but whose personalities and character structures remain essentially unchanged.

LIVING THROUGH VERSUS WORKING THROUGH

Working through in psychotherapy requires that a patient explore, with the therapist's assistance, the nature of his symptoms and problems and their antecedent emotional linkages. The reconstructive process is experienced differently by children and is more accurately depicted as *living through*.

Adolescent and adult patients maintain awareness of the professional identity of a therapist despite their unconscious emotional investment in the transference. Children, on the other hand, are not similarly concerned with, nor do they remain as sensitive to, or conscious of, a therapist's professional identity. Rather, they tend to experience the transference in a fused parent-therapist context. This accounts for a significant difference in the evolution of treatment in AGT as compared with adolescent and adult treatment.

In AGT, under the benign influence of the therapeutic transference, some of a child's emotional ties and typical responses to his parents become subject to change because of the partial identity fusion of parents and therapist. This occurs even in cases in which parental handling of a child may not alter significantly during the time the child is being treated. It is as if the following unconscious discourse took place in a child's mind: "I like (love) my therapist because he's made me feel happier. Grown-ups *can* be nice, not all bad as I used to think. My parents can't be *so* bad, after all!"

One effect of a child's improved attitude and his altered perception of parents—and adults in general—is manifested through improved behavior at home, in school, and elsewhere. This elicits better treatment from parents and teachers, who are pleased with the child's changed deportment. As unhealthy behavior patterns and character traits yield to more acceptable forms and become concretized over time, personality and character structure become modified. Even neurotic traits can be "sloughed off" through corrective experience in a noninterpretive treatment such as AGT.

ABREACTION AND CATHARSIS

Acting out in AGT (as in all methods of child therapy) represents a symbolic scenario of children's inner feelings, conflicts, and strong ambivalences. With the onset of positive transference, acting out becomes an expression of repressed and suppressed emotions, originally associated with parents and siblings, which now become displaced onto the therapist and other group members. Acting out thus acquires both cathartic and abreactive values, as these emotions are discharged in the partially fused transferences, through therapist-parents and group members–siblings associations. Thus, its content is a reenacted representation of blocked affect and repressed impulses, much of which can now be relieved, safely consummated in the treatment group.

This necessary acting out (which is evident during early group sessions and then abates) imposes rather severe stress on a therapist's forbearance, and can induce extraordinary countertransference feelings. Therapists inadequately trained for AGT. who lack understanding of its principles, often mistakenly construe such acting out as countertherapeutic, when in fact it constitutes their own countertransference reaction. They may then intervene incorrectly, thus modifying the intent of AGT. This will keep the children's acting out within sustainable bounds for the therapist, but it deprives the children of freedom to discharge feelings. Undetected, such countertransference errors may occasion unnecessary modifications of standard AGT. Failures in treatment are incorrectly attributed to the method employed.

Because of the unconscious nature of the fused parent-therapist transference, reenactments of repressed or inadequately expressed emotional conflicts in the group become psychologically homologous equivalents of "family" dynamics. However, their *reexperiential* expressions in the therapy group in no way replicate the harmful events in the families. Thus, the freedom to act out in the therapy group provides corrective recapitulation of earlier life experiences. It is this therapeutic experience which invests a noninterpretive activity method with the potential for effecting essential changes in children.

It is illuminating to compare the acting-out behavior of children with that of older patients. For children acting out is a symbolic "language" that reveals the nature of basic feelings; for older patients it is resistance. In adults, acting out may lack deliberation, as with children, and can often be impulsive, immature, and self-indulgent. Adults' acting out bears on their nuclear, unconscious problems, and has sexual, aggressive, sadistic, or masochistic qualities. An older patient, after sufficient working through, can eventually comprehend the underlying meanings of his acting-out behavior, but not until a therapist can bring him to examine it and probe its unconscious blocking of the therapeutic process will it become meaningful to him. In AGT, children's acting out, because of its abreactive, reexperiential nature, leads eventually to inner changes, with no need on their part to understand its symbolic meanings.

INSIGHT: DERIVATIVE VERSUS ANALYTIC

The development of insight (analytical) is a complex phenomenon. It evolves in a patient through the accretion of many separate and repetitive perceptions of the antecedents of his emotional disorder and its manifestations in symptoms and behavior; and also, through an awareness of the unique mechanisms of defense which come into being in order to cope with stress. Insight is a consequence of inductive discovery, which takes place over an extended period of time.... The foregoing elements of insight formation apply in the psychotherapy of adolescents and adults, varying in degree only with differences in the presenting problems and with idiosyncratic differences between patients. Most young children, however, are incapable of developing such insight; the elements involved are not in consonance with their intellectual and emotional capabilities.... Insight is an essential outcome for successful treatment of many emotional disorders of adolescence and adulthood, but it has no strict equivalent in the treatment of children.... [Schiffer, 1969]

In psychoanalytic treatment of a child suffering from *neurosis* (a form of pathology which in children is much less frequent than other problems, and which is counterindicated for treatment in AGT), it is necessary that the child be helped to discern the linkage between repressed material and symptomatology. But even in psychoanalysis or methods of therapy based in psychoanalytic principles, there is still a cognitive difference between children and adults in how such associative discovery of cause and effect is assimilated. Children may find emotional relief in acquiring psychological awareness, as do older people, but it is not necessary for them in all cases in order to find relief from symptoms.

In contrast to insight formation, which is necessary in analytic treatment of psychoneuroses, a child in AGT becomes increasingly conscious and pleased with changes in himself without having to work through resistances. While some ideational reflection may occur in AGT, children's reactions occur for the most part on the level of feeling and affect. The child is influenced mostly through sensate gratifications, and he is not impelled to reflect on them. He becomes less conflicted; he enjoys his advanced athletic ability and manipulative and creative skills newly acquired in arts and crafts; most of all, he enjoys interaction with peers and the social status derived from it. These changes are equivalent in effect to the insights and other gains achieved in successful therapy by older patients. In children treated in AGT, however, they represent a *derivative* (noncognitive) insight (Slavson and Schiffer, 1975).

Children with behavior disorders and character disorders, for whom AGT is the treatment of choice, are particularly disinclined to verbalize feelings or to ideate about the early experiences that led to their problems. Nor do they become intellectually preoccupied even when there are gratifications attending their successful treatment in AGT. Just as their original problems came into being reactively, noncognitively, defensively (as conditioned adaptations to their parents' mishandling of them), just so do entirely new feelings occur in response to the benign therapeutic experiences.

ACTION-BEHAVIOR-COMMUNICATION

In AGT a child's perceptions of a novel adult, the therapist, develops mostly through his *action-behavior-communication*. The therapist typically responds to interrogation, or he initiates conversation only as events necessitate his doing so. Otherwise, he is notably silent in his role. It is truly extraordinary how frequently a response can be made, correctly and sufficiently, with a mere affirmative or encouraging nod. When verbal intervention does become necessary, it should be accomplished in a neutral, moderate, matter-of-fact tone of voice.

For example: Pedro drew a stick figure of a human on a wall, using poster colors. It included obvious male genitalia. He giggled and called the attention of the other boys to his "art" work. Somewhat provocatively and challengingly, he called across the room to the therapist, "Hey, Morty, you know what this is?" The therapist looked up from his work, glanced to where Pedro was pointing, then commented briefly, "That's a big penis," and resumed what he had been doing. Other boys laughed, and Pedro was momentarily abashed by the mild, noncommittal response. He evidently had hoped to elicit a more dramatic effect, typical of that expected of adults when they are exposed to children's deliberately salacious behavior.

At the peak of boisterous acting out during an early session in another group, several boys locked one child out of the meeting room. For about five minutes he clamorously sought reentry by banging on the door and calling out loudly, but to no avail. When it appeared that the group was not yielding and the episode was acquiring an hysterical note, the therapist took possession of a waste pail, walked to the door, opened it, and left the room. "Don't let him in!" shouted one of the boys, belatedly. Of course, the object of their persecution rapidly took advantage of this opportunity and reentered the meeting room. Meanwhile the therapist took the refuse to the street, where he emptied it into a trash can. When he returned, a boy called out, "Why did you let him in?" The therapist replied, matter-of-factly, "I had to empty the pail downstairs." No further comment was made by anyone and the group soon engaged in other activities.

Two boys were struggling over possession of a saw, one tugging at the handle, the other resisting by holding on to the blade. The therapist, concerned that the boy might be cut should the blade slip through his fingers, stepped forward. "Tony, please hold this lanyard for me while I tie the end," he said, holding the clip end close to the boy's hand. Tony glanced at it, momentarily continued to tug at the saw, then released his hold on it to help the therapist. Suddenly freed, the other boy ran to the woodwork table with the saw, chortling triumphantly. When Tony finished helping the therapist he ran to the work table, verbally expressing his anger to the other boy about his taking the saw but allowing him to finish cutting the piece of wood. Tony then took the saw.

Two boys were facing each other in a standoff, one obviously intent on fighting; the other, a more passive child, was less inclined to do so. In the therapist's estimation, the situation required intervention. He obtained a water pitcher from the kitchen supply shelves and proceeded to cross the meeting room, in doing so deliberately passing between the boys. This act only momentarily distracted the more aggressive boy, but did not defuse the situation. Having filled the pitcher with water from the toilet sink, the therapist again crossed the room. This time, in passing once again between the boys, he "accidentally" spilled water on the floor. With a comment of dismay, he became occupied in wiping up the mess with newspaper and rags. This, in addition to the attention his "accident" had drawn from others in the group, provided enough distraction for the frightened boy to escape from a potentially bad confrontation.

A girl called out to the therapist, "Look what she's doing!"—referring to a group member who was aimlessly mixing all the available poster color paints at the easel, much of it slopping onto the floor. The therapist looked up from her work when addressed, but then returned to it without comment. "Don't you *see* what she's doing?" persisted the same girl. The therapist looked directly at her and said, "I see." Somewhat later, the therapist took some newspaper, walked to the easel where the girl was still messing, and without a word spread the paper under the easel.

THE NURTURANT TRANSFERENCE: ITS NATURE, EVOLUTION, AND EFFECT

Children's beneficent experiences in AGT, especially in the relationship with the therapist, is tantamount in its psychological influence to optimal, unequivocal "parental love." At no time is *unconditional acceptance* compromised by what the children might construe as rejection, disapproval, or punishment. The therapist's acceptance remains essentially inviolate and consistent. Even when an intervention is required, it is accomplished in the circumspect fashion described immediately above. No aspect of critical judgment is ever conveyed through his actions. This almost absolute acceptance of children and their behavior does not imply that the therapist sanctions acting out. Accepting children as they are is not the same as approving their behavior.

Since psychological nurturance is available to all members of a group, varying only in degree according to differences in children's personalities, problems, and readiness for transference, sibling rivalry feelings come into play. In families such rivalry may produce poor effects due to parental mishandling, but this does not occur in the therapy group. Rather, by virtue of the therapist's helpful, neutral ministrations to all children, sibling rivalry subsides and peer interactions of a more harmonious nature predominate. One exception to this may occur with children presenting with strong sibling rivalry feelings. Such children are counterindicated for exclusive AGT. They require individual treatment at first, and may be referred for supportive treatment in AGT once there has been a diminution of these feelings.

During normal child development, physical and emotional nurturance is supplied primarily through the mother's action communication. Its psychological counterpart in AGT, especially during the beginning and early phases, is provided by the ministrations of the therapist. This basic nurturance penetrates even further by virtue of the children's being fed during the latter part of every session. Foods children tend to enjoy are prepared and served, this oral gratification being given without reserve, regardless of whether the group has been "good."

What has just been described represents a sensitive, mostly unspoken "language." As described earlier, the basic therapeutic effects of AGT evolve in the main from interpersonal interactions that are largely nonverbal. These expose children's negativistic, ego-defensive feelings and behaviors and their general perception of adults to new, reconstructive influences. Their prior life experience and earlier perceptions, comprehensions, and ego-defensive adaptations become weakened, then ameliorated. The psychologically benign therapist becomes a significant libidinal object whom they now invest with implicit trust.

Thus, a therapist of either gender becomes unconsciously identified by the children as a maternal libidinal object (nonsexualized in AGT) during the early and middle phases of treatment. Initially the positive transference is operative psychologically on a preoedipal level, because of the dimensions of oral "feeding" inherent in the therapy. The corrective influence of such a transference is preeminent with behavior and character disorders as a result of their preoedipal etiology. While the maternal quality of the transference exerts its influence regardless of the therapist's gender, it undergoes change later in treatment, when the children respond to therapists' actual gender identities, using them as object models. It is primarily for this reason that activity therapy groups should be homogeneous with respect to gender: male therapists should work with all-boy groups, female therapists with all-girl groups.

POSITIVE AND NEGATIVE ASPECTS OF THE TRANSFERENCE

Early episodes of obstreperous behavior during the acclimatization phase of AGT have been incorrectly described by some therapists as negative transference. Actually, these are not transference phenomena at all; rather, they are conscious, deliberate "experiments" on the part of the group to test the actuality of an entirely novel and challenging perception—a permissive "new" kind of adult, one extraordinarily different from anyone previously encountered.

Initial acting out represents, then, a *conscious* enactment of children's negative feelings about parents, teachers, and other adults, displaced onto the therapist through already habituated behavior. This acting out, in addition to its primary purpose of testing the therapist, has cathartic value of a limited sort. Negative transference behavior, which has greater potential for abreaction and catharsis, comes into being only after a therapist is unconsciously invested as a significant libidinal object in the transference. When this relationship, which takes time to become established, is in effect, acting out, if present at all, is expressed symbolically, rarely against the person of the therapist. Thus, children may smear a wall, use materials improperly or wastefully, or waste or reject food which they may truly enjoy. These are unconscious, aim-directed challenges to the therapist. It is important to bear in mind that the entire setting of a group treatment room, its furnishings and equipment, are literally an extension of the therapist's persona.

Direct contact against the person of a therapist is forbidden. This is tantamount to a child's unconscious wish to destroy a cathected object. If such behavior were allowed, and should it persist, it would generate overwhelming anxiety and guilt feelings. In a psychologically balanced group, one whose members have been carefully and correctly diagnosed, such behavior is practically nonexistent.

Acting out as a manifestation of negative transference occurs for a relatively short time in AGT. It is a transitory condition in a properly constituted group. Should one child, or a group, act out persistently, with the therapist as a central focus, even symbolically, a technical error is indicated—improper selection of clients, an unbalanced group composition, or faulty role maintenance by a therapist. If a child infects the group without letup, he should be withdrawn and treated individually. Alternatively, he may be transferred to another activity group, one with slightly older children, where he may be more responsive to their limits. Should it happen that a well-constituted activity group acts out persistently, countertransference-induced behavior on the part of the therapist is usually accountable for this condition.

It is important to recognize that in AGT *the prevailing transference to the therapist is benign and positive.* Negative transference will vary in intensity from one child to another, and for a group as a whole, in accordance with the developmental phase in treatment; it may be quantitatively strong in the beginning, diminishing later. But positive transference is integral and permanent, and the beneficent, healing effects for children stem from this relationship. This is so because of the children who are eminently suitable for AGT—behavior disorders and certain character disorders.

Neurotic children, on the other hand, show persisting, deeper anxiety, and there is a sexual element in the transference. In view of this, there is a need for the working through of analytic psychotherapy. Exclusive AGT is counterindicated for such children.

Thus, the acting out of an activity therapy group is usually an initial, short-lived phase in treatment. It constitutes an experience of "discovery" by the children. The therapist's acceptance of them and his tolerance for antisocial (actually, antiparent and antiadult) behavior is what establishes the fundamentally positive transference that endures for the course of treatment.

With the passage of time and improvements in the children, the quality of the transference relationship changes from nurturant to affectionate; it becomes a relationship between friends. Having matured through the reconstructive influences inherent in the peer group, the children become stronger and more autonomous. Having experienced a sufficiency of unconditioned love, they become capable of reciprocating love.

CHILDREN'S CHANGING PERCEPTION OF THE THERAPIST

It is interesting how progressive improvements parallel pre- and postoedipal stages of normal development. The influence of the therapist's nurturant role predominates early in treatment, when children are in a regressive mode. Later, the attraction of the group as a whole, because of the status it affords each child and the many socialization opportunities it offers on a more mature level, lessens the dependency aspect of transference to the therapist. This is similar to a normal child's striving for social recognition in peer groups coincident with his movement away from dependence on the family.

In AGT there is minimal involvement of the sexual, libidinal elements focal during oedipal development. Sexual libido is not prominent in behavior and character disorders. Where neurotic anxiety is prominent, its roots lie in the sexuality attending the oedipal problem, and this is best dealt with in individual treatment.

EMERGENCE OF THE GROUP'S CORRECTIVE INFLUENCE

At its inception, an activity therapy group is only nominally a group; it is actually a mere assemblage of troubled children, however carefully chosen. In its composition and in the nature of early group sessions, a group reflects the idiosyncratic quality of each child's personality and problems. It is only when negative transference becomes expressed that the group becomes psychologically homologous to a family. Once it is so cathected, interpersonal interactions between the children acquire greater rehabilitative potential; they enable the children to work through feelings of sibling rivalry and other ambivalences. Later, the group as a whole acquires a nurturant influence reflective of the helpful therapist, this despite occasional episodes of rancorous, conflictual encounters between children.

As they become happier and more relaxed, and as improvement takes place in self-image, children are impelled, by the attendant satisfactions, to perpetuate and extend their gains. They also become more amenable to reconstructive psychological influences inherent in the group, supported always by the persisting, positive transference to the therapist and now, in dramatic increase, by more significant relationships with members of the group. At such an advanced phase of a group's evolution, the therapist deliberately distances himself further from interactions with the children, in order to maximize the group's corrective influence.

Dynamic changes in the psychological nature and influence of a therapy group fosters a subtle but extraordinary allegiance endowing the group with enhanced therapeutic viability. A maturing therapy group acquires a social imperative affecting each member in a positive, growth-promoting fashion. It is rare that a latency age child fails to respond to a group's penetrating influences, since compliance with peer group mores offers social status and recognition of the worth of each individual. This, for a child in latency, strongly supports identity formation.

Too casual a perusal of AGT by inexperienced therapists tends to focus them more on acting out behavior in a group, to the exclusion of broader, more significant therapeutic factors. Such superficiality is insensitive to the evolution of the extraordinary group gestalt, with its regulatory, corrective influence. It is this development in particular which constitutes the phenomenon of therapy of the individual *by* a group.

DIAGNOSIS AND SELECTION OF CHILDREN FOR AGT

In the diagnosis of young children, one must be guided more by syndrome than by symptoms. The variable and often diffuse nature of problems still in a formative state, as yet uncrystallized, requires this approach. Despite this, however, it is possible to elucidate primary, nuclear elements of presenting problems which can help determine an optimal treatment procedure.

In a gross fashion, children's emotional disorders may be grouped under four main categories: primary behavior (conduct) disorders, character problems, neuroses, and psychoses.

Primary Behavior Disorders

Children with behavior disorders or character problems are prime candidates for AGT. The high degree of success with these problems is understandable when one considers their etiology and how they respond to a purely activity, noninterpretive method of treatment.

Primary behavior disorders have been described as "reactive" disorders because hostile, aggressive, antisocial acting out is a characteristic pattern of response to mistreatment and nurturance deprivation experienced by the children during early development. Their parents are wont to impose maturational demands that far exceed the children's coping capabilities, and then subject them to punishments should they fail to meet these impossible standards. It is the actual conduct of the child which constitutes the essential problem—thus the term "primary." The problem, manifested as antisocial (initially antiparent) behavior, is not a consequence of organic, neurological disease or neurosis.

Of all troubled children, those with behavior disorders are the most suspicious and defensive towards adults, in conflict with peers, negativistic, and "deaf" to reasoning and verbal persuasion. They anticipate, almost reflexively, that adults, therapists included, will subject them to the same restraints and punishments as did their parents. Most behavior disorders originate during the preoedipal period, though there are also behavior disorders of oedipal onset.

The reactive conduct within the family is inevitably displaced to persons and situations outside. The child's combativeness and distrust is replicated with others because the pattern becomes ingrained as an antisocial adaptation. In a sense, these children behave as early experience has conditioned them to: spontaneously, thoughtlessly, impulsively, hurtfully, and without reflection as to causes and consequences. They tend to treat other persons as if they were objects rather than persons.

Children with behavior disorders are relatively inaccessible to dyadic therapy, which they construe as threatening and insincere.

Moreover, in individual therapy they are made increasingly anxious by the therapist's close proximity, which has the effect of further threatening already limited ego controls and perhaps triggering impulsivity. The presence of other children in the group provides insulation from the therapist, offering safety (and sufficient time) for a child to observe and learn about an adult who initially is viewed as an "enemy." The separation and safety provided by the group is enhanced by the therapist's typically tangential position with regard to activity, his noninterference. Thus, the child with a behavior disorder is permitted, as are all children in AGT, to make contact on his own terms, at his own pace. It is when the child manifests a newly acquired capacity for relationship—a transference (nonsexual in AGT)—that the corrective psychological influences are set seriously into motion.

The relative influence of adults' "deeds and words" was described earlier to emphasize how a therapist's *action communication* becomes the compelling force in AGT. This factor is critically important in the therapy of behavior disorders; children with such disorders possess an almost paranoid defensiveness. It is only absolute acceptance by a therapist, demonstrated in action, and his continuing ministrations to their needs, that eventually penetrates the hardened defensive core. Initially, during the acclimatization phase of a group, the child's conduct is qualitatively similar to the testing behavior of the group, except that it is expressed more energetically. However, as he becomes more conscious of the unusually permissive climate, he also becomes more demonstrative in acting out—he is thrown "off balance" by the behavior of a novel adult, a perception which challenges all his prior experience. Heretofore he has been altogether conditioned to punitive retaliations from adults. Should a therapist is constrained to intervene, he must do so adroitly and sensitively so as never to convey a sense of disapproval. Behavior disorders have an unforgiving attitude: at no time should a therapist's behavior resemble in the slightest that of parents or other adults.

Eventually the child confirms to his satisfaction that this "new" adult is "for real." His acting out will continue, though less intensely, but now it has cathartic value because expressed in a transferential relationship. Such emotional release is capable of modifying the pathological state.

It is this phase in the treatment of a behavior disorder which is the sternest test for the therapist, who must continue to tolerate the behavior and fulfill a preexisting nurturant need. In sufficient time—*minimally two years*—the restitutive value of AGT ameliorates the destructive conduct patterns acquired reactively as self-protection. Now the child has less need to defend himself. Unconditional love, experienced in the transference, becomes assimilated, and the psyche is altered. The child's ego is strengthened, his superego is restructured in a more benign way, an improved self-image emerges, and effective sublimations are acquired.

Such fundamental changes in a child are inevitably demonstrated outside the therapy group. Parents, other adults, and peers find him more acceptable and they change in their own responses to him. The previous cycle of abrasive interpersonal interactions is interrupted; no longer is it self-perpetuating. As this happens, further gratifications are experienced by the child in the form of recognition and acquired social status. These acknowledgments of the change in him sponsor and solidify sublimations.

Behavior disorders, for the most part, can be treated exclusively in AGT. In planning termination of treatment, it is wise to first affiliate the child with a supportive recreational program in his community, such as a settlement house, in order to broaden his social gains. Oedipal-type behavior disorders may require further individual therapy. This can be implemented following termination of AGT because of the newly acquired capacity to form a transference. It is not unusual to initiate individual treatment at some point during AGT, both methods used concurrently.

Character Disorders

The psychological effects of AGT are experienced somewhat differently by children with character disorders, or children with mixed problems in which characterological factors predominate. Among these are weak or defective sexual identifications (feminine boys and masculine girls); passive-dependent children; infantilized, overprotected, narcissistic children; nonpathological social isolates; children with inadequate egos; or "only" children. Such character-rooted problems are global personality defenses. The reconstructive effects of successful treatment of such children affects first their character structure and only then their behavior.

There are additional differences in the response to AGT between children with character problems and those with behavior disorders. In the early phase of treatment, the former do not test the permissiveness of the therapist with the intensity shown by the latter, nor do they require the same self-protective insulation from contact with the therapist. Most children with character-based problems, the isolated child excepted, are less threatened by proximity to the therapist. As a matter of fact, they are more inclined to seek him out. Infantile, dependent children actually try to monopolize his attention to gratify immature needs. Insecure children and others with weak egos seek support and praise.

A therapist must be mindful how the nurturant quality of his role can foster the dependency needs of children who have been overprotected and overindulged. An anaclitic child bonds too readily, because the maternal essence of a transference is syntonic with narcissistic character. An infantile child may try, unconsciously, to replicate with the therapist the debilitating bond which exists with one or both parents, most often the mother. Thus, an effeminate boy, motivated unconsciously by latent homosexuality, may attach himself to the therapist. In his manner of responding to insistent requests for attention from such children, a therapist needs to supply sufficient attention without at the same time indulging the dependency.

While a therapist is readily accessible to all children in AGT, his responses to their requests necessarily vary. In practice, he responds to an overly demanding child's request for assistance by merely explaining or demonstrating how a task is accomplished; he then turns the work over to the child for completion. The attention a therapist is forced to give to others in the group helps monitor the demanding child's ways. After momentary attention to an importunate child's requests, the therapist says: "Now I have to help him."

Children with confused sexual identities try to gain attention and please the therapist by taking over such routine chores as sweeping, cleaning, or serving food. The therapist relinquishes the task to the child without comment and applies himself elsewhere. He never conveys approbation for such volunteered behavior; to do so would have the effect of approving the child's covert seductiveness. In AGT praise is used with discrimination, and only when it has therapeutic merit. Thus, the finished product of an immature child will elicit a brief, appreciative smile from a therapist, or a nod, or a simple "That's good." The solicitations of approval of an effeminate boy are also briefly acknowledged in a neutral, noncommittal manner. Much later in treatment, when such children demonstrate growth and independence, a therapist may volunteer praise.

The advanced group exerts a paratherapeutic influence upon children with character problems much as it effects those with behavior disorders. It limits the excessive indulgences they seek from the therapist, and forces them to learn to share his attention. In addition, stronger children now serve as role models. In these ways, the group as a whole has a strong mutative influence. Especially affected are those fixated at infantile levels initially, who are now made more aware of the mores of the latency age peer group. Because they seek acceptance and status as therapy progresses, they learn to sacrifice narcissistic needs.

A therapy group is not averse to conveying negative judgments with vocal severity: "You're a baby!" "Stop asking him (the therapist) to help you all the time!" "Can't you see he's busy?" Toward an effeminate boy a group can be pointedly critical in its "analysis," yet instrumental in helping him change: "You act like a girl!" Or, more constructively: "Here, I'll show you how to *really* throw the ball!" Children who are exposed to a group's focused attention are rarely invulnerable to its pressures. It is, indeed, an unusual latency age child who can remain oblivious to, or untouched by, the social demands of the peer group. Such children are best treated individually.

During two or more years of treatment in AGT, children are exposed to an optimal gender model in the person of the therapist. It is this factor that recommends homogeneous grouping, with therapists of the same gender as the children.

MODIFICATIONS IN AGT

In the introduction to this chapter, reference was made to recently reported modifications in AGT. Ostensibly, these changes were necessitated by unusual clinical considerations, implying the inadequacy, or inappropriateness, of the standard AGT method. Attention is directed to several such methods to assess their psychological rationale.

In a published article, a therapist reported how, out of necessity, he converted a standard activity group into a "talking" group. The group had been acting out so severely and persistently that he questioned the wisdom of continuing it. He concluded that one boy in particular was instigating the group's manic deportment. He then directly confronted this boy, *forcibly* stopping him from acting out, and told him that such behavior was no longer acceptable. In addition, he informed the group that they could not continue as before; that henceforth their behavior would not go unquestioned; that they were now expected to talk about their feelings and the conflicts that arose in the group. In addition, they were informed that the therapist would continue to use direct interventions to insure that the group's conduct would be kept within reasonable bounds.

Several questions arise with respect to this sudden, dramatic change in the nature of the group. The unanticipated turnaround in the therapist's role literally shocked the boys' already established perception of him as noninterfering, tolerant, and helpful. What they then experienced was the precipitous conversion of a psychologically benign person into a manifest superego restrictor. Was their apparent acceptance of this change a conscious and unconscious response to feelings of guilt and remorse generated by what was tantamount to a criticism of them? If so, did their consequent "better" behavior represent a therapeutic outcome or simply a guarded and conditioned response?

It should be kept in mind that one boy acted as the focus of infection of the group, and he was responsible for generating a state of heightened acting out. It is also possible that psychological balance was lacking in this group. If so, this would have required reevaluation of the group's composition and its reconstitution. Was the instigator schizophrenic or psychopathic? Did he have an extreme behavior disorder or some other serious problem for which AGT is specifically counterindicated? In client selection the most seasoned therapist can at times be mistaken.[7]

It would appear that the group was precipitously altered in its fundamental method without sufficient consideration of its dynamics. Moreover, another question arises, one that tends not to be addressed objectively, whenever a therapist (even an experienced one) works without the opportunity for collaboration or consultation with another experienced person. Therapists engaged in any treatment modality are subject to countertransference feelings which, if left unexplored, lead inevitably to technical errors. The tenor of the report in question projects a countertransference quality, the failure to apprehend it and, consequently, a procedural error. It is not the first instance in which countertransference reactions have been responsible for the invention of purportedly "new" methods of psychotherapy. Not all

---

[7] An example of this can be seen in the film *Activity Group Therapy*, made by S.R. Slavson and myself. It can be rented from the film library of New York University, Washington Square, New York City.

those who departed from Freud's inner circle in the early days of psychoanalysis were motivated solely by objective differences with the "father" of dynamic treatment.

Another example of what actually constitutes a misconception of AGT: A noted training institute applied for and received a grant to attempt group therapy with emotionally disturbed young children in a public elementary school. It is relevant that, in its own training center, this institute employed group therapy only with adolescents and adults.

A male psychiatrist and a female social worker, as cotherapists, led a small group composed of six children five and six years of age. The physical setting was too small, poorly furnished with materials, and inadequately equipped. They employed a highly permissive, laissez-faire approach, allowing these disturbed children, most of whom were referred as notably hyperactive, to act out. Within the space of a few sessions, their acting out became manic and persistent, beyond control of the children or the therapists. Paints were smeared and paraphernalia of various sorts strewn about in such hysterical fashion that the school custodian, in helpless frustration, threatened to "report" this "crazy" situation (as he put it) to higher authorities.

What has briefly been described here is an uncritical application of permissiveness by therapists inexperienced in group therapy with an age group and problem types for whom such unrestricted freedom is counterindicated. Pertinent questions arise: What was their rationale for the use of cotherapists? It is conceivable that some of the children had problems that would respond favorably to this modification, given a well-formulated and properly implemented group method, but such questions were not addressed. Was it wise for the therapists to attempt such experimentation without prior training, supervision, or consultation? (See Slavson and Schiffer, 1975, Chapter 21.)

Another procedure that differs drastically from standard methodology with latency age children is to confine a group in a meeting room devoid of craft, play, or game materials. The therapist instructs the group that they are expected to talk about feelings, attitudes toward parents, siblings, and others, and circumstances affecting their lives.

The premise of this unusual method is that latency age children can tolerate and will respond to such direct intervention, and that this approach will in the long run afford them insight into their problems.

The assumption is that the therapist will be sensitive and alert to the children's tolerances for such direct, analytic treatment. It is assumed further that he will be skillful enough to help them cope with their anxieties and fears. Given such conditions, it is felt, there is no need for work or play activities to relieve tension.

This approach, I would argue, is a literal invasion of ego defenses. Such an aggressive method with latency age children is extraordinarily demanding on an age group which has, as one of its developmental tasks, a need to build adequate ego defenses and compensatory capabilities. Normal latency development is much involved with mechanisms of suppression, repression, and sublimation, and demands social interaction with peers. Such normal maturational requirements are even more crucial with emotionally disturbed latency age children. This nonstandard method of treatment actually challenges the resistances, and stresses the children to grapple with conscious and unconscious elements of their problems and the affective responses brought into the open by confrontation.

It is undeniable that children with neurotic problems require probing analytic treatment to make them aware of unconscious etiology and to assist them in making better accommodations in the light of such understanding. One wonders, however, about the necessity of so directly straining their tolerances. Latency age children are emotionally vulnerable; they are easily driven into flight when their defensive resources are stripped away. This method, purportedly, conveys to the children that they can and must talk to central issues affecting their lives; that in so doing they need have no fears; that they can place implicit trust in the therapist's ability to support them at all times; that eventually they will be helped; and that there is no need for even temporary relief, through work and play, from the analytic task at hand.

Perhaps so. It is possible that such a compelling, analytic approach can be employed with success, but only by therapists who possess formidable knowledge and extensive experience in psychoanalysis and psychoanalytic psychotherapy. Such therapists are uniquely talented in these respects. Only persons so endowed should attempt this highly specialized group treatment. The danger exists that others, less qualified, run the risk of further damaging already vulnerable children.

Another question: What recommends this aggressive form of group therapy when other standard group analytic methods exist, methods indisputably proven efficacious with this patient population? (Slavson and Schiffer, 1975, Chapters 15–16.)

Finally let us consider a method of group therapy that has borrowed conceptually some of the basic principles of AGT and has applied them with some success with a special patient population. In the writer's estimation, this modification represents a worthwhile therapeutic instrument for treating a very difficult problem.

The children with whom we are presently concerned are markedly impulsive; they possess minimal frustration tolerance; and they are capable of primitive, primary process behavior. They have been described variously as ego-deficient, ego-weak, and ego-impaired.[8] Their developmental histories reveal that they have been subject to severe nurturance deprivation during infancy and early childhood, and have been emotionally traumatized and physically abused by parents.

The number of such children has increased to a point where today they seriously tax the available clinical resources. They are not suited for individual treatment, and strongly resist it if it is attempted. They cannot tolerate the libidinal and aggressive elements implicit in a transference relationship with a symbolic "parent," the therapist, because they have limited compensatory and sublimatory capacities. If the children cannot flee from the threat implicit in a transference, they maintain an obdurate silence in treatment. Should they be pressed to communicate, they may become manic and very angry, and may act out explosively.

Such children have proved tractable when treated in modified AGT with others similar to themselves. The available crafts and games are appealing, and engagement with such activities "soaks" up restlessness and physical energy.

In establishing a corrective climate through which to alleviate the severe pathology of ego-impaired children, two conditions are essential. First is a careful selection and balance of candidates to ensure that a group complement possesses at least minimal capacity to modulate each child's behavior and to support the therapist's ministrations, thus permitting his interventions to work their effect on suspicious, defensive children. The second requisite condition concerns the role of the therapist, which differs notably from that in standard AGT. He remains permissive, sympathetic, and supportive, never critical or judgmental, but the climate of almost absolute freedom that typifies

---

[8] Such terms can be applied correctly in some degree, to all emotional disorders. With these children they denote *essential* ego pathology, a state of emotional primitivism.

standard AGT must be suspended in work with impulse-ridden children. Not to do so would be tantamount to sanctioning primary process behavior, the inevitable effect of which would be to shatter whatever minimal restraints the children may possess. This would altogether negate the possibility of fostering in them socially acceptable patterns of behavior.

An inevitable consequence of the indiscriminate use of permissiveness would be to elicit manic, unbridled acting out. Without conscious intent, the group would seek to destroy itself in order that the children might preserve their minimal coping abilities. Without these, they would be unable to sustain themselves in their families, in school, or in the community. Moreover, there is a danger, in the laissez-faire use of permissiveness, of deepening pathology, perhaps to a level of psychosis or criminal psychopathy.

It should be borne in mind that this patient population is developmentally fixated at an early preoedipal level, as early as the first or second year. No form of therapy with such children should be concerned with inducing regression to a point of fixation and then correcting ego function, a frame of reference fairly universal in other treatments. As we are concerned here with primitive fixation to begin with it would be folly itself to create even more chaotic feelings. In this special, modified AGT, children are accepted where they are emotionally and are then exposed to tolerable experiences designed to make the most of depleted egos.

A therapist cannot be neutral, nonintrusive, and tangential to such a group as in the classical model of AGT. He must literally be an alter ego for each child, supplementing and reinforcing ego capacities until there is enough improvement for each child to function more maturely and autonomously.

The therapist must be able to anticipate situations that might exceed the children's abilities to cope, and that might evoke acrimonious feelings leading to unduly aggressive interactions. This mandates that at psychologically propitious moments the therapist must take an active role in mediating conflicts, suggesting alternate solutions, and enhancing the children's abilities to reflect on their behavior and its consequences. This will assist them in acquiring new, more gratifying ways of accommodating to trial situations. At the same time, the therapist enhances the corrective influence of the group as a social modality. This has the effect of creating what can be termed a "group superego." Its therapeutic value is to promote the group as a monitoring, educational influence. By this point the group has taken on a paratherapeutic role that spares the therapist from acting as the sole intervenor during moments of stress.

Through his acceptance of the children, despite their rambunctiousness, the therapist provides at all times the symbolic equivalent of massive emotional nurturance. He is consistently helpful, mediates in a sensitive way, and shows that he acknowledges the worth of each child. Were such symbolic nurturance attempted in individual treatment with these children, it would be experienced as threatening and, for reasons given earlier, would lead them to terminate what for them constitutes a potentially dangerous libidinal transference. However, it is fascinating that these children can tolerate essentially the same symbolic nurturance when it is provided in a group. Moreover, in a relatively short time they become motivated to seek it out, provided the group is properly constituted and managed (Schiffer, 1984, Chapters 9–10).

Another significant question arises with respect to group treatment of ego-impaired children. If, in fact, a modified AGT method is helpful, would not a combined activity and interpretive method—such as activity-interview group psychotherapy—be even more productive, since it might bring the children to *explore* why they behave as they do?

Impulse-ridden children cannot tolerate in the least any exploration of inner motivations. They are governed largely by "fight or flight" considerations. Markedly narcissistic at a primary level, they are prone to seek instant gratifications on a simple hedonistic level. If one were to seek a parallel to such immaturity, its almost exact counterpart would be found in the normal biological and psychological constitutions of infants and very young children. Impulse-prone, essentially ego-deficient children are emotionally equivalent to the immature state characteristic of such early developmental stages.

During the first several years of normal child development, educative influences are brought to bear, and children acquire a degree of ego integrity and more advanced coping behavior. Depending on the diagnosis, most of those who become emotionally troubled have sufficient ego strength and the capacity to respond to therapy, whether individual or group. However, the ego-impaired children with whom we are presently concerned are insufficiently developed, unable to respond to treatment methods that depend on examination of the meanings of their behavior on a cognitive level.[9]

A therapist who attempts to encourage ego-impaired children to cogitate about themselves and their ways is literally asking them to recognize primary process phenomena, an analytic task that even a sophisticated adult patient must "sweat" through in classical psychoanalytic treatment. With these children, such an exploratory procedure assumes their potential ability to gain insight into formidable, utterly overwhelming primitivism. Need we wonder why children so severely impaired and driven to impulsive behavior and absolute resistance by analytic procedures? Such children relate to adults solely in terms of whether the latter will "hurt" them; whether they will gratify immature needs; and, with regard to therapists, whether they will accept them as they are and provide a corrective experience both tolerable and desirable.

When treatment in modified AGT successfully strengthens a child, it provides feelings of increased worthiness and a conscious sense of well-being. The child becomes more aware of the individuality of other persons, beginning first with the therapist and then fellow group members. He acquires a measure of sympathy, mostly through identification. While this is less mature than a capacity for empathy, it nevertheless represents a major change when viewed in the context of the original problems. Furthermore, such a child may develop, perhaps for the first time in his life, positive transference feelings toward others, starting with the therapist. It is conceivable at this point for him to be treated individually coincident with group treatment, preferably with the same therapist.

The diagnostic terms prevalent in reports on severely ego-impaired children—ego-deficient, ego-weak—are fairly accurate descriptions of the essential pathology. However, such children can be confused with others who are less disturbed yet whose behavior is similar. Among children identified as ego-impaired there are some who would be more accurately diagnosed as primary behavior disorders, social psychopaths (delinquent characters), and neurotic characters (Van Ophuijsen, 1961). These children are impulsive and belligerent, and they have minimal guilt and anxiety reactions. It is

---

[9] Margaret G. Frank (1983) has correctly pointed out the similarity of such children to those of nursery age. She draws parallels between the efficient ministrations of nursery school teachers with their young charges and therapists who treat ego-impaired children in a group.

conceivable that some children who have failed to respond to modified AGT are of these types and therefore were inappropriately selected. While they possess ego defects, they can be distinguished from children with *essential* ego impairment. Differential diagnosis is important to determine what constitutes such impairment, otherwise some children may be included in modified AGT who would be better treated with other methods.

The DSM diagnostic categories are of limited value in this regard. They altogether lack specificity in delineating children's emotional problems. Other diagnostic outlines and descriptive information, however, can be useful to child therapists (see Slavson, 1952; Hamilton, 1947; Group for the Advancement of Psychiatry, 1974).

As was described earlier, a primary behavior disorder is a reactive maladaptation caused by parents' gross mishandling of a child during early development. Such a child, however, has a more intact ego than one with essential ego impairment, and is not as fixated emotionally. Moreover, most children with behavior disorders have had an early nurturant relationship with at least one primary libidinal object. This again differs from the ego-impaired child, who has been massively rejected and mistreated during formative years, with little, if any, nurturance. Children with behavior disorders do manifest guilt responses in AGT, although they can also easily ignore them because of weak superego influence. Nevertheless, they do respond well in standard AGT.

Psychopathic children lack the capacity for compensatory behavior. They are intractable in both individual and group treatment. Experience has demonstrated that whatever correction is possible with them is accomplished best in institutional settings, in an environment that increases their awareness of social regulations and the consequences of transgressions. Unlike children with behavior disorders or ego impairment, psychopaths are very much aware of their behavior and its influence on others. They are quite alert and wary lest they be detected and suffer the consequences. Sometimes such children are inadvertently included in standard AGT or the modified method. Inevitably they subvert the treatment in insidious ways, destroying the group if undetected as "contaminants" of group psychodynamics.

An additional factor distinguishes the psychopath from children with behavior disorders or essential ego impairment. The psychopath has a character structure already crystallized as antisocial, asocial, and delinquent. By contrast, the others are amenable to therapy because their problems have not yet been fully assimilated into character. As a matter of fact, these children cannot be accurately assessed as to character formation. It is only later, if their problems remain unresolved, that character becomes substantialized, unfortunately to a pathological degree. This can be aborted if proper treatment is instituted early.

If behavior-disordered and psychopathic children are treated in modified AGT with those who are essentially ego-impaired, deleterious results will follow. Those with behavior disorders will begin to act out even more drastically, given the stimulation from less intact children. The psychopaths will use their studied skills to benefit themselves, to provoke others in underhanded ways, and to subvert the therapist.

There are, then, subtle diagnostic distinctions to be made between problems that may at first glance appear similar. If group treatment is to be effective, these clinical differences must be ascertained. While diagnosis of emotional problems is never as definitive with children as with adolescents and adults, the pathology of these children *is* detectable, even in the nascent state, and differences can be discerned. If they are not, children may needlessly be exposed to ineffective therapy and run the risk of having their problems exacerbated.

For these reasons, the selection of children for modified AGT must be monitored carefully. Close observations of the interactions during early group sessions, in addition to in-depth studies of the presenting problems, will help prevent errors in selection and grouping. Changes in the composition of a group should be made early if any doubts arise as to the suitability of this treatment for particular children.

Some therapists are prone to minimize the subject of clinical diagnosis of young children's emotional problems. "Diagnosis of children's problems is relatively unimportant, because they are only beginning," is a typical expression of this attitude. It is true that definitive diagnoses of latency children may be difficult. However, central elements of problems, both developing and developed, can be discerned in order to formulate optimal treatment programs. Merely dismissing out of hand the critical imperative for careful diagnosis is tantamount to malpractice.

Finally, a word of caution to therapists who anticipate treating essentially ego-impaired children: it should not be attempted until they have had sufficient experience with the standard methods of children's group therapy. Moreover, it is imperative that competent supervision be available from senior persons alert to the special considerations involved in treating this patient population. It should be borne in mind that these children are capable of arousing extraordinary countertransference feelings, which will challenge both the emotional equanimity of therapists and the efficacy of treatment.

As we have seen, the standard method of AGT has limitations stemming from the inapplicability of this noninterpretive method to certain problems. As noted at the beginning of this chapter, AGT must be used very carefully, with full awareness, and has little flexibility as to choice of patients or in its standard techniques. What some therapists consider limitations of AGT are in fact improper applications of this very subtle method of treatment. A purely activity method, one that does not require therapists to explore with children the meanings of their behavior, seems to the uninitiated a relatively easy clinical task. This is far from the fact.[10]

AGT has, for more than four decades, demonstrated unusual suitability in treating a wide variety of emotionally disturbed children. It is not my intention to discourage experimentation in children's group therapy; rather, it is hoped that readers will give careful consideration to proposed modifications in the standard method of activity group therapy, and also of activity-analytic methods, to assess whether the "new" procedures are based on psychologically valid premises.

There are many instances in which special circumstances affecting particular children, or an entire therapy group, require special interventions, deviations from standard techniques. This occurs in all psychotherapy, individual or group. It is said that an expert knows when—and how—to break a rule. However, a seasoned therapist realizes that a single departure from standard methodology represents a *situational* adaptation, a technique, and that it does not automatically merit elevation into "new" methodology.

We must recognize as a fairly common human trait, affecting therapists as much as anyone, the tendency to be inventive, to devise original procedures or alterations of proven methods. Some, of course, become latter-day Columbuses, rediscovering what is no

---

[10] A visitor from South America, a Freudian psychoanalyst, spent several weeks in New York with S. R. Slavson observing AGT through one-way mirrors and discussing his observations at length. Before returning to his country he said, "AGT is so complex that it makes psychoanalysis appear simple by comparison."

longer virgin territory. Fundamental methods of child group therapy have been around for a long time. It is unlikely that altogether new ones will arise to entirely supplant methods long proven fundamentally sound. If we are to improve the *practice* of group treatment of children, promote its use, and ensure its clinical validity, we shall have to monitor it more carefully. Otherwise, a less critical employment of groups will serve only to discourage the use of this valuable resource.

S. R. Slavson wrote:

> One cannot be unaware of the many obvious errors in the theory and practice of group therapy now extant. But a study of this situation reveals that most misconceptions are the result of confusion as to clinical assumptions, patterns of practice, possibilities and limitations. One is also impressed with the fact that much of the confusion and error does not stem from group psychotherapy per se, but rather, from inadequate clarity as to psychodynamics, the nature of psychopathology and the processes of psychotherapy generally.... Truth can be begotten from error, but seldom—if ever—from confusion. [1953, pp. 3–4]

REFERENCES

Frank, M. (1983), Modified activity group therapy with ego impoverished children. In: *Ego and Self Psychology*, ed. E. S. Buchholz & J. M. Mishne. New York: Aronson, pp. 145–156.

Freud, S. (1908), Creative writers and day-dreaming. *Standard Edition*, 9:143–153. London: Hogarth Press, 1959.

——— (1931), Female sexuality. *Standard Edition*, 21:225–243. London: Hogarth Press, 1961.

Group for the Advancement of Psychiatry (1974), *Psychopathological Disorders in Childhood*. New York: Aronson.

Hallowitz, E. (1956), Activity Group Therapy as preparation for individual treatment. *Internat. J. Group Psychother.*, 1:337–347.

Hamilton, G. (1947), *Psychotherapy in Child Guidance*. New York: Columbia University Press.

Herink, R. (1980), *The Psychotherapy Handbook*. New York: New American Library.

Klein, M. (1932), *The Psycho-Analysis of Children*. Rev. ed. New York: Delacorte, 1975.

Rosenthal, L., & Nagelberg, L. (1956), Limitation of Activity Group Therapy: Case presentation. *Internat. J. Group Psychother.*, 6:166–179.

Scheidlinger, S. (1965), Three group approaches with socially deprived latency children. *Internat. J. Group Psychother.*, 15:434–455.

Schiffer, M. (1969), *The Therapeutic Play Group*. New York: Grune & Stratton.

——— (1984), *Children's Group Therapy: Methods and Case Histories*. New York: Free Press.

Slavson, S. R. (1952), *Child Psychotherapy*. New York: Columbia University Press.
——— (1953), Common sources of error and confusion in group psychotherapy. *Internat. J. Group Psychother.*, 3:3–28.
——— Schiffer, M. (1975), *Group Psychotherapies for Children*. New York: International Universities Press.
Spitz, R. (1945), Hospitalism: An inquiry into the genesis of psychiatric conditions in early childhood. *The Psychoanalytic Study of the Child*, 1:53–74. New York: International Universities Press.
——— (1957), *No and Yes: On the Beginning of Human Communication*. New York: International Universities Press.
——— (1965), *The First Year of Life*. New York: International Universities Press.
Van Ophuijsen, J. H. W. (1961), Primary conduct disturbances, their diagnosis and treatment. In: *Modern Trends in Child Psychiatry*, ed. N. Lewis & B. Pacella. New York: International Universities Press, pp. 35–42.

Chapter 12
Innovative and Creative Approaches in Child Group Psychotherapy

IRVIN A. KRAFT, M.D.

The history of psychiatry demonstrates the power of creative innovation, beginning with Freud's modification of Charcot's and Bernheim's hypnotic techniques into what later became psychoanalytic therapy (Meissner, 1980). Once a pattern becomes established, it tends to remain paramount, although offshoots and modifications quickly appear and as rapidly fail to remain viable. Activity group psychotherapy and activity-interview group therapy of children have dominated the scene for decades (Charach, 1983). Early on, other techniques, such as the use of puppets or of doll families, would appear and become standard alternative techniques, but they did not in any way threaten the overall position of Slavson's innovations (1975).

In our world of mass communications, rapid change, concern over atomic warfare, and unemployment, we in the United States see the traditional nuclear family becoming a blended structure, if not a single-parent structure, for a number of years of a child's life. In the midst of their search for helpful and accurate information, parents and children feel buffeted by the welter of information that a relative insulation both temporal and spatial once helped monitor and filter. The daily bombardment of overt and covert stimuli contains less information for rational decision making than subliminal messages designed to influence rather than inform. The blended or nuclear family seeks to provide emotional support for its members. It attempts to train its children to be competent in age- and gender-adequate control of their bodies and of their symbolic environment, yet today it feels irresolute. Increased tension and a sense of decreased control (vividly portrayed by the repeated astonishment at the erosion of financial life by inflation) lead to familial disorganization and faulty communications, especially with respect to interpersonal functions. In systems terms, the family offers at its level of hierarchical organization the training for adaptation; survival there, however, may not be equivalent to health.

Children, to grow and develop healthily, must learn to operate in various subsystems, which call for rearrangements of equilibria. Therapy, in this view, offers settings and experiences allowing the patient to glimpse and to feel at varying levels of abstraction the role of the family, primarily as message center and information processor. The group leader and the group itself confront this aspect of their lives, primarily in the here and now of the session, rather than focusing on the intricacies of individual psychopathology. A recent exposition of this view by Sands and Golub (1974) "emphasized a developmental-environmental model in which the child's life stage, the continuous interactive influence of development and environment, and the thrust to health are underscored. The goal is not to resolve conflict but to make possible a developmental progression" (p. 664).

In latency a child processes energy, as nutrients of metabolism and of emotional growth, within a field of lessened drive urgency. He directs his energies outward to peers and to admired adults, usually as part of his learning to delay gratification. The latency child potentially thrives on his group investments. And, as Sands and Golub (1974) state, such a holistic overview "precludes viewing the treatment hour as either the primary or only treatment tool and points to a multifaceted form of therapy, with special use of groups, specific approaches to the familial environment, the use of community resources that fit into the psychic economy of the latency phase, awareness of the child's body, and concern with his entire life space" (p. 663).

To illustrate the great power of peer pressure, a report by Burgess, Groth, and McCausland (1981) described six child sex initiation rings involving 36 pubescent children:

> A key factor in the continued operation of the ring is the peer group membership dynamic. The cohesiveness of the children helps to guarantee that they continue going with the adult and submitting to the sexual activity. The peer pressure aids in developing group loyalty ("I didn't want them to think I couldn't

do it"), provides the child with a peer group, and pressures the child to earn peer approval ("Everyone else was doing it"). Games are a strong cohesive factor with children, and engage their competitive nature. Essentially, the children compete for the adult's attention and approval.... The continuation of the ring is dependent on it remaining secret [p. 113].

In contrast to the grisly story above, Suda and Fouts (1980) showed the effects of peer presence on helping in an emergency situation in extroverted and introverted children. Thirty-eight introverted and 38 extroverted sixth-grade children were tested in the presence or absence of a same-sex confederate peer, with the emergency being sounds of distress in an adjoining room. In the presence of a peer, more extroverts actively helped than introverts, with no difference occurring between the two types tested alone.

The group leader's assumptions and definitions of how people function control how he handles transactions. He demonstrates to the child and the group how a family system lurking in the background requires that the patient be upset in order to maintain the family's equilibrium. The therapist expects the child to replicate in the group arena the schisms, secret alliances, and power ploys of his family of origin (Melville, 1973). With children and adolescents, the built-in mechanism for identification as part of growth combats this trend. Modeling behavior plays an important role in personality formation (Bandura, 1969). Patterson and Anderson (1964) postulated that peers serve well as agents dispersing social reenforcers. Developmentally, as a therapy group anneals and grows, behavioral group values permeate the members, countering family-sponsored behaviors that have proved inadequate and maladaptive outside the family. Often a latency age child takes in from his social, educative, and group experiences sufficient information to enhance his industriousness and to lead him out of the family focus. Unless a child has developed neurotic traits or a full-blown psychoneurosis, he tries out behavioral changes in his group setting; when these meet with repeated success, he tends to maintain them, indicating that his detour from normal development has returned to the main course.

With this overview in mind, we can more systematically question the nature of "innovative approaches" to children's group therapy. An approach is a method used to accomplish a desired aim. It may be developed on the basis of a given theory or be pragmatically improvised and then explained ad hoc. "Innovative" implies novelty, something as yet untried, and in the context of group therapy we might think of boldness and a certain freshness of approach. It prompts the reader or observer to exclaim, "Why didn't I think to do that!"

Each of us in leading a group of children has experienced the urge to try something that just seemed to fit at that moment. We may not try it just then, but only later, upon reflection. Some techniques, then, arise from a synthesis within ourselves of the group's dynamics, its members, and our own involvement. We sense, intuit, and know it is right.

But how is an innovation disseminated? Do we learn of it through a formal presentation or published paper? Or by word of mouth, through the professional grapevine? And when we do learn of it, do we ask for results first, for assurances that it works? I suspect that initially we examine it from the standpoint of comfort: Does that fit me? Does it seem safe? Would my group go for it? What would their parents think of it? And perhaps only later, How does it fit with my theoretical position on group psychotherapy? Has anyone else used it? With what results? Has the originator effectively studied the tactic and its consequences? Does he still find it valuable? Is it something that takes a special leader, perhaps talented in a certain area?

Consider the factors to be taken into account in selecting children for the group and in tailoring techniques to meet their needs: age, gender, presenting problems, parents, and on and on. All of these go into the structuring of the group initially and into consideration of innovative approaches. Do we set goals for an innovation? Or do we try it out of curiosity and only later, by judging the results, think our way through to immediate and long-term goals? Hopefully, innovative technique for its own sake, just to be different, is not a frequent occurrence. Presumably, a skilled and experienced leader will use his knowledge to avoid anything that might be injurious.

The following table attempts to classify the basic configurations possible into which an innovative technique may be interpolated.

Since the literature presents for the most part one-time reports lacking replication, the following discussion will use this anecdotal material to delineate various tactics.

Let us begin with verbalizations. Often in group a special vocabulary must be devised for use by the children and the leader. One such attempt involved constructing with latency boys and girls in a day hospital a neuroanatomical and neuropsychological vocabulary

Table

I. Nonverbal
   A. Active
      1. Leader-centered
      2. Child-centered
      3. Group-focused
      4. Object-focused
   B. Passive
      1. Leader and group
         a. TV
         b. music
         c. mime
         d. other
      2. Group with very little action by leader

II. Verbal
   A. Active
      1. Leader-centered
      2. Child-centered
      3. Group-focused
      4. Object-focused
   B. Passive
      1. Child-centered
      2. Group-focused

III. Combination: nonverbal & verbal (varying with the flow of group dynamics)

IV. Activities primary
   A. Leader
      1. Passive
      2. Active
   B. Child—mostly active
   C. Group—Little emphasis on group as a whole

V. Combined therapies
   A. Group & individual therapy
   B. With family therapy
   C. With significant others: mother, father, peers, etc.

which would be descriptive, easy to use, and free of tension-producing associations. The leader gave talks of under five minutes on the evolution of the brain, using a three-brain model. The group members learned readily that the number one brain (forebrain) concerned itself with basic automatic functions; that the number two brain (midbrain) dealt with strong emotions (anger, love, hate, sex, etc.); and that the number three brain (neocortex) attempted controls over the first two brains, specifically with its ability to abstract, store, and process information and to use speech. They learned also the basics of the autonomic nervous system and its emergency functions, which tied them up in knots with anxiety and tension. These children, who showed extreme emotional disturbances and severe perceptual handicaps, made frequent and cognitively sharp use of these concepts. Sometimes this enabled them to point out, not only within their own group but also in staff members, those times when the number two brain had gained control over behavior.

Another group used a vocabulary provided by the transactional analysis model of five ego states: critical parent, nurturing parent, adult, adapted child, and free child. This mixed group had the *TA for Kids* text to refer to, and its typology readily caught their attention. Interestingly, like the group using the three-brain terminology, they took this home and started identifying the ego states of parents or siblings during stressful episodes or arguments. Parents pretended to be interested initially, but anger soon took over, as the somewhat calmer definition ("Mom, your adapted child is running you now!") contrasted strongly with the confusion and uproar which had until then been a major pattern of family life.

Another device of value was the use of a small battery-operated microrecorder by the leader. Toward the end of a session he would dictate an impressionistic summary of the session and of the group as a whole. Then he would describe each patient's career during that session in behavioral and psychodynamic terms. Usually the group quieted down and listened, often with winks and nudges and "I told you so's." Once one very timid lad, miserly with any verbalizations whatever, asked to use the recorder once the leader was finished. He then spoke, tensely and in a soft voice, of how sad he was that day, especially at not being able to speak up as the other boys did. The leader began to offer the recorder to others, who would sometimes break through their show-off poses to speak earnestly of their feelings during that session. Often they would correct the leader's summary by disputing certain statements or descriptions.

Another use of communication devices is the taping of sessions, video being much more frequent and prominent than simple audio (Corder, Whiteside, McNeill, Brown, & Corder, 1981; Mallery and Navas, 1982). The act of videotaping is itself an act of therapeutic involvement. Who runs the camera? Does the monitor stay on while the session is being taped? When, if at all, should a tape be made or reviewed? Does the group action stay spontaneous or does it take on a stagey quality? Each of these questions carries different implications for the group. Interactions with the camera become evident as the transference to it emerges: one child might be concerned with societal requirements of behavior, especially if the mother was watching. Another might challenge the equipment by going right up to the lens, while another might take himself out of range. Most of the time, even if the camera stands in the room (though not behind a one-way mirror), the children grow to ignore it if the monitor remains blank.

Then, toward the last fifteen minutes, the leader suggests replaying the tape and discussing the behaviors, the comments, and the psychodynamics displayed.

Another technique using television emerged when the leader had to excuse himself to take an emergency phone call. While his attention was diverted, one boy turned on the monitor to a late afternoon soap opera. The group gathered silently at first. The leader, a firm devotee of serendipity, joined them in watching the woes of wistful adults seeking peace of mind. He turned it off after a few minutes and pointed a discussion at what they had all seen of family life. Heated and loud comments followed. Each lad saw something of his family on that screen. Subsequently, watching soap operas became an occasional means of inolving the group, especially when it was failing to focus or was too hyperactive.

Girl groups in the latency period can make effective use of their transferences to a female therapist. In one group, each girl had previously been in individual therapy with the leader. The five girls sat in a circle with the therapist, either on the floor or on chairs, and each crocheted a design of her own selection. Meanwhile, each in turn talked of the major themes of the past week, with others chiming in, making for a lively discussion. And the needles clicked right along. Seemingly, they could with more safety verbalize and reveal their emotions individually and as a group if they were involved with a hand-oriented task. Building on that experience, the group baked cookies, designed things on paper, and engaged in other activities, while still referencing them to themes of family and other life dynamics.

Anatomically correct dolls proved a boon at a certain stage in a latency age girls' group. These Teach-a-Body rag dolls, twelve inches long and stuffed with nylon, are soft, flesh-colored, and warm and responsive to the touch. Each set includes a boy and a girl, male and female adults, and even a fetus, about an inch and a half long, with a red pull bag to represent the placenta. All body details are chain-stitched into the nylon casing except the hair, which is yarn sewn into the doll. The dolls foster discussion about sex and the correct naming of parts; they bridge to individual thoughts and experiences. In one group, Marie, while waiting for a group session to begin, had been looking at a magazine advertisement featuring a nude female body. She had brought the magazine with her from the waiting room into the group therapy room to discuss it. This child's behavior in regard to sex had been to withdraw into a corner, and she was indicating at this point, by this gesture, that it was okay now for her to talk about sex; she was ready. It so happened that the therapists did not discuss the advertisement at that session. At the subsequent group meeting, Marie, heretofore unable to give direct verbal expression to any of her feelings, confronted her therapists and demanded to talk about it with the dolls. Sometimes when the dolls are presented in latency age groups, the children throw them around with various derogatory, embarrassed comments. In avoidance, they may say, "Ugh, these are ugly!" The therapist intervenes by asking what each body part is called and if any of them have seen their parents naked. In a following session, the group leader will correctly name the parts, after the initial embarrassment has died down and the children are ready for accurate labeling. The therapist must be concrete because latency age children handle this better than abstractions. The dolls serve to connect them with their feelings, as in the case of Marie. Also, by virtue of their tactile and visual qualities, the dolls appeal to the learning mechanisms characteristic of this developmental stage.

Another object-centered technique that helps produce expressive play has been described by S. Fineberg (personal communication). In her boys' latency groups, she uses bean bag chairs as projective play objects. Fineberg suggests that these bean bags help children traverse the preaffiliation, power and control, intimacy, differentiation, and separation phases of group work. The multiple uses of the bean bags, as in building forts, making walls to exclude the therapists, and in conducting simulated warfare using bags as thrown weapons, are devices lending themselves equally well to active and passive pursuits encouraging interaction.

Group participation in certain types of athletics proves very productive of further insight into patients' overt behavior and their emotional responses to the vicissitudes of the game. One game, which requires an area suitable for a modified baseball diamond, involves using a kick ball from soccer instead of a bat and ball. The usual baseball rules obtain, with only slight modification. The pitcher rolls the ball to the "batter," who kicks it and tries to reach first base before the fielders can grab it and hit him with it by a throw or a kick. The children's emotional involvement in this game lends itself not only to expression during play, but also to discussion of it later in the group.

Our environments offer numerous situations that may elicit psychodynamic material from the children. In the city zoo, in a dim, red-lighted nocturnal animal room housing vampire bats, the animals' love of blood was very much evidenced by the contents of their feeding dishes. This safe but scary ambience offered the children a special opportunity to delve into body damage fears, separation concerns, and nihilistic, destructive fantasies.

Still another object-centered technique uses balloons filled with water, preferably in an outdoor setting. Paper is pinned to a wall or tree, and the children draw various figures or designs on it. Filling the balloons with water and tying off the neck, they throw them at the drawings, using expletives and other expressions in the effort of tossing the heavy balloons. The noise, the splash, and the mess provide a ready vehicle for catharsis, usually via expressions of anger.

Along with the more standard uses of TV previously described, some therapists use video games, either in the office or at a nearby location. Competitiveness emerges quickly, and how each child handles it becomes readily evident. Back in the office or at the next session, the leader focuses on the children's experiences with Pacman and other games. The destructiveness so pervasive in these games is also a major stimulus.

Modification of the usual group format offers creative openings, such as those Oberfield and Ciliotta (1983) report in their work with single mothers and their school age sons with moderately severe behavior problems. The five boys met as a boys' group every two weeks and in a group with their mothers the intervening weeks. They contracted for five months as a unit, with reevaluation at that point. This procedure helped clarify individual maladaptive responses among the boys and gave strong support to the mothers in their struggles with life generally, as well as with their sons.

Sometimes an event occurs in the life span of the group that calls for improvisation. A latency age girls' group encountered the unexpected hospitalization of their major therapist. When the group met, about four days after the surgery, they were obviously unhappy and uncomfortable with her absence. The cotherapist offered them the opportunity to call the senior therapist at the hospital. They took turns talking, and several got to their basic question: Are you going to die? They then returned to the group much more relaxed.

The combination of play therapy and discussion group therapy can be innovative, depending on the way each part is structured. Lovasdal (1976) utilized a large play room and a separate group therapy room. His group therapy focuses on well-planned discussions about anger, sorrow, love, fear, and other basic emotions.

Still other innovative techniques could be reported. Most of those described use creative modifications of standard techniques to encourage freedom of expression of pent-up feelings and to provide effective experiential opportunities for insight and change. The consistency, warmth, flexibility, and empathy of the therapist, coupled with adequate knowledge of personality theory and therapeutic technique, provide the ingredients for good group therapy in this age band. Innovation flavors the therapy and challenges both the therapist and his young patients.

REFERENCES

Bandura, A. (1969), Modeling and vicarious processes. In: *Principles of Behavior Modification*. New York: Holt, Rinehart & Winston, pp. 118–132.

Burgess, A., Groth, A., & McCausland, M. (1981), Child sex initiation rings. *Amer. J. Orthopsychiat.*, 51:110–119.

Charach, R. (1983), Brief interpretive group psychotherapy with early latency-age children. *Internat. J. Group Psychother.*, 33:349–364.

Corder, B., Whiteside, R., McNeill, M., Brown, T., & Corder, R. (1981), An experimental study of structured videotape feedback on adolescent group psychotherapy process. *J. Youth & Adoles.*, 10:255–262.

Lovasdal, S. (1976), A multiple theory approach in work with children. *Internat. J. Group Psychother.*, 26:475–486.

Mallery, B., & Navas, M. (1982), Engagement of pre-adolescent boys in group theory: Videotape as a tool. *Internat. J. Group Psychother.*, 32:453–467.

Meissner, W. (1980), Theories of personality and psychopathology: Classical psychoanalysis. In: *Comprehensive Textbook of Psychiatry III*, ed. H. Kaplan, A. Freeman, & B. Sadock. Baltimore: Williams & Wilkins, pp. 631–728.

Melville, K. (1973), Changing the family game. *Science*, 13:17–19.

Oberfield, R., & Ciliotta, C. (1983), A school-age boys/single mothers group. *J. Amer. Acad. Child Psychiat.*, 22:375–381.

Patterson, G., & Anderson, C. (1964), Peers as social reinforcers. *Child Devel.*, 35:955–960.

Sands, R., & Golub, S. (1974), Breaking the bonds of tradition: A reassessment of group treatment of latency-age children. *Amer. J. Psychiat.*, 131:662–665.

Slavson, S.R. (1975), Current trends in group psychotherapy. *Internat. J. Group Psychother.*, 25:131–140.

Suda, W., & Fouts, G. (1980), Effects of peer presence on helping in introverted and extroverted children. *Child Devel.*, 51:1272–1275.

Name index

Abramovitch, R., 216
Abramowitz, C. V., 173, 181, 190, 205, 216
Abramson, R. M. 176, 216
Achenbach, T. ., 173, 181, 188, 194, 197, 206, 207, 215, 216
Ackerman, N. W., 26
Adams, M. A., 100, 176, 216
Aichhorn A., 67
Allan, J., 176, 216
Allen, R. P., 107, 108, 109, 110, 111, 118
Altman, S., 47, 51, 67, 148
Amatea, E., 176, 179, 217
Amerikaner, M., 183, 201, 210, 216
Anderson, C., 265, 273
Anderson, R., 176, 179, 217
Anthony, E. J., 46, 63, 67, 72, 73, 79, 154
Apolloni, T., 184, 192, 196, 201, 208, 217
Arthur, B., 103, 121
Axline, V., 39, 42, 67
Azima, F. J., ix, xii-xiii, 139-155
Babigian, H., 108, 119
Baird, K. L., 115, 120-121
Bandura, A., 265, 272
Bardill, D. R., 111, 118, 176, 179, 216
Bardsley, P., 176, 216
Barlow, D. H., 215, 216
Barr, R., 103, 119
Barrell, M., 107
Barrett, C. L., 173, 190, 207, 209, 216
Barsky, M., 176, 198, 216
Barton, E. J., 217
Bednar, R. L., 179, 181, 189, 208, 210, 217
Bell, S., 183, 201, 217

Bellack, A. S., 107, 118
Bellucci, M. T., 117, 118
Belnap, K. L., 103, 119, 177, 218
Bender, 4
Bergman, A., 53, 68
Bernheim, H. 263
Berning, L. W., 185, 218
Berry, K. K., 183, 201, 217
Beswick, K., 117, 120
Bevirt, J., 217
Biegel, A., 98, 100
Bierman, K. L., 183, 190, 192, 195, 196, 201, 205, 211, 217
Blanck, G., 36, 67
Blanck, R., 36, 67
Bleck, B. L., 184, 201, 217
Bleck, R. T., 112, 115, 121, 184, 201, 217
Blick, L. C., 118
Bloch, S., 208, 217
Bornstein, B., 123, 135, 154
Bornstein, M. R., 107
Bower, S. 176, 179, 217
Bradshaw, E., 114, 118
Brinning, R. M., 100
Broekoff, J., 118
Bronstein, M. R., 118
Brown, R., 148, 154
Brown, T., 268, 272
Brunning, R. M., 86
Burgess, A., 264, 272
Burrow, T., 223
Butler, T., 208, 212, 217
Byrne, K. M., 103, 119, 177, 198, 218
Cantor, D. W., 112, 118, 177, 217
Cardarelle, J., 109, 121
Charach, R., 263, 272

Name Index

Charcot, J. M., 263
Cherbuliez, T., 178, 220
Churchill, S., 100
Ciliotta, C., 271, 273
Clement, P. W., 110, 111, 118, 184, 190, 192, 195, 198, 201, 208, 217
Clfford, M., 111, 118, 177, 217
Cobb, C., 178, 179, 198, 220
Cohn, A. H., 116, 119
Conger, J. C., 173, 212, 217
Cooke, T. P., 184, 192, 196, 201, 208, 217
Coolidge, J. C., 108, 119
Copeland, F., 90, 101
Corazzini, J. G., 179, 220
Corder, B., 268, 272
Corder, R., 268, 272
Cowen, E. L., 108, 119
Cramer-Azima, F. J., ix, xii-xiii, 139-155
Cratton, L., 79
Crawford-Brobyn, J., ix
Cross, T., 111, 118, 177, 217
Crouch, E., 208, 217
Crunebaum, M. G., 119
Cunningham, G. K., 185, 198, 218
Cunningham, J. M., 103, 104, 106, 119
Dana, N. T., 117, 120
Daniels, C. R., 100
Dannefer, E., 148, 154
David, L. J., 120
Davis, L. J., 104, 178, 198, 219
Dies, R. R., ix, 173-220
Downing, C. J., 184, 201, 210-211, 218
DuPlessis, J. M., 177, 179, 218
Durbin, D. M., 177, 179, 218
Durkin, H., 85, 100
Durlak, J. A., 109, 110, 119
Edelbrock, C. S., 207, 216
Effron, A. K., 100, 112, 114, 115, 119
Elkins, P. D., 173, 220
Elmer, E., 116, 119
Epstein, N., 47, 51, 67, 117, 120, 148, 154
Erikson, E. H., 34, 67, 102, 121
Erikson, M. E., 103, 121
Factor, D. C., 185, 190, 193, 196, 202, 205, 218
Feegan, L., 90, 101
Feinberg, S., 270
Fidler, J., 88, 101
Field, L. W., 72, 79
Fouts, G., 265, 272
Frank, M. G., 49, 51, 67, 123, 135, 257, 261
Franz, W. K., 185, 202, 218
Freedheim, D. K., 173, 199, 206, 218

Freeman, R. W., 219
Freud, A., 140, 154, 164, 170
Freud, S., 140, 261, 263
Frey, L. A., 108, 119
Fromm-Reichmann, F., 141, 155
Fuhriman, A., 208, 212, 217
Fuller, J. S., 125, 135
Fuller, M., 103, 104, 119
Furman, W., 183, 190, 192, 195, 196, 201, 205, 211, 217
Gabriel, B., 26, 65, 67
Gaines, T. Jr., ix
Gambrill, E. D., 123, 135
Ganter, G., 47, 100, 124, 135
Gardner, R. A., 112, 119
Garland, J. A., 127, 135
Ginott, H. G. 40, 42, 67, 97, 100, 193, 119, 234
Golden, M. M., 108, 120
Golub, S., 264, 273
Gonso, J., 107, 119
Gottman, J. M., 107, 111, 119, 120
Gratton, L., 73, 88, 100
Green, A., 141, 155
Green, A. H., 116, 117, 118, 119
Green, B. J., 112, 114, 115, 119
Green, R., 103, 104, 119
Greenson, R. R., 141, 155
Gregg, G. S., 116, 119
Gresham, F. M., 173, 195, 207, 218
Grossbard, H., 67
Groth, A., 264, 272
Grunebaum, M. G., 108
Guerney, L., 112, 114, 119
Gumaer, J., 110, 111, 120, 186, 203, 219
Gurman, A. S., 208, 218
Gustafson, J. P., 208, 218
Hadley, S. W., 206, 220
Hall, B. J., 84
Hall, E. T., 100
Hallowitz, E., 225, 261
Hamilton, G., 258, 261
Hampe, I. E., 173, 216
Hankins, G., 111, 120, 186, 202, 208, 211, 218
Hardt, P., 183, 217
Hargrave, G. E., 185, 202, 218
Hargrave, M. C., 185, 202, 218
Hayes, E. J., 185, 198, 202, 215, 218
Hayes, S. C., 216
Heaton, R., 107
Heckel, R. V., 210, 218
Heimann, P., 140, 141, 155
Henry, S. E., 186, 218
Herink, R., 261
Hersen, M., 107, 118

Name Index

Hiers, J. M., 210, 218
Hillman, B. W., 103, 112, 119
Hobbs, S. A., 173, 208, 218
Hock, R. A., 104, 121
Hoffman, L., 176, 177, 198, 216
Hoffman, T. E., 103, 104, 106, 119, 218
Holland, H., 67
Hops, H., 108, 111, 119
Howe, P. A., 210, 218
Hursh, L., 210, 218
Izzo, L. D., 108, 119
Jackson, D., 125, 135
Jackson, N., 125, 135
Johns, C. A., 176, 216
Johnson, W. G., 109, 110, 119
Jones, H. E., 127, 135
Jordan, L., 112, 114, 119
Junge, M., 100
Justice, B, 119
Justice, R., 119
Kalter, N., 112, 120
Kansky, E. W., 103, 121
Kauff, P., 61, 67
Kaul, T. J., 179, 181, 189, 208, 210, 217
Kazandkian, A., 187, 199, 203, 219
Kazdin, A. E., 179, 218
Keane, S. P., 173, 212, 217
Keat, D. B., 113, 120
Kelly, E. W., 109, 111, 120
Kelly, J., 121, 212
Kempe, R. S., 117, 120
Kendall, P. C., 173, 185, 192, 194, 195, 202, 208, 218, 220
Kern, R. M., 111, 120, 186, 202, 208, 211, 218
Kernberg, O., 38, 44, 45, 63, 68, 145, 155
Kernberg, P. F., ix, 71-79, 152, 155
Kiesler, D. J., 174, 218
Kilmann, P. R., 186, 202, 218
King, B. L., 73, 79, 100
King, C., 68
King, J., 177, 179, 219
Klein, M., 155, 234, 261
Kline, A., 120
Kline, G., 104, 178, 298, 219
Kolodny, R. L., 108, 119, 127, 135
Konstantareas, M., 216
Kosseff, J., 147, 155
Kraft, I. A., vii, ix, xii, 3-6, 41, 42, 43, 65, 68, 157, 170, 263-273
Ladd, G. W., 107, 120, 173, 197, 200, 209, 212, 219
LaGreca, A. M., 186, 190, 196, 202, 205, 206, 208, 211, 219
Lahey, B. B., 173, 218

Landgarten, H., 100
Lansing, C., 54, 57, 59, 62, 68, 88, 97, 101, 104, 121
Lantz, C. E., 184, 190, 217
Laughlin, J. E., 186, 218
Lawlis, G. F., 181, 217
Ledford, T., 183, 201, 217
Lemanek, K. L., 173, 195, 207, 218
Lemoncelli, J., 100
Leone, S. D., 110, 111, 120, 186, 203, 219
Leverton, B., 117, 120
Levin, S., 147, 155
Lewin, K., 140
Lewis, C., 90, 101
Liebowitz, J. H., x, 71-79
Lifton, N., 58, 59, 62, 68, 72, 79
Lloyd, R., 104, 120, 178, 198, 219
Lochner, L. M., 177, 179, 218
Lockwood, J., 148, 155, 186, 193, 197, 203, 214, 219
Lovasdal, S., 100, 108, 120, 177, 219, 272
Lucas, L., 26
Ludlow, B. B., 117, 120
Lynch, K. A., 117, 120
MacKenzie, K. R., 174, 197, 207, 212, 215, 218, 219
MacLennan, B. W., x, 68, 83-101, 130, 135, 170
Mahler, M., 53, 68
Mallery, B., 269, 272
Mann, J., 181, 219
Martin, H. P., 116, 120
Matthews, D. B., 109, 120
Matthews, K. L., 103, 104, 106, 119
McCausland, M., 264, 272
McFall, R. M., 108, 120
McKibbin, E., 177, 179, 219
McNeill, M., 269, 272
Meissner, W., 263, 272
Melnick, J., 208, 219
Melville, K., 265, 272
Meyer, M., 104, 120, 178, 198, 219
Michelson, L., 187, 192, 203, 214, 219
Miller, C., 27
Miller, L. C., 173, 216
Milne, D. C., 110, 111, 118
Mize, J., 173, 197, 200, 209, 212, 219
Moguin, L. E., 173, 218
Mondell, S., 219
Money-Kyrle, R., 144, 155
Monroe, C., 125, 135
Moreno, J., 223
Morocco, J., 187, 199, 203, 219
Mozenter, G., 176, 198, 216

Nagelberg, L., 225, 261
Nagi, S., 116, 120
Nagler, S., 67
Navas, M., 269, 272
Nelson, R. O., 215, 216
O'Leary, K. D., 173, 206, 207, 208, 219
Oberfield, R., 271, 273
Pasnau, R. O., 104, 120, 178, 198, 219
Pattak, S. I., 59-60, 61, 68, 97, 101, 178, 220
Patterson, D. R., 207, 219
Patterson, G., 265, 273
Patterson, G. R., 103, 120
Pattison, E. M., 181, 219
Pederson, A., 108, 119
Pedi, S. J., 187, 196, 203, 208, 209, 220
Penczar, J. T., 103, 119
Perry, E., 100
Pestalozzi, J. H., 4
Peterson, T. L., 109, 121
Pevsner, R., 103, 120
Phillips, L., 123, 135
Piaget, J., 115, 231
Pine, F., 45, 53, 63, 68
Polansky, N., 47, 100, 124, 135
Pope, L., 73, 79
Porter, F. S., 118
Pratt, J., 223
Putallaz, M., 107, 111, 120
Rachman, A., 141, 155
Racker, H., 140, 144, 155
Rank, B., 68
Rashbaum-Selig, M., 178, 219
Rasmussen, B., 107, 119
Ratusnik, C. M., 219
Ratusnik, D. L., 219
Redl, F., 68, 71, 79
Redl, R., 128, 135
Reibstein, J., 208, 217
Reilly, E. M., 185, 218
Rembar, J., 112
Rhodes, S. L., 101
Rickard, H. C., 173, 181, 220
Riester, A. E., x, vii, xii, 3-6, 173-220
Rizzo, A. E., 88, 100
Roberts, J., 117, 120
Roberts. M. C., 207, 220
Roberts, P. V., 184, 190, 217
Robinson, J. B., 185, 198, 218
Roff, M., 108, 120
Rose, S. D., 103, 120
Rosen, B., 130, 135
Rosenberg, J., 178, 220
Rosenthal, L., 68, 141, 155, 158, 170, 225, 261
Ross, A. O., 191, 194, 220
Rousseau, J. J., 4
Russ, S. R., 173, 199, 206, 218
Ruttenberg, B. A., 220
Rutter, M., 173, 181, 192, 194, 196, 197, 199, 210, 220
Safer, D. J., 107
Samit, G. J., 101
Sands, R., 264, 273
Santogrossi, D. A., 186, 190, 196, 202, 205, 208, 211, 219
Sarnoff, C., 33, 68, 155
Scarbro, H., 186, 218
Schamess, G., x, 29-69, 124, 135, 141, 155, 164, 170
Scheidlinger, S. R., vii, xi, 52, 59, 61, 68, 72, 79, 123, 135, 147, 155, 164, 170, 225, 261
Schiffer, M., x, 3, 40, 42, 65, 68, 84, 97, 101, 103, 120, 155, 157, 158, 170, 223-262
Schilder, P., 223
Schilmoeller, G. L., 185, 190, 196, 193, 202, 205, 218
Schindler, W., 147, 155
Sechrest, L., 207, 219
Sells, S. B., 108, 120
Selverstone, R., 114, 120
Sgroi, S. M., 117, 120
Silvern, L. E., 210, 218
Slavson, S. R., x, 3, 5, 9-27, 39, 42, 65, 68, 71, 78, 79, 84, 85, 97, 101, 120, 124, 135, 141, 155, 157, 158, 170, 223, 224, 225, 229, 251, 252, 253, 258, 260, 261, 263, 263, 273
Slawson, J., 227
Sloman, L., 216
Smolen, E. M., 58, 59, 62, 72, 79
Sonnenchein-Schneider, M., 115, 120-121
Soo, E. S., x, 68, 108, 121, 141, 155, 157-171
Speers, R. W., 54, 57, 59, 62, 68, 88, 97, 101, 104, 121
Spitz, R., 231, 233, 262
Stedman, J. M., 109, 111, 121
Steward, M. S., 103, 119, 177, 198, 218
Stover, D., 86, 100
Strupp, H. H., 206, 220
Suda, W., 265, 273
Sugar, M., 41, 42, 43, 65, 68, 141, 155
Sullivan, H. S., 140
Summerlin, M. L., 183, 201, 210, 216
Tanner, D. L., 187, 193, 203, 210, 220
Tasem, M, 100
Ticho, E. A., 155
Tiktin, E. A., 178, 179, 198, 220

Name Index

Tower, L. W., 155
Trafimow, E., 59-60, 61, 68, 97, 101, 178, 220
Tramontana, M. G., 220
Trost, M. A., 108, 119
Tucker, L., 90, 101
Turkewitz, H., 173, 206, 207, 208, 219
Turone, R. J., 183, 217
Tyler, F. B., 219
Tyroler, M., 173, 218
Urbain, E. S., 173, 220
Van Ophuijsen, J. H. W., 257, 262
Vroom, A. L., 103, 121
Walker, C. E., 207, 220
Wallerstein, J. S., 111, 121
Ward, A., 107
Watson, M., 100
Waxenberg, S., 88, 101
Weidemann, C., 88, 101
Weigel, R. G., 179, 220
Weill, A. P., 68
Weisselberger, D., 108, 121
Wenar, C., 220
Wender, L., 223
Westman, J. C., 103, 104, 121
White, A., x
Whiteside, R., 269, 272
Wiedemann, C., 101
Wilkinson, G. S., 112, 115, 121
Williams, J., 90, 101
Wilson, D., 114, 121
Winemen, D., 68, 128, 135
Winnicott, D. W., 44, 68-69, 140, 141, 147, 155
Wodarski, J. S., 187, 196, 203, 208, 209, 220
Wood, R., 187, 192, 203, 214, 219
Woods, M., 200, 219
Yalom, I. D., 195, 210, 220
Yeakel, M., 47, 124, 135
Zigler, E., 123, 135
Zilbach, J., 123, 135
Zuelzer, M., 117, 121
Zupan, B. A., 185, 192, 194, 195, 202, 208, 218

Subject index

Abreaction
    activity group therapy and, 236-237
    therapeutic value of, 22
    see also Aggression
Abused child(ren), 17, 116-118
Acceptance
    craving for, 11
    unconditional, 241-242
Acting out
    activity group therapy and, 236-237, 242-244
    child versus adult, 237
    primitively fixated child and, 62
    training group and, 166
    see also Impulse-ridden child(ren)
Action as communication, 238-241, 247
Active restraint, 23
Activity group therapy, 223-262
    abreactions and catharsis in, 236-237
    action as communication in, 239-241
    analytic methodology and, 228-230
    behavior disorders and, 246-248
    character disorders and, 248-250
    child's experience and, 230-232
    child's perception of therapist in, 244
    diagnosis and selection of children for, 245-250
    ego-impaired impulse-ridden child and, 225
    energy flow in, 17-18
    furnishings and, 97
    group's corrective influence in, 244-245
    insight and, 238-239
    intermediate level of character pathology and, 39-40
    internalization of corrective experience and, 235
    limitations of, 260-261
    living through versus working through in, 235-236
    modifications of, 225, 250-261
    ego-impaired child and, 51, 254-258, 259-260
    inappropriate, 250-254
    role playing and, 49-50
    psychopathic child and, 258-259
    transference in, 241-244
    origins of, 4-5, 227-228
    primary behavior disorders and, 246-248
    as restitutive experience, 234-235
    social changes and, 226
    space requirement and, 96
    therapist's influence in, 233-234
    training and supervision and, 162-163
Activity-interview group, 41-42
Adolescent group therapy, training and supervision in; see Supervision and training
Adult
    acting out and, 237
    child group therapy versus adult group, 30
    countertransference in, 142
Age, 9-27
    aggression and, 22-23
    discipline and, 13
    fire and, 23-24
    five- to seven-year-old, 20-21
    four- to five-year-old, 21-22
    group associations and, 10-12
    infant, 12-13, 18-19
    interference with normal growth and, 9-10

279

Subject Index

materials and, 25
nine- to fifteen-year-old, 23
nursery age child, 18-20
overmature activities and, 22
seven- to twelve-year-old, 24
stage of helplessness and indulgence, 13-14
value of group and, 25-26
Aggression, 17, 107
  diagnostic play group and, 75, 76
  five- to seven-year-old and, 20-21
  generalization and, 196
  impulse-ridden child and, 132-133
  intermediary group treatment and, 48
  inversion of, 14
  concealment of, 35
  physical environment and, 32
  primitively fixated child and, 62
  release of, 22-23
  sexual, fire and, 23
  see also Acting out; Impulse-ridden child(ren)
Alternatives, objectal, 61
American Psychiatric Association Task Force, 98
Anaclitic child, 249
Analysis
  insight and, 238-239
  activity group therapy and, 228-230
Anatomically correct dolls, 270
Anecdotal reports, 175-180
Anger, fear and, 22-23; see also Aggression
Antisocial behavior, generalization and, 196; see also Impulse- ridden child(ren)
Anxiety
  diagnostic play group for child with, 74, 75
  models for treatment of, 52-53
  neurosis and, 14
  performance, 159
Assertiveness training group, 110
Assessment
  multiple, research and, 180
  outcome, 199-207
Association, craving for, 11
Athletics, 271
Attention-deficient child, 107-108
Attention-placebo group, 211
Autistic child(ren), 53-63
  first group therapy for, 54-57
  overview of, 61-63
  relationship group therapy for, 58-59
Avoidance behavior
  diagnostic play group and, 75

modified nondirective play group and, 41
Balloons in group therapy, 271
Behavior
  antisocial, generalization and, 196
  as communication, 239-241
  see also Behavior disorder(s)
Behavior disorder(s)
  activity group therapy and nondirective play group for, 39-40
  activity-interview groups and interpretive group therapy for, 41-44
  character disorder versus, 14, 248-249, 258
  modified nondirective and therapeutic play group for, 40-41
  overview of, 42-44
  primary, 246-248
Behavior modification, 108-111
Biologic function, interference in, 18
Blind spots, countertransference and, 152
Borderline conditions, 44-53
  Common-Sense Club for, 47
  intermediary group treatment for, 47-49
  modified activity group for, 49-50, 225, 254-258, 259-260
  modified experiential group for, 52-53
  overview of, 50-52
  small room technique for, 46-47
  two-stage model for, 123-135
Boredom, countertransference and, 149
Boy(s)
  autistic, 57
  bean bag chairs for, 270
  effeminate, 249, 250
  impulse-ridden, two-stage model for, 123-135; see also Impulse-ridden child(ren)
Case-finding, 86
Catharsis, 236-237
Character disorder or pathology
  activity group therapy and, 248-250; see also Activity group therapy
  behavior problem versus, 14, 248
  higher level, 63-67
  intermediate, 38-44
  lower level, 44-53
Common-Sense Club for, 47
  intermediary group treatment for, 47-49
  modified activity group for, 49-50
  modified experiential group for, 52-53

Subject Index

overview of, 50-52
small room technique for, 46-47
two-stage model for, 123-135
realistic situations and, 15
Child abuse, 17, 116-118
Child care worker, 130
Child development
  activity group therapy and, 230-232
  phases of, 12-14
Child guidance agency, 87
Child versus adult group therapy, 30
Child-therapist relationship, 209
Classroom teacher, outcome assessment and, 100, 201-203, 205
Clinic
  medical, 91
  public service, 6
Clinical agency, 188
Coaching, 108
Coeducational therapeutic play group, 65
Cognition, 33
  ego-impaired child and, 257
Combat, 22-23, 132-133; see also Aggression
Common-Sense Club, 47, 57
Communication
  developmentally appropriate medium of, 33-37
  group and, 6
  importance of, 233-234
  innovations in, 266-269
  latency age child and, 35-37
  modified nondirective play group and, 40
  nonverbal, 34-35, 239-242, 247
  physical surroundings and, 32
  see also Communication modes
Communication modes
  intermediate level of character pathology and, 39-44
  lower level of character pathology and, 46-53; see also Impulse-ridden child(ren)
  neurotic child and, 64-65
  psychotic child and, 54-63
  first group therapy and, 54-57
  overview of, 61-63
  primitively fixated child and, 59-61
  relationship group therapy and, 58-59
Compensatory models, 36-37
Competence, social, 108; see also Peer relations
Complementary identification, 144-145
Compliance, 33
Concordant identification, 144-145
Conduct disorder(s)

activity group therapy and nondirective play group for, 39-40
activity-interview groups and interpretive group therapy for, 41-44
character disorder versus, 14, 248-249, 258
modified nondirective and therapeutic play group for, 40-41
overview of, 42-44
primary, 246-248
Confrontations, 47
Constricted child, 41
Contingency management, 108
Contrast Mother Group, 198
Contrast Peer Therapist Group, 198
Controls
  research design and, 180
  group, 24
  waiting-list, 211
Corrective experience
  group and, 244-245
  internalization of, 235
Cotherapist(s)
  male, 152
  primitively fixated child and, 61
Countertransference, 139-155
  acting out and, 237, 243-244
  definition of, 141-143
  examples of, 148-152
  sources and process of, 143-146
  techniques for reducing, 152-153
  training and supervision and, 159-160, 159-160
  treatment network and, 146-148
Crafts, 129; see also Equipment and materials
Cravings, oral, 25
Creative approaches in child group psychotherapy; see Innovations in child group psychotherapy
Crisis groups, 94-95
Culture as basis of understanding person, 9-10
Curiosity, 230-232
Defaulting techniques, 42
Deprivation, sensory, 231-232
Derivative insight, 238-239
Development, child
  activity group therapy and, 230-232
  phases of, 12-14
  deviations of, 38-44
Diagnosis, differential, 29-69
  activity group therapy and, 245-250
  importance of, 259
  communication medium and, 33-37
  group structure and, 30-32; see also

282 Subject Index

Group structure
  intermediate level of character pathology and, 38-44
  lower level of character pathology and, 44-53
  models in, 37-38
  neurosis and higher level character pathology and, 63-65
  psychosis and, 53-63
  see also Diagnostic categories; Diagnostic play group
Diagnostic categories
  anxiety-ridden child and, 52
  impulse-ridden child and, 46
  intermediate level of character pathology and, 38-39
  limitations of, 258
  neurotic child and, 64
  psychotic child and, 54
  see also Diagnosis, differential
Diagnostic play group, 71-79
  advantages of, 78-79
  aggression and, 75
  anxious child in, 75
  avoidant personality in, 74
  clinical example of, 74-78
  encopresis and, 75
  history of, 71-74
  see also Diagnosis, differential
Didactic approach to supervision, 163-164
Differential diagnosis; see Diagnosis, differential
Direct restraint, 23
Discipline, 13-14
Discussion
  Common-Sense Club and, 47
  primitively fixated child and, 60
  problem talk as, 41
  talk therapy and, 252-253
  see also Communication; Interpretation
Divorce, 111-116
Dolls
  anatomically correct, 269
  clothed family, 32
DSM diagnostic categories
  anxiety-ridden child and, 52
  impulse-ridden child and, 46
  intermediate level of character pathology and, 38-39
  limitations of, 258
  neurotic child and, 64
  psychotic child and, 54
  see also Diagnosis
Dyad for impulse-ridden child, 125, 126-129
Dynamics, intergroup, 84-85
Early-object stage, 60
Eating
  activity group therapy and, 241
  autistic child and, 56
Effeminate boy, 249, 250
Ego
  damage and, 48; see also Impulse-ridden child(ren)
  function and, 38
  inadequately developed, 36
  integrity of, interpretation and, 43
  primitively fixated child and, 61
  structure and, age and, 18
Ego alien symptomatology, 63-65
Egocentric trends, 24
Ego-impaired child; see Impulse-ridden child(ren)
  activity group therapy and, 225, 254-258, 259-260
  behavior disorder and, 258
Emotional experience, corrective, 30
Encopresis, 75
Energy
  activity group therapy and, 17-18
  processing of, 264
Environment
  group structure and, 31-32
  modified experiential group and, 52
  primitively fixated child and, 60
  protective, 44
  relationship group therapy and, 58
  social, 11
  therapy failure and, 33-34
Epistomophilic drive, 230-231
Equipment and materials, 32
  age of child and, 23
  autistic child and, 55
  behavior and, 19
  disorganization and, 21-22
  evocative, 42
  gradation of, 25
  primitively fixated child and, 60
Evaluation, 180; see also Diagnostic play group; Research on child group therapy
Evocative play equipment, 42
Experience
  activity group therapy and, 230-232
  corrective, 15, 235
  restitutive, 234-235
Experiential therapy
  activity group therapy as, 232
  modified, 52-53
  training and supervision and, 169

Extraindividual factors in maladjustment, 14-15
Extratherapy process measures, 213
Failure
  fear of, countertransference and, 145-146
  of therapy, physical environment and, 33-34
Family
  group as, 164, 235
  therapy for, 6, 95-96, 99
  treatment results and, 197-198
  see also Parent(s); Parent group psychotherapy
Fantasy, 33
Fear
  anger and, 22-23
  of failure, 145-146
  of self-disclosure, 151
Feeding
  activity group therapy and, 241
  autistic child and, 56
Fees for therapy, 98-99
Female(s); see Girl(s)
Fighting, 132-133
  frightened child and, 23
  see also Aggression
Financing of program, 98-99
Fire
  playing with, 23
  sexual meanings and, 25
Five-year-old child(ren)
  activating materials and, 21-22
  explosive behavior and, 20-21
Fixation
  ego-impaired child and, 255
  primitive, 59-61
Follow-up of treatment effects, 191-194
Food
  activity group therapy and, 241
  autistic child and, 56
Format of group for training and supervision, 157-158, 165
Foster care for abused child, 117
Four-year-old child(ren)
  activating materials and, 21-22
  value of group for, 19
Frightened child, fighting and, 23
Frustrated child, 17
Furnishings for therapy room
  importance of, 31-32
  primitively fixated child and, 60
  requirements for, 97
  see also Equipment and materials
Games, 129
Gender identity disorder
  activity group therapy and, 249
  modified nondirective play group and, 41
  see also Sexual issues
Generalization of therapeutic gains, 194-197
Girl(s)
  hand-oriented tasks and, 269
  hospitalization of therapist and, 271
  modified activity group and, 49
Gratification, guided, 53
Group(s)
  activity; see Activity group therapy
  activity-interview, 41-44
  autistic child and, 57
  contraindications to, 24-25
  corrective influence of, 15, 244-245
  age of child and, 25-26
  as ego, 61
  diagnostic play; see Diagnostic play group
  dynamics of, 84-85
  modified nondirective, 40-41
  nondirective play, 39-40
  parent; see Parent group psychotherapy
  parent-child, 106-107
  personality development and, 10-13
  process of, 131
  resistance of, in training and supervision and, 159-160
  rewards and, 130-132
  seven- to twelve-year-old and, 24
  structure of; see Group structure
  as superego, 57
  use of, 11
Group structure, 29-69
  diagnoses and models in, 37-38
  intermediate level of character pathology and, 38-44
  lower level of character pathology and, 46-53
  neurosis and higher level character pathology and, 63-65
  psychotic child and, 53-63
  training and supervision and, 165
  two-stage model and, 129
Growth
  needs of, 9-10
  orderly, 12
Guided gratification, 53
Habit training, 13
Handicapped child, 91
Hand-oriented tasks, 269
Helplessness, 13
Higher level of character pathology, 63-

67; see also Neurosis
Hilarity, 21
Historical overview of child group psychotherapy, 3-6
Hospital settings, 90-92
  financing of programs in, 98
Hyperactive child
  early stage of treatment and, 21
  intermediary group treatment and, 48
Hypothesis testing, 174
Identification, countertransference and
  with child, 149-150
  double, 144
  with parent, 150-151
Impulse-ridden child(ren), 46-52, 107
  Common-Sense Club for, 47
  intermediary group treatment and, 47-49
  modified activity group and, 49-50, 225, 254-258, 259-260
  overview of, 50-52
  small room technique and, 46-47
  two-stage model for, 123-135
Inadequate personality; see Impulse-ridden child(ren)
Inanimate objects, 57
Individual supervision, 160-161
Individual therapist, 163
Infant
  nurture and, 12-13
  as part of mother, 18-19
  sensory deprivation and, 231-232
Infantile autism; see Autistic child(ren)
Infantile child
  group and, 17
  bonding and, 249
  omnipotence and, 55
  see also Impulse-ridden child(ren)
Inhibited child(ren)
  fighting and, 23
  group therapy and, 16
Inhibition, removal of, 17
Innovation in child group psychotherapy, 263-272
  anatomically correct dolls and, 269-270
  athletics and, 270
  balloons and, 271
  bean-bag chairs and, 270
  communication and, 266-269
  hand-oriented tasks and, 269
  special vocabulary and, 266-268
  tape recorder and, 268
  television and, 269
  video games and, 271
  videotape and, 268

Inpatient settings, 90-92
  financing of programs in, 98
Insight
  derivative versus analytic, 238-239
  self-observation and, 131
Insurance, 99-100
Intake procedures, 86-87
Integration of program, 98
Intellectualization as countertransference, 148-149
Intergroup dynamics, 84-85
Intermediary group, 47-49, 51
Intermediate level of character pathology, 39-44; see also Conduct disorder(s)
Internalization of corrective experience, 235
Interpersonal skills
  development of, 5
  generalization and, 195
Interpretation
  corrective emotional experience versus, 30
  intermediate level of character pathology and, 41-44
  primitively fixated child and, 62
Interview, screening, 161-162
Interview group therapy
  energy flow in, 17-18
  neurotic child and, 65
Intratherapy process measure, 213
Introjection, 145
Joint sessions, 106-107
Language, importance of, 233-234; see also Communication
Leader, role of, 165
Learning
  elements of, 4
  relationships and, 17
Libidinal countertransference, 145
Libidinal object, maternal, 242
Limits for impulse-ridden child, 129
Literature; see Research on child group therapy
Living through versus working through, 235-236
Long-term residential setting, 91
Lower level of character pathology, 44-53; see also Impulse-ridden child(ren)
Maladaptation, social, 11; see also Conduct disorder(s)
Male(s)
  autistic, 57
  bean bag chairs for, 270
  effeminate, 249, 250
  as cotherpists, 152

Subject Index

impulse-ridden, 123-135; see also Impulse-ridden child(ren)
Materials and equipment, 32
   age of child and, 23
   autistic child and, 55
   behavior and, 19
   disorganization and, 21-22
   evocative, 42
   gradation of, 25
   primitively fixated child and, 60
Maternal libidinal object, therapist as, 242
Maturational tasks, 36
Medical settings, 91
Model(s)
   compensatory, 36-37
   intermediate level of character pathology and, 39-44
   interview, 65
   lower level of character pathology and, 46-53; see also Impulse-ridden child(ren)
   neurotic child and, 64-65
   psychotic child and, 54-63
   tripartite, for understanding therapeutic gain, 206-207
Modification, behavior, 108-111
Modified activity group, 225, 250-261
   ego-impaired child and, 51, 254-258, 259-260
   inappropriate, 250-254
   role playing and, 49-50
   psychopathic child and, 258-259
Modified experiential group, 52-53
Modified nondirective play group, 40-41
Mother
   autistic child and, 54-55
   of young child, 19
   see also Parent(s)
Mother Therapist Groups, 198
Multiple assessment, 180
Multiple-family groups, 106
Narcissism, 231
Need-gratifying stage, 60
Negative transference
   activity group therapy and, 242-244
   private practitioner and, 89-90
Network, treatment, 146-148
Neurosis, 63-67
   analytic therapy and, 229
   anxiety and, 14
   insight and, 238
   transference and, 15, 243-244
   universal complaints in, 11
Nondirective play group, 39-41

Nonverbal communication, 34-35
   activity group therapy and, 241-242
Nursery age child, 18
   awareness of others in, 19-20
Nurturance
   character disorder and, 249
   problems in, 12-13
   symbolic, 256
   transference and, 241-242
Object relations
   intermediate level of character pathology and, 38
   training and supervision and, 164
Objectal alternatives, 61
Objective countertransference, 160
Observer(s)
   generalization and, 196
   independent, 205
Omnipotence
   autism and, 55
   countertransference and, 151
One-way screen room, 152-153
Oppositional personality disorder, 41
Oral cravings, 25
Outcome assessment, 199-207
Overidentification, countertransference and, 149-151
Overmature activities, 22
Panic, 55
Parent(s)
   autistic child and, 57
   Common-Sense Club and, 47
   group treatment for, 103-107; see also Parent group psychotherapy
   outpatient groups and, 86
   overidentification with, 150-151
   resistance of, to child abuse group, 118
   therapist as ideal or symbolic, 233, 234
   treatment results and, 197-199
Parent group psychotherapy, 95-96
   advantages of, 105-106
   autistic child and, 54-55
   countertransference and, 153
   divorce and, 115-116
   lower level of character pathology and, 50
Parent-child groups, 106-107
Parent-therapist transference, 237
Passion, 34-35
Passive restraint, 23
Pathology
   character; see Character disorder or pathology
   developmental, 35-37
Patient selection, 6

activity group therapy and, 245-250
  training and supervision and, 161
Peer relations
  generalization and, 196
  importance of, 123
  pressure from, 264-265
  problems in, 107-111; see also Impulse-ridden child(ren)
  treatment results and, 211
Peer pressure, 264-265
Peer-sociometric evaluation, 196
Perfectionism, 151
Performance anxiety, 159
Permissiveness
  activity group therapy and, 252, 255
  ego-impaired child and, 255
  older child and, 24
Physical environment; see Environment
Planning, sequential, 153
Plastic materials, 19; see also Materials and equipment
Play group therapy
  coeducational therapeutic, 65
  furnishings and, 97
  intermediate level of character pathology and, 40-41
  modified nondirective, 40-41
  nondirective, 39-40
  space requirement for, 96-97
  materials for, 25, 32, 55; see also Equipment and materials
Play Therapy Observational Instrument, 210
Positive transference, 242-244; see also Transference
Postsymbiotic child, 60-61
Power
  therapist and, 47
  training group and, 166
Praise, 249-250
Prenursery age child, 18
Preoedipal behavior, 17, 38
Prepsychotic conditions, 44-53
  Common-Sense Club for, 47
  intermediary group treatment for, 47-49
  modified activity group for, 49-50
  modified experiential group and, 52-53
  overview of, 50-52
  small room technique for, 46-47
Preschool age child, 18, 193
  awareness of others in, 19-20
  social skills training and, 193
Primary behavior disorders, 246-248; see also Behavior disorder(s)

Primitively fixated child, 59-61
Private practice, 88-90
  research and, 188
Problem talk, 41
Process
  research and, 180, 207-213
  small group, 84-85
  training group, 165-168
  two-stage model for impulse-ridden child and, 131
Program integration, 98
Psycho-osmosis, 19-20
Psychopathic child, 258-259
Psychosis, 53-63; see also Autistic child(ren)
Public service clinic, 6
Punching bag, 32
Rage and autism, 55
Reconstituted family, 164
Recorder, tape, 268
  intermediary group treatment and, 48
Recruitment, differential, 188
Regression
  autistic child and, 56
  training group and, 166
Reinforcers, 130-132
Rejection, 5
  relating to others and, 14
  stages of nurture and discipline and, 13-14
Relationship
  child-therapist, 209
  group and, 26
  peer; see Peer relations
  supervisor-supervisee, 163-164
Relationship group therapy, 58-59
Replication of research, 179-180
Representation, symbolic, 164
Repression
  intermediate level of character pathology and, 38
  neurotic child and, 63
Research on child group therapy, 173-220
  anecdotal reports in, 175-180
  research reports in, 180-213
  contribution of group treatment and, 197-199
  deficiencies in, 181-182, 190
  definition of treatment in, 207-213
  generalization of therapeutic gains and, 194-197
  outcome assessment in, 199-207
  quality of, 190
  recommendations for, 179-180
  setting in, 183-187

treatment effects and, 191-194
Researcher versus practitioner, 174
Residential treatment, 90-92
  financing of programs and, 98
  intermediary group treatment and, 48
Resistance
  group, 159-160
  subgroup, 168-169
  training group, 165-168
Resistivity of materials, 25
Restitutive experience, 234-235, 248
Restraint, 23
Rewards, 130-132
Rivalry, sibling, 241
Role playing, 49-50
Room
  importance of, 31-32
  impulse-ridden child and, 129
  shape of, 97
  space requirements and, 60, 96-97
Rules, 129
Scapegoating, 162-163
Schizophrenia, 58-59; *see also* Autistic child(ren)
School, 92-94
  divorce group in, 112
  financing of programs in, 98
  outcome assessment and, 200, 201-203, 205
  phobia and, 75
  research and, 188
Screen, one-way, 152-153
Screening interview, 161-162
Security
  needs of, 9-10
  young child and, 18
Selection of group members, 6
  activity group therapy and, 245-250
  training and supervision and, 161
Self-disclosure, fear of, 151
Self-esteem, interpretation and, 43
Self-expression, inhibition of, 17
Self-indulgence, 13
Self-observation, insight and, 131
Self-report, 100, 196, 201-203
Sensory deprivation, 231-232
Sequential planning, 153
Seven-year-old child, 20-21
Sex of therapist
  countertransference and, 152
  two-stage model and, 130
Sexual issues
  autistic child and, 56, 57
  countertransference and, 150
  fire and, 23
  group makeup as, 42, 65

identity confusion and, 41, 249
  longings and, 35
  primitively fixated child and, 62
Short-term groups, 99
Shyness, 107
Sibling
  group as symbolic, 234-235
  rivalry and, 241
Single-sex group, 42
Six-year-old child, 20-21
Skills
  social, 108-111, 123
  treatment results and, 211
Small group process, 84-85
Small room technique, 46-47
Smothering, 149
Soap operas, 269
Social change, 226
Social environment, 11
Social hunger, 24
Social skills
  development of, 108-111
  generalization and, 195
  maladaptation and, 11
  treatment effects and, 193
Social superego, 226
Social worker, 130
Somatizations, 152
Space requirements, 96-97
Speech
  importance of, 233-234
  level of character organization and, 36
  see also Communication
Splitting, 46
Structure, group; *see* Group structure
Subgroup resistance, 168-169
Subjective countertransference, 160
Superego
  group, autistic child and, 57
  intermediate level of character pathology and, 38, 44
  social, 226
Superego-bound child, 41
Supervision and training, 157-171
  clinical example in, 162-163
  countertransference and, 159-160
  format for, 157-158, 165
  group, 168
  individual, 160-161
  leader's role in, 165
  member selection and, 161
  object relations and, 164
  process and resistances in, 165-168
  reduction of countertransference by, 153
  screening interview and, 161-162

subgroup resistance in, 168-169
supervisor's task in, 160
supervisor-supervisee relationship, 163-164
symbolic representations and, 164
trainee and, 158-159, 163-164
Supervisor
role of, 165
task of, in training and supervision, 160
see also Supervision and training
Surgical problems, groups for, 91
Symbiotic child(ren), 53-63
first group therapy for, 54-57
overview of, 61-63
relationship group therapy for, 58-59
Symbiotic relationship, 19
Symbolism, 33, 34-35, 164
nurturance and, 256
Systems theory, 5
Talk therapy, 252-253
Tape recorder, 268
intermediary group treatment and, 48
Teach-a-Body doll, 269
Teacher, outcome assessment and, 200, 201-203, 205
Team, cotherapy
male therapist and, 152
primitively fixated child and, 61
Television
playback of, 153
groups and, 269
Termination of treatment, 248
Testing of therapist, 21
Therapeutic change
meaning of, 191-194
generalization of, 194-197
tripartite model for understanding of, 206-207
see also Treatment
Therapeutic play group
intermediate level of character pathology and, 40-41
neurotic child and, 65
Therapist(s)
activity group model and, 40
age of child and, 26
change in role of, 18
child's perception of, 244
Common-Sense Club and, 47, 51
countertransference and, 139-155; see also Countertransference
direct contact against, 243
as ideal parent, 233
identification of, in research reports, 214

influence of, 233-234
male, 152
as maternal libidial object, 242
modified experiential group and, 52
neurotic child and, 65
older child and, 24
permissiveness of, 252, 255
primitively fixated child and, 61
ratio of, in outpatient setting, 87
recognition of, 100
relationship with child and, 209
as superego restrictor, 250-251
testing of, 21
third, reduction of countertransference by, 152
training of, 88; see also Supervision and training
transference and; see Transference
transition of, from individual to group, 163
two-stage model for impulse-ridden child and, 130
Therapist-child relationship, 209
Therapist-parent transference, 237
Third-party reimbursement, 99-100
Three-year-old child, 19
Time
requirement for, in different settings, 97-98
of treatment, research and, 214
Time-out
third therapist and, 152
two-stage model and, 129
Toilet training, 56
Touch, 133
Toys
autistic child and, 56
young child and, 18
see also Equipment and materials; Play group therapy
Trainee(s)
reaction of, to supervision, 163-164
training group and, 158-159
see also Supervision and training
Training
habit, 13
toilet, 56
supervision and, 157-171; see also Supervision and training
Transactional analysis, 268
Transference
acting out and, 236-237
activity group therapy and, 233, 236, 242-244
depth of, 15-16
group and, 16

maternal quality of, 242
negative, 89-90, 242-244
neurosis and, 15
nurturant, 241-242
parent-therapist, 237
training and supervision and, 159-160
two-stage model and, 130
see also Countertransference
Transportation requirements, 97
Treatment
  effects of, 191-194
  generalization and, 194-197, 207-213
  identification of, in research reports, 214
  network and, 140-148
  termination of, 248
Tripartite model for understanding therapeutic gain, 206-207
Tutoring in ego capacities, 49
Two-stage model for impulse-ridden child(ren), 123-135; *see also* Impulse-ridden child(ren)
Unconditional acceptance, 241-242

Variables, 180
Verbal communication
  autistic child and, 56
  group and, 6
  importance of, 233-234
  innovations in, 266-268
  latency age children and, 35, 36
  modified nondirective play group and, 40
  see also Communication; Discussion
Video games, 271
Videotape, 268
Vocabulary, special, 266-268
Water, sexual meanings and, 25
Wild behavior, 21
Withdrawn child, 52-54, 107
Worker; *see* Therapist(s)
Working through versus living through, 235-236
Young child
  authority and discipline and, 20
  fighting and, 23
  as part of mother, 18-19

Date Due

DEC 14 1993		
DEC 23 1993		